The lives of gay people are shaped not only by laws, but by the treatment they receive every day from their families, from their neighbors. Eleanor Roosevelt, who did so much to advance human rights worldwide, said that these rights begin in the small places close to home – the streets where people live, the schools they attend, the factories, farms, and offices where they work.

Those who advocate for expanding the circle of human rights were and are on the right side of history, and history honors them.

United States Secretary of State Hillary Rodham Clinton
Geneva, December 6, 2011

Praise for
Out & Equal at Work:
From Closet to Corner Office

"*Out & Equal at Work* speaks to the power of cultivating an environment that celebrates diversity, and ensures employees can bring their whole selves to work every day. Not only is this the right thing to do, but I believe it has profound benefits on employee engagement, retention, productivity and, ultimately, business results. Sexual orientation and gender identity are differences that should not matter. The only things that truly matter are the content of one's character and the unique talent a person brings to the organization."

Don Knauss, Clorox CEO

"There are business books that reinforce the business imperative of diversity. This book is not just one of those. It's a collection of authentic stories from real people — authentic, successful role models — whose stories are both moving and educational. More than that, they're *inspirational*, because they demonstrate how LGBT employees can contribute and prosper at the highest levels in the inclusive workplace."

Harry van Dorenmalen, Chairman, IBM Europe

"Every American deserves to be treated fairly and equally in and out of the workplace. *Out & Equal at Work* is both educational and inspirational for employers and employees regardless of sexual orientation or gender identity. With moving personal stories, *Out & Equal at Work* puts a human face on the benefits of diversity in the workplace and the rewards of being open and honest about who we are."

Congresswoman Tammy Baldwin (D-WI)

"Part of the way we each find the strength to bring our whole lives into the workplace is to learn about the experience of others who have taken that step. We not only can succeed, but we can contribute to the work environment in a more substantive way and lead a more fulfilling life. These stories of leadership and courage serve as a real inspiration."

**Rick Welts, Chief Operating Officer,
Golden State Warriors**

"These are the stories that executives around the world should hear, coming from the brave voices of smart, successful executives who are making important contributions in business, in government and in the ways they conduct their lives with dignity and integrity. Even more so, these are the stories that all companies should want to be part of, showcasing how creating inclusive workplaces equates with creating a business culture where all of us can bring our mind and heart to work."

Sophie Vandebroek, Xerox Corporate Vice President

"When I started my career at Ford Motor Company, and ultimately served as Ford's Vice Chairman, what strength and insight *Out & Equal at Work* would have offered. Each personal narrative here is a reminder how important it is to celebrate diversity and openness in every workplace — and to lead by example."

**Allan Gilmour, former Vice Chairman, Ford Motor
Company and President, Wayne State University**

"The aim of the Nation's best employers is to implement policies that make every workplace as equal, welcoming and purposeful as it can be. Selisse Berry's new book, *Out & Equal at Work*, will help managers and employers everywhere understand why these fair-minded values make a real and lasting difference."

The Honorable John Berry

Out & Equal at Work

From Closet to Corner Office

Selisse Berry, Editor

Published by Out & Equal Workplace Advocates
155 Sansome Street, Suite 450, San Francisco, CA 94104
www.OutandEqual.org

Cover design by Uptown Studios and layout by 1106 Design

Library of Congress
Berry, K., Selisse.
Out & Equal at Work:
   From Closet to Corner Office / Selisse Berry, M.S., M.Div.
p. cm.
Includes references and index.
ISBN 978-0-9881898-0-5 (softcover: alk. paper)
1. Corporate Culture 2. Lesbian, gay, bisexual and transgender people 3. Workplace Equality 4. Diversity and Inclusion 5. Workplace Issues 6. LGBT Rights 7. Corporate Social Responsibility I. Berry, Selisse II. Title
HD58.7.H38 2012
Printed in the United States of America
FIRST EDITION
SC Printing

This book is gratefully dedicated to lesbian, gay, bisexual, and transgender people who help create a world in which everyone can be fully out and equal.

Table of Contents

Acknowledgments

Like Out & Equal itself, the book you hold in your hands is a labor of love. It is written on behalf of the lesbian, gay, bisexual and transgender community everywhere, especially those who have experienced discrimination because of who they love.

The world is changing and the stories you will read here are at the heart of this transformation. Our work will only be complete when every member of our community can bring his or her whole self to work with pride.

I am profoundly grateful for the visionary leaders who have courageously shared their stories in these pages. Some have been pioneers in the work for justice; others have more recently joined the front lines of this movement. All of them are fearless leaders committed to freedom and justice.

Many thanks to the *Out & Equal at Work* team. April Hawkins has been instrumental in facilitating the telling of the contributors' stories. April has worked tirelessly to edit and gently shepherd this wonderful project. Stanley Ellicott managed much of this project with a calming, positive perspective. Marina Bennett was willing to help out whenever and wherever needed.

A huge debt of gratitude to Nancy Ferguson who helped me tell my story. Nancy's patience, wisdom and friendship have been an integral part of this process. Julia Randall shared her stellar talents and expertise editing this book. Cindy Solomon lends her smart advice and good humor to everything Out & Equal.

Deepest thanks to Deputy Director, Kevin Jones, and the entire Out & Equal team, whose hard work and dedication make our difficult days bearable and the good ones a joy.

I am very fortunate to have an incredible, supportive and committed Board of Directors, with a resounding thank you to board president, Tom Johnson and president emeritus, Kayla Shell. A heartfelt thank you to Mike Feldman, Julie Hogan, Angie Wilson, Patrick O'Donnell, Eleanor Mercado, George Kalogridis, Donna Griffin, Bobby Wilkinson, Claudia Brind-Woody, Scott Beth and Charles Lickel.

My fellow Executive Directors, Jody Huckaby of Parents and Friends of Lesbians and Gays (PFLAG) and Rea Carey of the National Gay and Lesbian Task Force are peers I know I can always count on. Their friendship and support as we meet the challenges of this important work are invaluable to me.

Christie Hardwick has been a fabulous mentor and coach, and a remarkable facilitator of the Executive Forums. She is one of the reasons we have these stories to tell.

A special thank you to Kate Clinton for her support of Out & Equal and for her friendship. Kate's brilliant humor and astute political perspective have been such a gift to our community for many years. May it continue.

I want to say thank you to the indefatigable Secretary of State Hillary Clinton, whose mandate to state departments around the world to support LGBT efforts is changing the global landscape of our community.

My dad, Jack Berry, is not only my biggest fan, but also a vocal supporter of Out & Equal. I am so grateful to have him close by and to know he is proud of who I am and what I do.

My beautiful wife, Cynthia Martin, has made my life, my work, and this book so much better. She is my rock, and the one who makes my heart sing.

Selisse Berry

Foreword by Kate Clinton

In the 1970s during my eight years of high school English teaching, after nights creating lesson plans, correcting papers and doing grades, I would spend free time quilling or doing pen and ink. The first and only time I ever tried quilling, an art form using strips of paper rolled and glued into delicate filigrees, I spent months creating an intricate cornucopia of fruit. Degree of difficulty: ten.

The first and only time I took an evening art class, and while students were dashing off drawing after drawing, I spent the entire semester doing a pen and ink of a stand-alone shadowy old farm house with tattered curtains fluttering in the darkened windows. The time I spent on the detail of the roof finials caused my teacher to remark that I was putting eyelashes on eyelashes. She encouraged me to loosen up. After that class, I did another overly detailed pen and ink of a bleak, boxy old country church floating in blank white space.

I was trying not to be a lesbian. I knew there would be no place for me in the school where I taught. I didn't dare visit the home of the known lesbian couple, or go to the wild dances sponsored by the anti-war commune, or go to the Women's Center. I kept my head down and made myself cross-eyed with projects, so that I couldn't really see or be who I was. At a distance of thirty plus years, I call the three pieces my "Trying Not to Come Out" series.

I had not thought of those cramped, stark art works until I read the stories in this collection. Joining the stories of allies are the stories of lesbian, gay, bisexual, and transgender people who struggled to come out and then used the lessons of their struggle to make a better world. Coming out stories are often pooh-poohed in this so-prematurely-called "post-gay" world, but the narratives gathered here are not only important LGBT history, including the story of the founding and growth of Out & Equal, but also the stories of courage, being honest and still rising to the top and organizing for change in the workplace and beyond.

Courage is in the story of Dr. Louise Young, a Senior Software Engineer at Raytheon, who tells of growing up in Oklahoma, losing her beloved teaching job because she was a lesbian and then founding the first LGBT employee resource group at Texas Instruments.

Being honest is in the story of Maggie Stumpp, Senior Advisor to Quantitative Management Associates, who tells of her transition from male to female while working at Prudential and her acute insights on transgender integration in the workplace. Honesty is in the story of Vice President and Chief Diversity and Inclusion Officer at Campbell Soup Company, Rosalyn Taylor O'Neale, who shares her experience of being an African American, a woman and out lesbian and all the moments of truth that come with those identities in the workplace.

Rising to the top is in the story of George Kalogridis, president of the Disneyland Resort, who tells of rising through the Walt Disney Company, coming out and the continued fears of LGBT people coming out at work in a pro-LGBT company.

And relentless organizing is in the story of Selisse Berry, Founding Executive Director of Out & Equal Workplace Advocates, who tells of her Oklahoma roots, the mid-wiving of Out & Equal, its vision and values and its global growth.

Compared to the larger legislative and judicial tale of the LGBT movement, the chronicle of the incremental transformation of the workplace for and by the frontline work of LGBT people is an under-told and under-the-radar story. This book is not only about coming out but also about the hard grind of making change in the workplace. I admired and learned from the strategies and daring patience of each narrator. They are creating a world where lonely quilling is replaced by joyous community quilting bees and black ink crosshatching is replaced by bold colorful strokes in all the colors of the rainbow.

Introduction

Around the world, attitudes, laws and policies relating to lesbian, gay, bisexual and transgender people have improved at a remarkable pace over the past fifteen years. The business community has had a significant impact on this phenomenal social transformation. *Out & Equal at Work* tells the inspiring story of change from the perspective of the movement's visionary leaders.

This anthology shares the story of Out & Equal Workplace Advocates, the world's largest nonprofit organization specifically dedicated to workplace equality for lesbian, gay, bisexual, and transgender people; its founder Selisse Berry; and the corporate leaders with whom Out & Equal has collaborated. Selisse conceived of this book through Out & Equal's work with employee resource group leaders and senior executives who are leading change in the world's largest companies.

In *Out & Equal at Work*, openly lesbian, gay, bisexual, and transgender executives and leaders tell their personal coming out stories and share firsthand accounts of how they work to bring lasting change to their workplaces. Many of them discuss their initial fears and the transformation and support that was needed to ensure their company was a safe and equitable work environment.

Along their incredible journey, a few of these champions lost their jobs. Some lost family and friends. Some nearly lost their lives. While it's clear there is much more work to do, the stories in this book give us hope.

Many of these visionary leaders discovered that being their authentic selves at work helped their careers blossom. Some executives like Kayla Shell of Dell and Tom Johnson of Clorox found that advancing LGBT rights in the workplace helped them in advancing their careers. As a result of being out and equal, they achieved more than they dreamed possible.

Several pioneers from various global locations provide unique perspectives on the state of workplace equality around the world. Tracie Brind-Woody, Citi, shares her coming out experience in the United Kingdom. Adrian Balaci, European Business Forum, discusses the challenges he faces in advocating for equality in Hungary. Silvy Vluggen, IBM, is based in France and discusses her daily work to pass diversity initiatives in Southeast Asia, the Middle East, and China.

Powerful allies, from Intuit's CEO Brad Smith to the Chief Diversity Officers of Citi and Merck, relate the profound stories of how they became avid supporters for the LGBT community. They discuss the challenges they face in educating peers and managers, and share their greatest successes in advocating for equal rights.

You will also read stories of people who were bullied as youth who have become wildly successful adults living authentically and openly. Their stories serve as a true testament to the fact that *it really does get better.*

This anthology is designed to empower employees who have not yet found the courage to live and work authentically, provide guidance to Diversity and Human Resources professionals seeking to improve workplace climates, and inspire corporate leaders to continue making substantial progress toward equality at work. This volume also serves as a resource for students and allies so that they can better understand the journey of LGBT people who occupy corner offices, cubicles and work in businesses of all types and sizes.

Many thanks to the visionaries in this book who have come out boldly and shared their stories of challenges and success. May their stories inspire you and give you hope that one day everyone on the planet will be fully *Out & Equal at Work!*

Selisse Berry

Selisse Berry is Founding Executive Director of Out & Equal Workplace Advocates. Under her leadership, the organization has grown significantly with dramatic increases in attendance at the annual Workplace Summit and the expansion of programs and global initiatives. Selisse is a frequent speaker on workplace equality and has spoken across the United States and abroad including  recent conferences in London, Amsterdam, Rome, Canada, and Mexico. Her most recent awards include the Outstanding Hero Congressional Recognition from Congresswoman Nancy Pelosi; the Parks Award in Rome, Italy; and the KQED Local Heroes Award in San Francisco, California. Selisse and her wife, Cynthia Martin, live in the San Francisco Bay Area.

From the very beginning of Out & Equal, I knew how important it was to showcase high profile people to speak at our annual Workplace Summit. It took me a while to understand that adding my own voice to the discourse was essential and an important aspect of the Out & Equal Workplace Summit. Before my first speech, I struggled with self-doubt about telling my personal story. I thought the audience would expect me to know everything, including all the statistics and policies relevant to our movement.

At the same time, I knew that facts and figures often put people to sleep, but stories serve to engage and inspire. With this realization, I went from dreading public speaking to sharing from my heart: telling the story of my life, talking about the remarkable people I have met along the way and the amazing things we have accomplished together. This book is a tribute to all those who have inspired and encouraged me — and our collective stories of advancing workplace equality.

Out of the Closet and into the Seminary

The full realization that I am a lesbian came to me in my car early one morning as I was driving back to graduate school from my semester break. The good news was that I felt such relief and joy — and suddenly felt so lucky! The bad news was that the school I was heading back to was a seminary.

> **"** *In the archaic spirit of "Don't Ask, Don't Tell," I would need to hide my authentic self if I wanted to fulfill my dream.* **"**

In my first semester at San Francisco Theological Seminary, I had learned the drill: students who were lesbian, gay, bisexual, or transgender (LGBT) were essentially required to lie about their sexual orientation or gender identity if they wished to be ordained upon graduation. In the archaic spirit of "Don't Ask, Don't Tell," I would need to hide my authentic self if I wanted to fulfill my dream of working as a Presbyterian minister to better the world. My gifts, my commitment, and my passion for the ministry would be deemed meaningless without the "correct" sexual orientation. If I chose to live openly as a lesbian, my dream of ordination as a minister would be shattered.

Bible Belt Beginnings

Of course, the real beginning of my lesbian life came much earlier. Born in a small town in Oklahoma, I am the second of three daughters. My mother was an artist and a true Francophile. She loved all things French and even spent a summer in Paris when I was in middle school. Mother was a free spirit living a provincial existence. Looking back, I realize that she was essentially unhappy, and while she tried to be a good mother and do special things for her girls, nurturing didn't come naturally.

On the other hand, my sisters and I thought our Dad was perfect. He was easy-going, accepting, and adored by his daughters and his students alike. My father taught high school, and by the time I was entering middle school, he had been promoted to State Director of a vocational program, and we moved to the bigger small town of Stillwater, Oklahoma. There, I watched with admiration as he deftly organized statewide conferences for high school students.

As my parents' marriage became more difficult, Dad traveled more, and we were left to deal with our mother's increasing unpredictability. Her mental health was fragile and declined over time. I learned to create my own network of friends, my alternate family. While the battles raged at home, I had a steady stream of friends drop by to pick me up. Perhaps my passion for people finding their rightful place in the workplace — and in the world — stems in part from my own struggle to find my rightful place in my childhood home.

Eventually, my parents divorced and moved on with different lives, but each of them gave me much for which to be grateful. From my mother, I learned to love beauty and adventure, to pursue dreams, and to look beyond the picket fence to worlds unknown. From my father, I learned kindness, love, and how to work hard. They both valued spiritual awareness and believed in social justice. All those traits, to the extent that I have them, have stood me in good stead on my own path.

My network of friends and early penchant for organizational leadership inspired me to become a student leader in high school and in our Presbyterian youth group. Throughout high school, I went on many mission trips during spring breaks, but my idea of social justice may have had more to do with fitting in and having friends. In that regard, it pains me to say, I was "typical." I joined in the teenage practice of demonstrating horror for anyone who was different or "queer," one of our favorite epithets for people who did not fit into what we considered "normal."

> " My unexamined homophobia traveled with me, but so did my stowaway attractions to my boyfriends' sisters. "

I specifically remember a girl who was being fostered by one of my teachers. She dressed and behaved like a boy, and any encounter with her sent my friends and me into tizzies of giggling disgust. We even had a derogatory, if unofficial, song about "lezbifriends" that guaranteed a laugh and a nice, warm feeling of superiority in belonging to the right group. When I left Oklahoma for college in Texas, my unexamined homophobia traveled with me, but so did my stowaway attractions to my boyfriends' sisters.

Talking About Who You Love

Applying the strong work ethic I'd learned from my father, I went on to earn degrees from the University of Texas and the University of North Texas. After graduating, I taught school and worked as a guidance counselor in Dallas. I had joined an Evangelical Christian church, and I struggled over my strong crushes on women, which I tried desperately to pray away. I know now that when you are running away from yourself, you go where others say you "should" be, not necessarily where you want or need to be.

I enjoyed teaching school, but my true passion was to pursue a career in social justice. In the world where I grew up, which is part of the Bible Belt, social justice was synonymous with the church. If you wanted to work to change the world or heal society's ills, you became a minister.

So I set my sights on the seminary, where I thought I might finally find a community in which I belonged. I planned to become an ordained Presbyterian minister and hoped to make real change in the world. All my questions would be answered and my frustrations put to rest. As I headed west to pursue this dream, little did I know how dramatically my life would change.

Finally coming out to myself during my first semester in seminary left me with many more questions than answers. I spent the first two years of a four-year seminary program closeted and fearful. I dated a few women — always in secret. But I withheld my true self from most of my peers for fear of discovery by the church. The people who could and would have been my community had to be off-limits. Outwardly, I was fun-loving; I joyously embraced student life and my schoolwork. But inside, I was often lonely and anxious.

As a part of my studies, I had signed up for a program that provided opportunities to visit various urban ministries that were being run or had been started by Presbyterian ministers. There was a halfway house for women prisoners and another one for runaway youth. I elected to make one of my visits to the LGBT Center in Marin County, where I met Reverend Janie Spahr.

Unlike many of our site visits where over-worked volunteers gave quick, uninspiring tours, Janie met us with enthusiasm and joy. I remember hanging around a bit after her presentation in order to set up a time to speak with her and risk opening up a conversation about my personal situation.

To my relief, she was extremely supportive and encouraged me to visit churches and organizations that were open to the LGBT community in order to explore who I was and my place in the world. She also invited me to a women's spirituality group that she had organized. Janie would wait in her car behind my apartment building so I could slip away secretly to these affirming evenings. The group helped me eventually identify as a "Lesbyterian" and gave me the courage to begin to feel more comfortable with myself.

> " The group helped me eventually identify as a "Lesbyterian" and gave me the courage to begin to feel more comfortable with myself. "

In my third year of seminary, I was required to do an internship and secured one in Boston working with women prisoners. My first order of business in Boston was to find a place to live. Anonymity in a new city allowed me the freedom to drop by the LGBT bookstore where I saw a notice on a bulletin board for a lesbian household seeking a roommate.

I moved onto a beautiful street in Jamaica Plain and openly dated women for the first time. I became involved with a women's group and attended a Unitarian Church. It was finally okay, even wonderful, to just be me! And while my work that year with women prisoners was both illuminating and gratifying, even more rewarding was my personal experience of letting my guard down, exploring my identity, and discovering a community. With my new lesbian life, I relished a freedom I had never felt before.

> " With my new lesbian life, I relished a freedom I had never felt before. "

Perhaps the most defining moment of my time in Boston occurred during a conversation with the pastor of the Unitarian

Church I attended. I was struggling with the most pressing question that so many churches have imposed on talented, passionate and committed seminarians who do not identify as straight: Do I honestly share who I am with the church and lose my planned career completely? Or do I, as others were doing, lie about who I am in order to be ordained? The wise pastor looked at me and answered with a question that went straight to my heart and to the heart of the matter: "*Selisse, how do you plan to talk about love as a minister, if you can't talk about* **who** *you love?*"

That simple query was a wakeup call. I knew the answer at once and with intense clarity. So when it came time for me to leave Boston, I left as an out, proud lesbian. It was exhilarating and terrifying. I was more myself than I had ever been, and I was coming out to the people in my life.

> " *Selisse, how do you plan to talk about love as a minister, if you can't talk about* **who** *you love?* "

Telling My Truth

On my cross-country trip back to San Francisco for my final year in seminary, I took a circuitous route and stopped in Texas to visit my Dad and his wife, Roberta. The long hours in the car had given me plenty of time to obsess about this conversation. I tried hard to believe that no matter what the outcome, it was imperative to tell my truth.

Tense and overwhelmed by anxiety, when I got there, I simply blurted out, "I'm a lesbian." I think they were both surprised but worked hard at being understanding. I could tell that Roberta was concerned about what people would think. Dad referenced a cousin of mine who's gay and said, "If your Uncle Jack can deal with his gay son, I guess I can handle my lesbian daughter."

Both my Dad and Roberta made giant strides after that initial conversation. Years later, they surprised me by showing up at the 2003 Out & Equal Workplace Summit in Minneapolis. The prior evening, they had dined with friends and revealed their destination. Their friends were supportive and even spoke of numerous relatives and friends of their own who were lesbian and gay. That experience seemed to relieve any lingering sense of unease Roberta had about me.

When they surprised me at the hotel, we all had a wonderful time together. In fact, Roberta was a big hit in the sparkly jacket she had chosen to wear; she was constantly being stopped by gay men telling her how fabulous she looked. She and Dad also attended the 2008 Workplace Summit in Austin — a bittersweet memory, as Roberta suffered a stroke and passed away soon afterward.

As I continued my coming out process, I remember being nervous and obsessing again about the right way to tell my older sister. I planned to say either, "I date women," or "I'm a lesbian." When the right moment came, I stammered and finally said, "I date lesbians!" Not terribly smooth, but, while surprised, she was accepting, and I'm sure our happy relationship helped prepare her for her own daughter's similar announcement several years later. Unfortunately, my younger sister did not take the news as well. With her conservative political and religious views, she has never accepted me for who I am and is unhappy that our Dad is supportive of my partnership with my wife, Cynthia.

After retiring, my father left Texas and now lives near Cynthia and me in the San Francisco Bay Area. The loving man of my childhood continues to demonstrate his support for me. Recently, he was featured in a newspaper article about LGBT diversity training in retirement communities, and he spoke with evident pride about Cynthia and me and my work with Out & Equal. He makes *me* proud.

Seminary Lesbians Under Theological Stress

One of my greatest realizations after coming out as a lesbian has been that when we are comfortable with who we are, other people tend to be comfortable as well. It was my newfound ease with my lesbian identity that led me to my first organizing effort. During my last year in seminary, I came to know several out lesbians in the Graduate Theological Union. We befriended one another and talked about making a place for ourselves in the community. To that end, I began to organize lesbian gatherings. A few potlucks and bottles of wine later, we founded SLUTS: Seminary Lesbians Under Theological Stress. We were a committed constituency, but as you can imagine, rather limited in scope. It was a fun group of women, smart and creative, with whom I felt totally free to be myself. We

> **"** *When we are comfortable with who we are, other people tend to be comfortable as well.* **"**

affirmed and supported one another and talked about issues that affected the larger community. We also marched in the San Francisco LGBT Pride Parade several years in a row — wearing our "SLUTS" T-shirts, of course. I was always surprised and pleased to discover how many LGBT people had been to seminary or had a religious background in our broader community.

After earning my four-year postgraduate degree and moving toward what should have been one of my life's most joyous accomplishments, I was denied ordination as a Presbyterian minister because of my sexual orientation. Even though I had known it was coming, the official denial made me burn with frustration and disappointment. That little girl from Oklahoma still believed strongly in fairness, and this was simply unfair. I had completed the coursework and had the passion and skills to do the job, but I was denied the opportunity, simply because of who I loved.

> **❝ I had completed the coursework and had the passion and skills to do the job, but I was denied the opportunity, simply because of who I loved. ❞**

Eventually, that thoroughly educated gal got up, brushed herself off, and started looking for a new way to put all that learning and experience to work for the good of the world. I was offered the opportunity to direct a small nonprofit organization committed to lesbian visibility in mainline religious denominations. I found another part-time job with the Religious Coalition for Reproductive Choice, which advocated for women's reproductive freedom. During that time, I began dating a San Francisco attorney, and we eventually moved in together. While I had dated a number of women, she was my first real partner. Together, we created a home and a sense of family with each other and our two cats.

My bank balance may not have been impressive, but what I learned in those years provided a rich and formative basis for what was to come. I didn't know it then, but I was honing my skills as an organizer. While these part-time jobs were not quite what I'd envisioned upon entering seminary, they gave me the opportunity to learn about nonprofit administration on a shoestring budget — skills that were definitely useful in my next adventure.

A Passion for Building Bridges

Not far from my office, a promising program called Building Bridges[1] had begun to offer LGBT diversity training for nonprofit organizations supported by United Way of the Bay Area. Because of what I had gone through in seminary, the Building Bridges concept fueled a fire that had been smoldering inside me since I

---

1   See History Section

had been denied ordination. I believed in my heart that no one should ever have to go through what I did.

No one should ever have to choose between a career they love and living their life with authenticity and integrity. Building Bridges presented the opportunity for me to turn that personal passion into tangible social change. So, in 1996, when the opening for the Director position was announced, I interviewed for the position and fought hard to get it.

> **"** *No one should ever have to choose between a career they love and living their life with authenticity and integrity.* **"**

Early in my tenure as Director, I realized that the best way to ensure the success of Building Bridges — and maximize our impact on Bay Area workplaces — would be to move beyond nonprofits and offer the program to local businesses and larger companies. I began conversations with small volunteer-led organizations, Progress, Colleagues, and AGOG: A Group of Groups, and leveraged our exceptional relationship with the United Way to build a successful program that offered LGBT diversity training, provided networking events and supported LGBT employees in Fortune 1000 companies in the San Francisco Bay Area and beyond.

We spent two years involved in conversations and collaborative work. During that time, the United Way generously provided us with office space and essential support. At the Seattle Workplace Summit in 2000, we announced our merger and our new name: Out & Equal Workplace Advocates.

Creating Community

Since the beginning, Out & Equal has had its share of ups and downs, but our success has increased and the organization has grown significantly year after year. We have added staff, broadened our impact, and garnered new corporate support. As Founder and Executive Director, my role transitioned from volunteer management to executive management of full-time employees.

As a founder, letting go of "my way" and being open to what others envisioned or how they approached problem solving was difficult at first. After all, Out & Equal was in many ways my "baby," and trusting others with its care and sustenance did not come easily. At the same time, it was clear from the beginning that Out & Equal was far bigger than one person and had a life of its own. Through the years, I have worked hard to create a strong leadership team within Out & Equal, both on the staff and on our board.

Today Out & Equal has a team of over twenty staff members whose capabilities and competence exceed what I would have imagined possible when I hired my first part-time assistant in 2000. Through the years, thousands of people have participated in the Out & Equal Workplace Summits and we have seen increasing numbers of leading corporations stepping up as sponsors and partners. Each year, we've enjoyed high profile speakers and celebrity entertainment.

Yet the heart of Out & Equal lies in its daily operations: meetings, maintaining connections, email, networking, developing outreach, providing resources, community support, fundraising, and diversity training. All our activities focus on making the workplace better, safer, and fairer for the LGBT community.

I am still driven by my desire to create community, even beyond the work sphere. I think coming out is such an individual and often lonely experience. For those of us who reached adulthood before *Will & Grace*, *Ellen* and other cultural phenomena helped to smooth the way, real fear of loss continues and is too often confirmed by difficult experiences with friends and families.

I want all people, especially our constituents who spend so much of their lives at work, to be able to be themselves and have access to a wider, open community. I want them to know that they are valuable and that they are not alone. People who are not out yet are not proud of who they are and can't focus on their jobs. I know personally about the energy that gets lost in hiding

> **"I want them to know that they are valuable and that they are not alone."**

the true self — energy that could be spent feeling pride in who we are and what we bring to our work.

The Out & Equal Workplace Summits

Out & Equal is best known for the Workplace Summits, annual conferences that focus on lesbian, gay, bisexual, and transgender workplace equality. Bringing together participants from the United States and — increasingly — abroad, they're unifying, heartening events that offer training, networking, and support for allies and LGBT employees at every company level. Well-known celebrities and business leaders deliver keynote speeches to a warm and supportive audience.

The Out & Equal Workplace Summits started out small, with our first national Summit in Atlanta in 1999. I was the only paid staff person in the mix, with everyone else doing this as their "night job." We relied on a network of phenomenal volunteers from the corporate world who had a real understanding of customer service. There was a buoyant sense of camaraderie. We were all in it together, doing something bigger than all of us.

We spent most of a year working together on the phone. This was before the emergence of social media, so although we'd spent hours in conference calls, none of us knew what each other looked like. Arriving in Atlanta, we finally clapped eyes on each other for the first time, and it was, "Oh, I thought you'd be tall with dark hair!"

Another aspect of those early days that now seems quaint was that most people would register for events by sending checks, and if they wanted to put the expense on a credit card, they would tell me their credit card number over the phone, digit by digit. I'd walk down the hall to United Way's finance department, enter the number manually and shred the receipts to maintain privacy. Just another part of hands-on organizing.

Prepping for the event also meant I had to conquer my fears and learn how to ask for sponsorships. I still remember the excitement of landing our first sponsor in 1999. That year, HP and one community organization supported us as our first conference exhibitors, and we simply had the hotel bring out two tables to set them up. It's amazing to think back — now that we have over a hundred exhibitors, sometimes with cars and airplanes on display.

About two hundred people attended our first Summit, and we started to build momentum. When attendance exceeded five hundred, I knew our vision was becoming a reality. Since our 2007 conference in Washington, D.C., registration numbers have exceeded two thousand. With significant growth in attendance, hotels began wooing us. Suddenly I began seeing my name and "Welcome Out & Equal" on the marquee of the Convention and Visitor's Bureau when I visited a potential venue.

> **"Since our 2007 conference, registration numbers have exceeded two thousand."**

One of the many outstanding dimensions of the Summit is being able to meet iconic people like Billie Jean King, Ann Richards, and George Takei. We typically invite featured celebrities to sign books or autographs, and attendees line up to talk to them. The speakers have always been very impressed with the warmth and support of the audience and with the number of LGBT people and allies who have gathered together.

Every year, people tell me that their lives have been changed by the Summit. There are a number of couples who first met at the Summit, and many people have come out through Out & Equal. I can think of one instance where an executive learned that his company was one of our major sponsors. He researched their involvement, came to a conference, and then felt safe to come out at work — after many years in the closet at his company. People's first Summit experience is often very powerful, and because they've had an experience in which they're no longer an isolated minority, they're very proud to be able to bring their colleagues and senior executives to the Summit.

> " Every year, people tell me that their lives have been changed by the Summit. "

Making a Global Impact

From early on, I knew that it would be imperative to expand our work beyond the United States. I was committed to having a global presence for a number of reasons. For one thing, our constituents requested it. But even more importantly, I believe we have a duty to help change the world for lesbian, gay, bisexual, and transgender people who live in parts of the world where homosexuality is still a crime. If

> " I believe we have a duty to help change the world for lesbian, gay, bisexual, and transgender people who live in parts of the world where homosexuality is still a crime. "

we could start by improving the work environment for LGBT employees around the world — and ensuring that global companies offer LGBT-friendly policies in their global divisions and businesses — then we could begin to effect broader cultural change.

Every year, global participation in our Summits continues to increase. More and more of our constituents are asking for advice about best practices in the global arena. More business leaders are asking about the best ways to roll out global policies and what to do, for example, to protect an LGBT employee being offered an assignment in a country with local anti-LGBT laws. Our way of providing best practices guidance has always been to find people who have expertise and bring them together. In 2010, we started a Global Advisory Committee and held our first meeting during the Out & Equal Workplace Summit in Los Angeles. We developed a thoughtful discussion among corporate participants with input from members of various nonprofit LGBT advocacy groups.

> **❝ More business leaders are asking about the best ways to roll out global policies and what to do, for example, to protect an LGBT employee being offered an assignment in a country with local anti-LGBT laws. ❞**

In the summer of 2011, we gathered in Rome for the LGBT Business Forum. During the Global Advisory Committee meeting it was determined that Out & Equal would be the leading convener of the LGBT Workplace Summit coinciding with World Pride in London in 2012. We were daunted, but up for the challenge.

I have met many incredible people in Asia, Europe, Africa, Latin America, and other regions who want to organize but are often the only openly lesbian, gay, bisexual, or transgender people in their companies. The challenges they face are tremendous, and our goal is to support them and stand with them in this important work.

> **"** *The challenges they face are tremendous, and our goal is to support them and stand with them in this important work.* **"**

Global Summit in London

One step in that direction was our 2012 Global LGBT Workplace Summit in London. From our hotel, we could look across the Thames towards Big Ben or upriver to the London Eye. The first night we held a dinner at the House of Lords, a centuries-old building and the upper house of Parliament. Propertied, white, presumably straight men have been making significant decisions there for hundreds of years, and there we were with our LGBT and ally conferees, listening to keynote speaker, Anna Grodzka, the first openly transgender member of Poland's Parliament — and the third nationally elected transgender politician in the world.

Some of the highlights of the Global Summit included an onstage interview with Martina Navratilova and keynote speeches by Harry van Dorenmalen, Chairman of IBM Europe. During lunch, people talked about how the business community can influence the broader society, especially in countries that still criminalize homosexuality and the importance of civil society organizations working with the private sector to engage in dialogue, especially in the Middle East, Asia, and Africa.

> **"** *We had a wonderful Gala, and afterwards people were dancing in the aisles not wanting the experience to end.* **"**

In session after session, there was such a buzz in the room. People were excited to be there, networking and enthusiastically discussing the workshops, speakers and entertainers. We had a wonderful Gala, and afterwards people were dancing in the aisles not wanting the experience to end.

The Work That's Left to Do

Of course, my ultimate hope is that by organizing LGBT employees and allies within companies around the world, Out & Equal will have an impact not only on the workplace, but also on the surrounding social climate. When the international business community refuses to build facilities and make investments in nations that criminalize LGBT individuals, we will begin to see change that promises to help realize our dream of true global equality.

> " We will begin to see change that promises to help realize our dream of true global equality. "

In our San Francisco office, we are encouraged daily to carry out our mission by the presence of our colleague, Danny Katende. Danny was born in Uganda. When he realized he was gay, his family disowned him, yet he went on to become an outspoken advocate for LGBT rights in an unwelcoming country.

In 2009, an anti-gay Evangelical Christian organization from the United States collaborated with Ugandans who wanted to outlaw homosexuality. They paid the media to start exposing members of the LGBT community. Danny was publicly outed by a newspaper that published his name and photograph. Danny continued to speak out, even on the radio, in an effort to educate people. After leaving a radio station one day, he was kidnapped at gunpoint by security officials, beaten and tortured for three days, and left for dead on a roadside, simply because he's gay.

A courageous soul took Danny to the hospital, and when released, he escaped to a refugee camp in Kenya. Later granted refugee status by the United Nations High Commissioner for Refugees, he eventually moved to San Francisco and now works with us at Out & Equal. Danny reminds us that there are men and women in similar jeopardy all over the world, and it is for them that Out & Equal demands justice.

I grew up during the American Civil Rights movement and saw broadcast coverage of people being beaten and arrested because they stood up to demand fairness and dignity. My parents instilled in me that fairness and equality is worth standing up for.

Both here and abroad, I believe the civil rights movement for the LGBT community is about having the freedom to be who we are and to love who we love. That is the message and the mission of Out & Equal. One day soon, the efforts that we are making now will reach places like Iran and Uganda, so that our lesbian, gay, bisexual, and transgender brothers and sisters will be able to live their lives with integrity, hope, and freedom.

> **The civil rights movement for the LGBT community is about having the freedom to be who we are and to love who we love.**

In 2011, I was honored to be invited to give a keynote speech at the LGBT Hungarian Business Forum in Budapest, another relatively conservative setting. During my speech, I introduced my lovely wife, Cynthia, to the audience. I spoke about workplace equality, and when it was time for the Q&A, all anyone wanted to discuss was that I had used the word "wife" to introduce Cynthia. They had not heard that language used before for LGBT couples and were amazed and delighted to even consider the possibility that the dream of real equality could one day come true. Many of their questions were about our wedding and what it felt like to

> **"** Together we are working toward the day when marriage equality will be a reality everywhere. **"**

be legally married. Together we are working toward the day when marriage equality will be a reality everywhere.

My Lovely Wife, Cynthia

I met Cynthia Martin at a national LGBT business council meeting in 1999. She was representing Kodak, and I was there with Out & Equal. It was a dry meeting on a stifling day in an inadequately ventilated room. I remember wondering if there was anyone fun in the room, and that's when I noticed Cynthia. We sat together at dinner that evening. We were both in relationships at the time, but we really enjoyed each other's company.

In 2001, we reconnected at the LGBT leadership program at the University of California, Los Angeles. A month later, Cynthia and I both spoke at a *Reaching Out* conference for LGBT MBA

> **"** My lesbian niece and Cynthia's gay nephew spoke and contributed to the magic of the celebration. **"**

students in San Francisco. I was single then and soon learned that she was, too. We began a long-distance relationship, as she was living in Rochester, New York, and I was in San Francisco. That fall, Cynthia took an early retirement from Kodak and moved to the Bay Area so that we could be together.

Cynthia and I decided to celebrate our relationship with a commitment ceremony in 2007. My dad had just had a stroke, and her dad had undergone heart surgery, so we felt the timing to be somewhat urgent. My lesbian niece, Mandy, and Cynthia's gay nephew, Kirk, spoke and contributed to the magic of the celebration. Reverend Janie Spahr, who has been a mentor and friend, performed a beautiful ceremony for us, surrounded by friends and family. Of course, we had no idea that marriage equality would be legalized in the state of California just one year after our commitment ceremony. On our first anniversary, we married again in 2008 in San Francisco City Hall. I initially thought the legal wedding would feel redundant, but I was quite moved by the historic nature of this basic human right.

In that simple ceremony, we shared a victory not just with our closest friends, but also on behalf of all loving souls who had been denied this basic right for so many centuries. While our gathering was small, it felt as though there were hundreds of people there smiling with us.

> **In that simple ceremony, we shared a victory not just with our closest friends, but also on behalf of all loving souls who had been denied this basic right for so many centuries.**

The fact that Cynthia and I met doing this work means a great deal to me. In addition to being the love of my life, she has substantial experience as a corporate leader and as an activist, and her wealth of knowledge has enriched my role with Out & Equal immeasurably and has made me a better leader. She understands the corporate culture, and she shares my passion for justice. Cynthia also appreciates my gift and need for community, and together we have brought that gift into our home.

Our community includes many of the extraordinary people Out & Equal has brought into our lives. We have a "chosen" family in which we give and receive a sense of belonging — the belonging I dreamed of as a girl, as a disenfranchised seminarian, and as a young adult struggling to find her place in the world. In so many ways, with Cynthia, our friends, and our extended family, I feel like I have come home.

Coming Home to Ourselves

In my keynote address at the 2011 Summit in Dallas, I spoke about coming home… to a place, to a community, to ourselves.

> " I spoke about coming home… to a place, to a community, to ourselves. "

To some degree, I believe the journey home is part of all of our stories, and it certainly lies at the heart of mine. Since I was a small girl growing up in the red hills of Oklahoma, I have sought the kind of meaning and connectedness one can only find in a loving, supportive community. Now, I not only have that sense of community in my own life, but I am also privileged to do the work of helping bring it to the wider world.

> " We really are changing the world, one cubicle, one workplace, and one corner office at a time. "

With each new success Out & Equal celebrates, and with each new challenge we take on, we remain true to our vision of workplace equality for all and to our belief in a committed community that is far greater than the sum of its parts. As we all work together, we really are changing the world, one cubicle, one workplace, and one corner office at a time.

Brad Smith

Brad Smith became Intuit's president and chief executive officer in January 2008, capping a five-year rise through the company in which he successfully led several of its major businesses. Intuit is a leading provider of business and financial management solutions for small and mid-sized businesses, financial institutions, consumers, and accounting professionals, and the company is consistently ranked as one of the most-admired software companies and best places to work. Smith joined Intuit in February of 2003, having previously served as the senior vice president of marketing and business development at ADP, as well as holding various sales, marketing, and general management positions with Pepsi, Seven-Up, and Advo, Inc.

> *"You're probably wondering what a white male from West Virginia knows about diversity. I asked the same thing when I was asked to join Intuit's Diversity Council, a cross-functional team focused on creating a shared understanding of diversity. But I recalled a moment early in my career when an employer*

sent me to a communications school to drill the West Virginia accent out of me. They thought it would be good for business. But I was being asked to hide a part of who I am. I've maintained the accent as well as an appreciation for individual talents and contributions. Throughout the years, I've heard many similar stories of hiding from ourselves, especially from the lesbian, gay, bisexual and transgender community."

—Keynote speech, 2010 Out & Equal Workplace Summit

I became an ally when I was twelve years old when a close friend confided to me that he was gay. We lived in a close-knit, small community in West Virginia with a population of about thirty one hundred. I suspect that number includes the cows and horses. My friend and I spent a lot of time together, riding bikes, watching movies, playing in the neighborhood. Assumptions were made. Ignorant comments were thrown around. And let's face it: the preteen years are already pretty rough. I didn't know what to say or how to respond.

My parents helped me find the answer. They valued diversity and difference and taught me that we are all equal, regardless of our gender, our skin color, our sexual orientation or our religion. My father used to say that he believed in the Elvis Presley religion: he was going to wear one of everything around his neck and not be kept out of heaven on politics.[1]

My father sat me down one day for a serious discussion about my friend. "At this point in your life, Brad, you are going to have to make a decision," he said. "Do you want to spend your energy protecting your image and worrying about what others think? Or

---

[1] Elvis constructed "a personalized religion out of what he'd read of Hinduism, Judaism, numerology, theosophy, mind control, positive thinking and Christianity." Steve Turner, *Hungry for Heaven*, (Westmont, Illinois: InterVarsity Press, 1995) p. 143.

do you want to defend the friendship that you value?" The choice was easy. I stood by my friend — and continue to stand by him decades later.

Work eventually led me away from West Virginia, but the experience I'd had when I was just twelve years old gave me great insight and has helped shape how I lead a global company. At Intuit, diversity and inclusion is part of our DNA. We celebrate and respect our differences. We foster a safe culture where employees can bring their whole selves to work. I'm proud of our ten employee networks, started through grassroots efforts in 2002, which harness our diversity to connect with each other, our customers and the marketplace. Diversity, inclusion and diversity of thought build better outcomes.

Here's an example. In 2007, our TurboTax team was committed to creating a product to address the needs of the growing number of same-sex couples. Many of these people lived in states that recognized their union and allowed them to file as married on their state tax returns. But they were still required to file as single on their federal returns. Volunteers from our Pride Network provided the feedback and insight we needed to fine-tune the domestic partner section in our TurboTax products. This partnership between a business unit and an employee network demonstrates the value that diversity of thought brings to the workplace.

I had a similar experience a few years later as I prepared my 2010 keynote speech at the Out & Equal Workplace Summit. Christie Hardwick, founder of Spirited Contribution, joined me and many Intuit LGBT employees in a candid discussion about their experiences.

Many shared how it felt to live or work in environments where they had to filter their self-expression and self-presentation on a daily basis. Some of them were not out of the closet. They also had to avoid inviting the people they loved to special occasions related to work because they did not feel safe. Their stories broadened my perspective. I heard how some people faced discrimination from their former employers, friends, and even their families.

It was a powerful session, one that heightened my awareness of the issues facing the LGBT community. I was honored that these employees had the courage to share their stories openly without fear of repercussion. It reinforced my commitment as an ally and as an executive to continue to make Intuit a comfortable environment where we can unite in our similarities and respect our differences, be it West Virginia dialect like mine or sexual orientation.

I also discovered that when we relate our personal struggles to the challenges of other communities, we develop a deeper understanding of their experiences and become advocates because we know that we can make a difference. Allies can use their voices to help people reconsider their belief systems.

> " Allies can use their voices to help people reconsider their belief systems. "

We have seen some great progress at Intuit. We began by thinking about diversity. Over time, we realized that diversity has led to an even more powerful outcome: inclusion. The result has been a strong cohesion across the company. Some employees participate in more than one employee network. I've seen members of the Christian network attend Muslim network events, and I've witnessed some members of the religious networks attend the LGBT network as allies. This reflects an increased awareness and empathy. We have also seen some dual memberships that indicate the variety of identities each of us can have, as Latin American and Christian, or LGBT and Muslim or Christian, for example.

I still see being an ally the same way that I did when I was twelve years old: it means being a human being and a good friend who fully accepts the people I care about. I'm proud to be an ally for the lesbian, gay, bisexual, and transgender community. I've stood up for a childhood friend, and I've stood up to the vocal minority who were against the creation of a Pride Network at Intuit. I encourage other allies in the workplace to be authentic. Create a culture where employees can be themselves. Engage employees, so they can't imagine working anywhere else. And above all else, don't be afraid to do the right thing.

> **"** *Create a culture where employees can be themselves. Engage employees, so they can't imagine working anywhere else. And above all else, don't be afraid to do the right thing.* **"**

Kayla Shell

Kayla Shell is the Executive Legal Director for Dell's Commercial Business Unit. Since 1998, she has managed several Dell legal teams and served on executive management staffs supporting sales, IT solutions, marketing, advertising, and e-commerce. She previously worked for Shell Oil Company in Houston, Texas. For several years, Kayla co-chaired the Executive Advisory Board of Pride, Dell's lesbian, gay, bisexual, and transgender (LGBT) employee resource group. During Kayla's leadership of Pride, Dell became an Out & Equal Summit sponsor and consistently scored 100% on the Human Rights Campaign's Corporate Equality Index. Kayla is currently the Vice Chair of Equality Texas and previously served as President of the Out & Equal Board of Directors. Kayla and her partner, Randi Shade, recently won HRC Austin's Bettie Naylor Courage Award. Kayla and Randi live in Austin, Texas, with their two children.

I remember first hearing about the gay rights movement when I was in the third grade. My hometown, Hamburg, Arkansas, is a small town of about three thousand residents. My family has lived and run a family farm there for more than three generations now. Growing up, I did not know any gay people, but I remember certain friends being called "sissies" who were later rumored to be gay. I also heard some negative comments at church, as I recall, but not much more than that. I learned more about the gay movement from reading *Time* magazine and newspapers. So I knew at an early age what "gay" was, but rarely encountered any gay people in my small town. I realized when I was a teenager that I was different, but I thought that I should just keep it to myself. I had boyfriends. My mother told me once that she overheard someone calling me a "dyke"

> " *I realized when I was a teenager that I was different, but I thought that I should just keep it to myself.* "

when I was playing in a tennis tournament. I remember thinking that was weird, since I had never told anyone that I thought I was a lesbian.

I finally came out to my family in my early thirties. It was gut-wrenching and terrifying for me, but my mother said, "You are our daughter. We love you, and we don't want this to impact our relationship at all." My parents are my best friends, and telling them the truth about my life was very liberating. I was working for Shell Oil at the time. My mother urged me not to say anything to my colleagues, because she knew how hard I had worked to get there, and she was concerned that being openly gay would hurt my career. I followed her advice, which was given out of concern and love.

I became an in-house attorney with Shell Oil in Houston, Texas, right out of law school. The first three years of my career were a blur, because I did nothing but work. At some point, I realized that I had some extra time to devote to my personal life.

I had a lesbian friend who was also in the closet, and we started to venture out into the social scene in Houston.

I was never out of the closet at Shell Oil, but I was out of the closet from day one when I joined Dell. I simply decided that if my coworkers wanted to know me personally, then they would also know that I was a lesbian. I was completely accepted, and it turned out that some of my coworkers were also gay men and lesbians.

In 2001 when I returned from an expatriate assignment in Europe, I joined Dell's newly formed LGBT employee resource group, Pride: Partnering for Respect of Individuality in the Dell Environment. In 2003, Dell decided to drive more executive involvement across all employee resource groups (ERGs). The leadership team established an Executive Advisory Board for each ERG. Trisa Thompson, one of Dell's Legal Vice Presidents, suggested to the Chief Diversity Officer, Thurmond Woodard, that he invite me to serve on the Pride Executive Advisory Board and help build the Board. I was the only executive at Dell who was out and willing to serve at that time. Since I have always been an introvert, I had never considered taking on a leadership role with Pride. I agreed to do it, however, because I realized that I was the only openly gay executive willing to serve and felt that if I stepped up, others would, too.

I recommended that we involve allies to fill the other Executive Advisory Board (EAB) positions in order to build broad support for Pride. I served as the Chair of the EAB, and we had a lot of success in those early years. We expanded our internal EEOC policy to include sexual orientation and gender identity. Dell signed up to support the federal all-inclusive Employment Non-discrimination Act. We developed a toolkit for HR professionals to help our transgender employees through transitions. We also expanded our health benefits for

> **It is so important for all of us — now and in the future — to be treated equally.**

transgender employees. We have had eight consecutive years of 100 percent scores on the HRC CEI. We were able to enact progressive policies that supported LGBT employees and were essential for establishing expectations for how employees should behave at work and for demonstrating that Dell values diversity.

It was not hard to get these policies enacted at Dell, but it is hard to change worksite culture and to create acceptance. We continue to work to ensure that we are creating a respectful and accepting workplace. While I can get tired and feel that progress is slow, I remind myself of how many great things have happened and why it is so important for all of us — now and in the future — to be treated equally. We have to keep working, keep pushing, and keep talking, because to me, equality is not a "nice to have," but a "must have." Equality does not just happen. We have to work for it every day.

> *Equality does not just happen. We have to work for it every day.*

The work that we have done through employee resource groups like Pride has made a huge difference. Employee resource groups have been on the forefront and instrumental in creating workplaces in Corporate America that are welcoming environments. Most of Corporate America now says, "Yes, we want LGBT employees. We want the best and brightest people." Many companies have made it easier for people to be out and open; consequently, more people know coworkers who are LGBT. This has increased acceptance in the United States. Knowing and working with people who are different and who come from different backgrounds help create an accepting and respectful environment, both at work and in our communities.

We have learned that engaging allies is one of the best ways to improve the workplace climate. Teaching allies to use — and model — more respectful and accurate language is a great tool.

We took a great idea from Out & Equal and developed placards for cubicles that say, "Dell is an Out & Equal workplace." The placards provide allies with tips on how to interact with LGBT employees and how to show their support for the LGBT community. Allies were encouraged to place the placards in their cubes, so that LGBT employees would know they could come out to that person if they wanted to do so. We also have made sure to invite our allies to workshops and panels around LGBT diversity issues.

> " Each person who is out of the closet at work has an immense impact on everyone in the organization. "

Each person who is out of the closet at work has an immense impact on everyone in the organization. Being open about my sexual orientation has allowed me to share my experiences with executives all across the company. I have made presentations to Michael Dell, Founder and CEO of Dell, and have also discussed LGBT issues directly with other executives. Dell has been very supportive of my serving on the board of Out & Equal Workplace Advocates and my work for LGBT equality.

Being a leader for workplace equality has contributed to my success at Dell. The leadership role that I took within the Pride group taught me to speak up more easily and helped me become comfortable speaking to large groups of people. The importance of the message overrode my natural reticence and my reluctance to speak publicly.

More than anything else, my family inspires me to make a difference. My partner of nearly ten years, Randi Shade, campaigned for election to the Austin City Council — with our children and me very publicly at her side. Randi was the first openly gay person elected to the Austin City Council. People ask Randi what her strategy was to run publicly as a lesbian, and she replies that our strategy is to live our lives openly and honestly. If people have an issue with our relationship and family, then we hope that we demonstrate that their issues are non-issues. We received very few negative comments or slurs except from "anonymous" bloggers who were obviously trying to be controversial or were too embarrassed to use their real names.

We have had a supportive experience living in Austin. Our six-year-old son and four-year-old daughter go to school and take classes in the community. The staff at these places has always been very accepting and accommodating. They recognize that today's children have all kinds of families. We have not had any issues with other parents, either. Our children have playdates, kids come to our house, and we socialize with other parents, gay and straight alike.

I am very lucky to have such a beautiful family and supportive community. Sometimes I look back on those years before I came out and realize that it has been an amazing journey. I consider myself a late bloomer. I could look back and wish that I had been out sooner, but we all have different journeys and learn to accept and be who we are at different times.

In my hometown of Hamburg, Arkansas, our community of friends has been incredibly supportive of my family and me over the years. When our son, Ethan was born, our friends in Hamburg hosted a baby shower for us. I put together the list of friends to be invited based upon whether I thought they would be comfortable coming to the baby shower — probably the first baby shower ever in Hamburg for two mommies. For a year after the shower, my mother would see people who would ask why they had not been invited.

" I decided that if I could speak up at work and talk to executives about LGBT issues, then I could learn to use my voice to speak before the state legislature. "

Obviously, the list that I had made was too short. Clearly, small-town Arkansas is no longer what it was when I was in the third grade.

For many years, I focused my direct participation in the LGBT equality movement at work. Now, I am committed to help change happen by participating directly in the broader political process by advocating for changes in federal and state law. Many laws in Texas are not supportive of our community and certainly not LGBT families. I decided that if I could speak up at work and talk to executives about LGBT issues, then I could learn to use my voice to speak before the state legislature and contribute to changing public opinion in a broader way.

For instance, Texas laws do not allow same-gender parents to be recorded on a birth certificate. Randi gave birth to both of our children, and I was able to do a second parent adoption. Although I am their legal parent now, too, Randi's name is the only one on their birth certificates. Your birth certificate follows you throughout life and is required in many situations to prove who you are. Our children deserve to be protected and have an accurate record of their birth and who their parents are. Randi and I are working to have the law changed by writing to state legislators and regularly testifying in front of the Texas Legislature's public health committee.

Through Equality Texas, I am also working to pass an all-inclusive state employment nondiscrimination act in 2013. I am working on these issues with Anne Wynne, the first straight ally to chair Equality Texas, and other committed LGBT leaders and allies in Texas. We are working to form a statewide business alliance with Dell and other major corporations with brand names in order to demonstrate to the public at-large and, in turn, state legislators that equality is good business and good for the state.

Sadly, Texas passed a constitutional amendment in 2005 defining marriage as between only a man and a woman. We are trying to form coalitions, raise money, and prepare to repeal this unfortunate, discriminatory amendment so that we can truly make a difference in Texas. In a recent Equality Texas poll, results showed that people are moving quickly to adopt a favorable stance towards marriage equality and employment nondiscrimination — even in Texas. However, the laws currently on the books do not reflect these public views. Again, you have to work for equality.

I am very grateful for organizations like Out & Equal that are working to bring workplace equality to companies across the United States and abroad. Being part of the Out & Equal network and having the opportunity to learn and discuss LGBT issues with other openly gay corporate leaders has been one of the greatest experiences I have had that supports the work that I do for equality. I am grateful for the opportunity to learn from other corporate leaders.

It is so important to work for change. If we do not ask for change, there will never be any progress. It is amazing how many people become supportive and engaged when they are invited to make a difference. I found my voice at Dell because of the diverse and accepting environment here. I am inspired by my coworkers and by having mentors like Selisse Berry, the Founding Executive Director of Out & Equal, Christie Hardwick of Spirited Contribution, and Anne

> " It is amazing how many people become supportive and engaged when they are invited to make a difference. "

Wynne, the founder of Atticus Circle. I am very lucky to be supported by family, friends, and Dell, so that I can try to make a difference and work for LGBT equality each and every day.

George A. Kalogridis

As president of the Disneyland Resort, George Kalogridis oversees a workforce of twenty-three thousand Cast Members at the five hundred-acre resort, which comprises the world-famous Disneyland Park, Disney California Adventure Park, the Disneyland Hotel, Disney's Grand Californian Hotel & Spa, the Paradise Pier Hotel, and Downtown Disney. George is active in the local community and currently serves on the Out & Equal Board of Directors, CHOC Children's Hospital of Orange County Board of Directors, and the University of California, Irvine Paul Merage School of Business Dean's Advisory Board. George lives in Orange County, California, with his partner, Andy, whom he met in 2000 at Disney.

My career at Disney began in a seemingly endless line in the sweltering heat of central Florida. It was 1971, and I had just finished high school. I needed a job to support me through college. Walt Disney World was opening soon and had set up a group of trailers in a cleared-out palmetto thicket to process job applications for a massive recruitment drive. The line stretched for miles, full of hopeful applicants waiting to get into a trailer and obtain a card to mail back to Disney in hopes of an interview. The Apollo Space Program had just concluded, and thousands of people had been laid off. The guy in front of me and the guy behind me were both engineers who had recently lost their jobs.

So, I thought to myself, here were two men who had just sent people to the moon, and I had just finished high school. I imagined that my odds of getting a job were pretty slim, but I took my chances and waited in that line. I finally got the card and filled it out. A couple of weeks later, I received a call for an interview. The interviewer looked at my last name and said, "You must be Greek. You'd probably be good in food and beverage." Today a comment like that would be completely inappropriate, but at the time I was just thrilled to get a job.

The next thing you know, I'm working as a busboy, and a whole new world was opening up for me at Disney. Not only had I started a job that would turn into a career, but I was gaining my first exposure to people from all over the country. Most important, I encountered other gay people. Before I met gay colleagues at Disney, I didn't even know what the word "gay" meant, and I certainly didn't know any gay people. I knew something was different about me, but I didn't know how to define it.

I met my first partner at Disney in 1977, and we moved in together. We didn't announce anything, but we didn't hide our relationship either. I would take him to company events all the time, but we both worked for Disney, so it didn't really raise any eyebrows. My coworkers were part of the entertainment industry, and sexual orientation wasn't an issue from a social perspective. However, sexual orientation definitely wasn't discussed from a business angle during the seventies.

The first time it came to light that everyone at work was aware that I'm gay occurred during the late nineties. I was working at Walt Disney World at the time and in a meeting with the president of our division and a lot of senior executives. In the middle of the meeting, the president pulled the VP of public affairs and me aside to tell me that the company was very concerned for my personal safety. Organizers were gearing up for the annual Orlando Gay Days event and several right-wing Christian groups were planning to protest with roadblocks. Disney security became aware of a message posted on a website belonging to an extreme-right Christian group, advertising the fact that I was gay and telling people how to get into my office. At the time, entry was only through a backstage area, past a specific number of doors and along a secured path that could only be navigated with precise instructions.

The overwhelming support I received from Disney touched me. In response to this threat, the president said, "George, first of all, you need to know that the company will not tolerate this kind of activity happening to any cast member. We're going to support you 100 percent, and you have nothing to worry about." Because police officers had to be stationed outside of my office for a while, I had to have a conversation with my colleagues explaining the situation. There were no surprises. People were infuriated that someone would put a coworker in danger. We found out that a Disney cast member had shared the information, and he was fired on the spot. He filed a grievance with the employee's union, but the union refused to pursue it because his actions were illegal and because he had put another employee in danger.

> **"** The overwhelming support I received from Disney touched me. The president said, We're going to support you 100 percent. **"**

The local sheriff also stated that there would be a zero tolerance policy for any violence. His response demonstrated an important evolution in the local community. At first, people had been somewhat resistant to the idea of Gay Days. By the late nineties, the entire Orlando area had realized that a quarter of a million people were attending the event and spending a lot of money over the course of three or four days. The business case far outweighed any potential homophobia.

By 2011, when we aired our Disney *It Gets Better* video, I received hundreds of emails from employees from throughout The Walt Disney Company expressing that they now felt like they had the courage to be able to come out at work. It makes me proud that Walt Disney Parks and Resorts is leading the way in this regard. The company has certainly made it clear that we do not tolerate discrimination. I remember in the seventies and early eighties, the word "faggot" was in frequent use. If that happened in the business environment today, the person would be fired. There really is zero tolerance for homophobia, or any other type of discrimination for that matter.

> *"The company has certainly made it clear that we do not tolerate discrimination."*

We've worked really hard to address the different dimensions of diversity and have committed to create diverse applicant pools from which all hiring decisions are made. We have diversity resource groups in various locations across our company, and we work hard to ensure their voices are heard, and we rely on them for counsel on many business decisions that affect the diverse populations we serve, as well as decisions that affect them.

What's fascinating about our business is that we welcome our guests into our house every day. As the faces of our guests change, we need to continue to focus on ensuring that we're aware of that changing dynamic and to keep providing content and experiences that are important to them. This is really important to us.

Disney has accomplished so much since the 1970s in bringing equality to the workplace, and I know that we will continue expanding our diversity and inclusion initiatives for all communities.

My career with Disney over the last 40 years has been a journey and an enriching learning experience. When I think of my first role as a busboy, and the evolution of my career, it helps me to never forget what was important to me during those early days. This helps me better understand the needs of my cast members. I look back on the security threat I faced in the early nineties and the way that it pushed me into coming out at work, and I am so thankful for the support and acceptance I've received from my colleagues at Disney. As we continue working toward equality in the workplace and beyond, it is so important for us to remember our similarities and the things that tie us together within the human community. As Maya Angelou said in *Human Family*, "We are more alike, my friends, than we are unalike."

> " When I think of my first role as a busboy, and the evolution of my career, it helps me to never forget what was important to me during those early days. "

Bobby Wilkinson

Bobby Wilkinson is an Executive Director of Client Marketing at USAA Insurance. Prior to that, he served as the Head of the California Zone Marketing Department at State Farm Insurance. Bobby has led a very successful career, is openly gay, and mentors other employees in coming out at work. Bobby was active in State Farm's LGBT employee resource group and guided State Farm California in creating marketing strategies and tactics specifically tailored to the lesbian, gay, bisexual, and transgender community. He currently serves on the Out & Equal Board of Directors.

I grew up in a tiny town of two thousand people in the Bible Belt of Kentucky, where my grandfather was the Deacon and my grandmother played the piano at one of the only Black churches in the community. Growing up African American in a predominantly White community wasn't all that bad because my neighborhood was mostly Black. What was more challenging was growing up knowing that I was different than the other guys. I've always been an extrovert and made friends easily, so while many of my friends were White, I had two very close African American friends, and the three of us melted into our town, mostly by being involved in sports. I loved going fishing with my grandfather, playing baseball and riding skateboards with my friends.

> " I grew up in a tiny town of two thousand people in the Bible Belt of Kentucky, where my grandfather was the Deacon and my grandmother played the piano at one of the only Black churches in the community. "

My mom, dad and grandma worked together at a furniture production company for most of my time in elementary school. My mom and grandma were seamstresses who made the cushions and pillows for the couches. My dad worked in the furniture framing production area, building furniture. My parents also opened a side business in our garage, where they reupholstered old furniture.

In 8th grade, I had my first crush on a guy, and something inside of me told me it was "wrong." I tried to suppress those feelings and like girls. Of course, that wasn't successful. It was a difficult realization for me to digest because it was so far from the norm in our community. I had no idea how my friends and family would react, and so I kept this secret to myself for a very long time. I can't think of another kid I grew up with who was gay. By the time I finished high school, I had become convinced that I could push my feelings for other men aside, and I became engaged to a very dear friend of mine. I cared deeply for her, but realized after some time that I really was gay, and so I broke off our engagement. I didn't tell anyone why I made this decision, and I moved to a different state. Twenty years later, I reconnected with my ex-fiancée and explained what I had been going through during those years. Amazingly, she was more than understanding of my situation.

I joined State Farm twenty years ago in a minority internship program. One of my early mentors was the first African American man who had made it to our Chairman's Council, State Farm's executive management team that oversees all operations. A few years later, I fell in love with a man who worked at State Farm, and we moved in together. I wanted to share this beautiful part of my life with my family, and so I brought him home for Christmas and family reunions. My relatives and I never had a clear discussion about my relationship with this man, but they understood that he was more than my roommate. I introduced him to some of my friends as my partner. They accepted us completely and told me that I should have told them earlier because they already knew I was gay. I felt so relieved and blessed that the closest people in my life supported me. I wished that I had shared our relationship with all of my friends earlier.

> **They accepted us completely and told me that I should have told them earlier because they already knew I was gay.**

Even though I had a very positive experience with my family and friends, I wasn't sure how people at work would react to my sexual orientation, and so I kept it to myself for some time. I thought that this part of me had nothing to do with my work. The truth is, though, that before I came out at work, I was keeping my partner and an important part of myself hidden. I was afraid to share my whole self.

I had a strong foundational start at State Farm, working in the Claims Department. Then in 1998, State Farm hired an executive from outside of the company as Vice President of Advertising. She became my mentor and friend, and she later asked me to join the marketing team. I knew she was an ally of the LGBT community, and so I came out to her before I accepted the job offer. I felt some comfort in knowing that she was an ally. I didn't know how other people at her level in the organization would react, but she guided me through the process, telling me to be myself and deliver a sound work product. She taught me that doing great work and building your personal brand are the two most important things; the rest will take care of itself.

I had a very visible position, interacting with some of State Farm's most senior executives. My partner at the time would travel to events with me, and in the slow process of introducing him to my colleagues, I came out at work. Once the burden of hiding who I am was lifted, I could be myself and deliver stronger results and be a much better leader. I was pleasantly surprised at the level to which people were accepting of my partner and me. Over the past thirteen years that I've been out at work, I have not encountered a single person who has rejected me for being gay. My only regret is that I wasn't open with more people earlier. There is such power in being authentic and sharing our individual stories.

> " Once the burden of hiding who I am was lifted, I could be myself and deliver stronger results and be a much better leader. "

Even though I'm open about my sexual orientation with my coworkers, there are some business settings in which I don't come out until we've developed a strong business relationship. For example, I had an interesting experience once while golfing with my friend, Mike, and a sports vendor named Jim, who we work with on a regular basis. I overheard Jim make a tacky comment about something being "gay." Mike immediately went over to him and told him that his remark was inappropriate and offensive. Jim was embarrassed and apologized to Mike and me. It's so meaningful to have those allies who will stick up for you. Jim had no clue that

I'm gay: he had a preconceived notion of what gay "looks like," and I didn't fit that picture. Now Jim knows that someone he's comfortable with is gay, and I hope he will be the one to speak up the next time he hears a homophobic comment. I'm now happy to consider Jim a friend, and I've even received a Christmas card from his family. People's stereotypes and preconceived notions really can change.

> **" People's stereotypes and preconceived notions really can change. "**

If there's one thing I have learned in my coming out process, it's that I should continue to have faith in people. The first thing I say to people whom I mentor is that no matter what organization you work for, you have to come to work and deliver your very best, and then everything else will fall into place. You have to be true to yourself. If, after giving your best, you realize that there is discrimination, then you can address the issue.

God's grace, mercy, and His faith in me are the three things that help me be confident and be a mentor to people. I'm proud to be Christian and a member of a wonderful church called Christ Chapel of the Valley in North Hollywood, California. Our congregation is ninety-five percent LGBT. Having that community strength really helps me feel more comfortable in who I am. I realize that we can each do anything we want, if we put our minds to it. I work every day to give back to our community, encourage and inspire others, and provide support and guidance to other LGBT folks.

When I was with State Farm, I really advocated for the company to provide services to the lesbian, gay, bisexual, and transgender community to make sure that we have the best service, products, and protections. I felt that I was promoting my brand and also doing something good for other LGBT people. State Farm's Chief Marketing and Sales Officer, Rand Harbert, is a mentor and friend who always provided unconditional support in me being who I am. Again it's important for all of us to have straight allies! From a business perspective, providing products and services specifically directed to the LGBT population is simply smart business; we are a financially powerful community and any brand should want our $800 billion in annual spending behind their brand.

I believe that to whom much is given, much is required. We should all "reach back" with a helping hand to those who are less fortunate in their coming out process. In the current business climate, employees represent the largest expense at any company. Some economists estimate that companies could see as much as a tenfold return out of their LGBT employees by providing specific partnership benefits, career advancement protections, and LGBT diversity training. Each organization receives a higher return from its investment in employees by simply giving them a safe place to work, where they feel they can have long-term careers regardless of their race, religion, gender, sexual orientation, or gender identity. How can anyone think "outside the box" if he or she is hidden inside of one? Allowing employees to bring all of who they are to work helps them think more creatively, which equates to better products, services and revenue growth.

> **"** How can anyone think "outside the box" if he or she is hidden inside of one? **"**

Maggie Stumpp

Margaret Stumpp is the Chief Investment Officer at Quantitative Management Associates (QMA), a subsidiary of Prudential Financial, Inc. She is the first openly transgender employee at Prudential, a company with a workforce of more than forty thousand. In February 2002 at age forty-nine, Maggie transitioned from male to female while maintaining her role as an executive with  QMA, a position she has held for over two decades. She also continues to be actively engaged in investment research, and her work has appeared in a number of academic journals, including: the *Financial Analyst's Journal, The Journal of Portfolio Management,* and the *Journal of Investment Management.* Margaret earned her B.A. in Economics from Boston University and a Ph.D. in Economics from Brown University. While continuing in her investment career, Maggie has also made numerous presentations and held meetings with corporate executives across the U.S. to help increase the awareness and acceptance of transgender people in the workplace.

As far back as I can remember, I wanted to be a girl. It was not a coming of age thing, and it had nothing to do with sexual orientation or attraction to other people. My parents were fairly conservative; they sent me to Catholic school, and we attended church every Sunday. We did not discuss things like sex, and I certainly did not feel comfortable talking about my gender identity. My parents caught me cross-dressing one day when I was in third grade, but we did not discuss it.

> " My parents caught me cross-dressing one day when I was in third grade, but we did not discuss it. "

I always imagined that I would grow out of it. I didn't, of course, and so I tried to understand my feelings as an adult by going to a therapist. This was during the early eighties, and most people were not aware of the concept of gender dysphoria. The therapist I saw was convinced that I was just gay and in denial. I finally stopped going to therapy.

Over the next ten years, I tried to understand my situation by seeing various professionals and consulting all of the research I could find. I learned about others who had gone before me, like Renée Richards, and I began to understand, "Perhaps this is who I am." I eventually started seeing a therapist with the intention of actually transitioning. It was a long process that involved a lot of starts and stops and quite a bit of contemplation.

At the age of forty-nine, I decided it was time for me to transition. I had been working at Prudential for about fifteen years. One afternoon, I was sitting in my office with the co-founder of our business, chatting about research, and I told him bluntly that I was planning to transition and wanted to be called Maggie. He stared at me silently for a long time. Finally, he mumbled something like, "Well, Maggie, we love you, whatever you want to do." He was out of my office in seconds, and I am pretty sure he went directly to the nearest bar. I realized that the conversation had not gone particularly well.

A couple of days later, I brought in a letter from a therapist and a business plan with various options for moving forward. From then on, we approached my transition as a business issue, which was more comfortable for everyone. My associate's reaction went from shock to, "Okay. We'll be supportive. Let's figure out how to deal with this." He worked with others at Prudential, including executives in human resources, law, marketing, and a sizable cast of other stakeholders.

I was pleasantly surprised with the acceptance and support I received from everyone. The people I worked with were all incredibly kind while I was out having surgery, and many sent me supportive emails. It was quite pro-found to receive all those notes of encouragement.

> **The people I worked with were all incredibly kind while I was out having surgery, and many sent me supportive emails.**

I went through a lot when I transitioned. Life takes on a very different color when you change gender, because you start to see things through a different set of glasses, and it takes a lot to get used to what you are seeing. Until you are comfortable in your new skin, little things can really surprise you and throw you for a loop.

For example, one time I went into a Chinese restaurant that I'd been going to for a while, and one of the ladies looked at me and said, "Can I ask you a question?" I thought, "Ugh! This is going to be about my prior life." Then she blurted out, "Were you once a model?" I laughed in relief. It was funny and very sweet.

I experienced a lot of self-doubt through the process. There was a protracted interval during which I could not pass a mirror without checking to make sure I looked passable. I would not even go to the grocery store without putting on makeup. It took years to get my feet on the ground and to come to terms with myself. This naturally affected how well I could focus on work.

When I transitioned, it was a clear and irrevocable move. I used to wear a suit and now suddenly wore skirts and lipstick. I could not be selective about who I came out to.

There were many personal issues that came along with transitioning. I had to navigate some difficult situations with my family and friends. Initially I had to do a lot of soul-searching to cope with this, and it did affect my workplace performance. It was a big distraction, and so I worked harder to compensate for it.

Although my colleagues were extremely supportive, there were questions about how clients would respond to me. One of my first client meetings was with a fairly conservative union. They decided to meet me at a restaurant on neutral territory. We all sat down, took one look at each other and ordered a round of stiff drinks. After a few minutes, the guy sitting next to me leaned over and said, "You know, you don't look so bad for a guy." It was probably the best offhand compliment I've ever received. The meeting turned out to be fun, and the business relationship continued.

We have a global client base, and I have to be sensitive to other cultures when dealing with international clients. Some prospective clients are fairly conservative. There are certain countries to which I will not travel and certain meetings in which I will not participate. This is both because I am transgender and often simply because I am a woman. I consequently face two forms of discrimination.

After transitioning, I have seen that women face an uphill battle. In fact, one of the biggest challenges I have faced is the impact of being female in a male-dominated

> " One of the biggest challenges I have faced is the impact of being female in a male-dominated profession. "

profession. There are only a handful of female chief investment officers for large financial institutions. Men sometimes have trouble dealing with female investment professionals, possibly because they perceive women as being less aggressive and have lower expectations for what a woman can accomplish.

I transitioned in 2002. At that time, gender reassignment was a fairly new phenomenon in the business world. I used my position as an executive to demonstrate to other companies that someone transitioning on their staff can be a huge success. I'm happy to say that Prudential was quite supportive of this effort.

Over the last ten years, the corporate world has changed immensely. In 2012, I feel that it is safe to say that most of the larger corporations have had an employee transition or have seen someone transition at one of their competitors. Any large corporation with a mind towards diversity will keep an employee after he or she transitions. The person's career prospects may suffer, but they will still have a job. I do not believe that this is true for smaller companies and in certain parts of the country. Smaller corporations can learn by looking at the larger firms they aspire to become, and they will realize slowly that having transgender people on the payroll is not a bad thing. It will not cause employees or customers to abandon the company.

Large companies are willing to stand up for people that they've already hired, but even the most diverse companies are not going out and hiring transgender employees. Transgender people face higher unemployment rates than any other population in the United States. I have witnessed this in my own work. My firm has been wildly successful, and I used to receive calls all the time from headhunters. Those calls almost completely

> **Transgender people face higher unemployment rates than any other population in the United States.**

stopped after I transitioned. Even now, a decade later, I rarely receive calls from recruiters. When I do, I often suggest that the caller Google me. I usually don't hear from them again. Most transgender people I have met have accomplished a lot in their lives; they either have advanced degrees or have done incredible work, and yet many of them can't find employment.

In order to make change in this area, we need to find ways to overcome the hurdles that transgender people face during the hiring process. It is always easy for a hiring manager to build a defensible case for why a particular transgender person was not hired. Even if the manager does not realize that the individual is transgender, he or she may pick up on a subtle vibe that makes him or her uncomfortable, and then the transgender person is passed over for another candidate.

The solution is for people to work alongside transgender individuals and gain direct experience that counters any preconceptions. People seem to be more accepting after working with me. I doubt very much that anyone in my office would react to a transgender person today the way that they might have before they'd experienced working with me. I imagine that if they met a transgender person, they would say, "My boss is trans, too." And that would be it.

> " I imagine that if they met a transgender person, they would say, "My boss is trans, too." And that would be it. "

The problem today is that there are so few of us, and such little exposure. The number of people in the country who have worked alongside a trans person is so small that the issue remains unknown to most. The lack of knowledge leaves people afraid, and why would anyone hire someone who is unusual to them? I think that people also project how others might react. Often, the story I hear when I raise these issues is, "Oh, I'm fine with transgender people. It is my coworker who might have a problem." Or, "You might make the clients uncomfortable." I think that the more society understands that transgender individuals are ordinary people trying to earn a living and live our lives, the less of an issue it becomes.

I have been involved with various diversity efforts at Prudential, including our LGBT employee resource group. Prudential has always been an organization that values all of the people who work here. QMA, which operates within Prudential, has one of the lowest turnover rates in the industry, and that is often one of the reasons clients cite for retaining us as an investment manager. People who work at Prudential accept each other, and it has always been a very collegial, respectful environment, which is a true reflection of Prudential. It has always been an open place to work, but I would say that people are even more sensitive to diversity issues now than they were a decade ago.

It is certainly helpful to have organizations that pave the way for companies to become more diverse. Out & Equal has been an excellent resource for connecting me with other executives. It has been pleasant to go to the annual meetings and the workshops. The annual Summit gives me the opportunity to have discussions with diversity professionals from around the country and make sure that they are aware of the range of issues that transgender people face.

In closing, there have been many positive aspects to my transition. There are also many aspects that have been incredibly difficult. It is a very different life than I would have had. Had I not transitioned, I would probably be wealthier. I would certainly be healthier. I would have fewer issues about self-doubt in public. It is not all a bed of roses after transition. It is not good, it is not bad; it is just different. But it was something I had to do. My life was going down

The question is not where you will end up; the question is how you got there.

one path. I came to a fork in the road and chose. As travel writer Paul Theroux once wrote, "It's the journey that matters, not the destination. It's the voyage, not the landing." The question is not where you will end up; the question is how you got there, what you've learned and shared, and how you carried yourself during the trek. So far, I have no big regrets.

Ana Duarte-McCarthy

Ana Duarte-McCarthy has been Citigroup's Chief Diversity Officer since 2002 and a dedicated ally to Citi's lesbian, gay, bisexual, and transgender employees. She led the efforts that resulted in the creation of employee resource groups, the addition of gender identity and expression to Citi's nondiscrimination policy, and the securing of Citi's endorsement of the Domestic Partner Benefit Tax Equity Act and the Employment Non-Discrimination Act (ENDA). Ana was chosen as one of Hispanic Business Magazine's "25 Elite Women for 2009" and in 2007 received Out & Equal Workplace Advocates' Champion Award for her support and advocacy of LGBT workplace equality.

Fairness matters. I learned this as a young child watching my parents navigate the difficulties of being immigrants and people of color in predominantly white, suburban communities. I'll never forget one early experience: my whole family was having breakfast in a diner in South Carolina, and my father asked the waitress for more coffee. Her service had been lackluster, and she threatened

> " *Fairness matters. I learned this as a young child watching my parents navigate the difficulties of being immigrants and people of color.* "

to throw eggs in his face because, we understood, she did not want to serve a darker-skinned man.

While growing up, I discovered that some people perceived me differently simply because as a Latina, I was not from the majority white culture. It was always surprising that someone could have a problem with me because of who I am, and it was very hurtful.

During graduate school, I learned that people who are lesbian, gay, bisexual, or transgender face similar challenges. My perspective on the LGBT community really underwent an awakening during this time period because I came into contact with a lot of people who were "out." I made some very dear friends, who shared many stories of how they were mistreated at times and disrespected because of their sexual orientation. The fact that they were not treated fairly simply because they were gay was not right.

Each time that I came home from school for vacation, I talked a lot about my new friends with my family. My parents finally took me aside and asked, "Are you trying to tell us that you're gay?" I laughed and responded, "No, I am not." I thought it was pretty funny that they assumed that I could be a lesbian simply because I had friends who were gay. My father, who is of Dominican heritage, referred to gay men as "*maricóns*"[1] before that time. I think that my conversation with him may have opened the path for him to reconsider his opinions. Many years later, my lesbian sister-in-law was the real agent of change for my father; he ended up becoming very close to her and her partner. Knowing someone who was gay and part of the family made the issue very personal for him, and I

---

[1] Colloquial Spanish language slang expression for a homosexual individual.

was so proud of the way he embraced my sister-in-law.

Gay rights always felt like the great civil rights fight to me, and I have always wanted to help in any way possible. Once I started my career, I sought to understand equality, inclusion, and diversity on both a personal and professional

"The fact that they were not treated fairly simply because they were gay was not right."

level. I took advantage of a faculty perk at the New School that allowed me to attend courses for free, and I soaked up everything I could about gender identity, racism, and women's studies. During the same time period, I collaborated with a group of professors to write a white paper on diversity and inclusion. We researched several of the New School's student minority groups, including the lesbian, gay, bisexual, and transgender community. Our work revealed that these students did not feel like a valued part of the academic community and that giving them a stronger voice in curriculum development would allow them to be better represented.

One of my favorite diversity initiatives was working with economically and academically disadvantaged students at the New School. I led the Higher Education Opportunity Program (HEOP), a New York State program that provided economic and academic aid to help these students fulfill their potential to succeed. One of their struggles involved dealing with the perceptions of professors, who at times assumed that people who came to the New School through the program were not good students. As part of HEOP, we held meetings with professors to reshape their preconceptions and help them better understand the quality of the students' work. Creating a dialogue around the disadvantaged students' experiences and demonstrating their hard work made a real and measurable difference in the students' relationships with their professors. In the end, these discussions dramatically improved the HEOP students' university experience and ability to succeed in school.

Many years have passed since I made the transition from the academic world to the corporate world. In retrospect, I would say that one thing rings true in both settings: most people express negative bias in subtle ways. A coworker once remarked to me, "You're very literate for a Latina." I quipped, "And I ski, too. What's that supposed to mean?" Because I am the head of Diversity for Citi, and in light of our policies, people do not generally tell me that they do not want to support the LGBT community — or any other community for that matter. When I perceive there is a gap on being fully inclusive, it may be more subtle.

This was apparent in a discussion that occurred around the creation of our affinity group for lesbian, gay, bisexual, and transgender individuals. By the time I became chief diversity officer, good progress had already been made towards creating affinity groups, but no policy was in place to allow these groups to actually form. I worked with committed colleagues to implement the necessary policy. The first group ready to form was the LGBT Pride Network. Some people were hesitant about this group being recognized first because, as a network focused on lesbian, gay, bisexual, and transgender issues, they thought it would raise more eyebrows about the employee network program overall. I explained to them that it would seem inconsistent with our practice of inclusion to deny the Pride Network the right to form first simply because it was LGBT. In the end, the group launched, and it was successful and well embraced by the Citi community.

We faced similar concerns a few years later when we added a voluntary question about sexual orientation and gender identity to our annual employee opinion survey. The decision to add the question had been reviewed by the highest levels at Citi. Even after it was approved, there were some who did not understand why Citi was adding the question. Someone approached me at work, claiming that a lot of employees had a problem with the fact that a question about sexual orientation and gender identity appeared in a workplace survey. As the manager further considered whether it should be removed, I offered another suggestion. "Let's talk to the people who have a problem with it," I suggested, "so that they better understand why we're doing it." I took a firm stance on the issue, because I felt that removing the question would send the wrong message to our teams. I also believed that discussing the issue would help create more comfort around differences.

Creating employee network groups and facilitating conversations around diversity have been the two most powerful tools in developing an inclusive environment here at Citi. There are now seventy employee networks that bring employees together to work on common interests, including gender, multicultural identity, sexual orientation, generations, women, military veterans, people with disability, and work life strategies. Everyone is welcome to participate in any group, regardless of whether they are members of that community. The affinity groups have achieved wonderful things for Citi by helping to shape the culture.

> " Creating employee network groups and facilitating conversations around diversity have been the two most powerful tools in developing an inclusive environment here at Citi. "

Our core belief at Citi is that diversity makes us better able to meet our business imperatives. A diverse workforce provides us with diversity of thought, which is critical in supporting our goals, among others, on product innovation. One of the indications of Citi's progress is the fact that there was strong support when we recommended adding gender identity and gender expression to the nondiscrimination policy in Citi's global code of conduct, which outlines Citi's values and standards of behavior. We partnered with various LGBT workplace advocacy groups to build the business case for offering these protections. The request was reviewed by Citi's most senior leaders, including the board of directors, as is customary for changes to the code of conduct. People just understood that it was the right thing to do. Citi's code of conduct now includes a nondiscrimination policy that includes sexual orientation, gender identity, and gender expression. The same policy is applied in each of our offices in all of the one hundred and sixty countries in which we operate.

Citi also implemented a diversity annual report beginning in 1999, which brings diversity issues to the attention of shareholders and decision makers within the organization. The report includes metrics with an overview of Citi's workforce, our diversity governance structure, and the different areas we're working on relative to diversity. In it, we outline our core priorities and discuss our actions to accomplish them. We also include our various practices supporting diversity, including recruiting, hiring and leadership development. The report creates transparency and real accounting for Citi's work. Citi took the lead by becoming one of the first businesses to implement this type of accounting.

As I mentioned before, some people had initially expressed concerned about an LGBT affinity group forming before any other back in 2002. One of their primary concerns was that LGBT issues had not been discussed in the workplace. I have taken a strong position as an ally and had the opportunity to facilitate high-level discussions to change this dynamic. One example was having the LGBT Pride Affinity Group meet with members of our business leadership team to talk about all of the challenges and opportunities in the gay community at Citi. This conversation had not taken place before, and some of the actions that came afterwards were a direct result of those meetings.

One very visible result of this discussion was that Citi became a lead partner with LGBT organizations on a national level, including the work that we do with Gay Lesbian Straight Education Network (GLSEN), the Human Rights Campaign and Out & Equal. Part of my role has been to facilitate this decision and create visibility around the work we do both internally and externally. As a group, we determined that we needed to be more focused and have a more significant partnership with Out & Equal. In 2004, we started to contribute by sending more employees to the Workplace Summit and offering various workshops. Sending employees to the Summit is always beneficial because it offers a great opportunity for them to hear about best practices and core focus areas, including policy and new initiatives to promote an inclusive workplace.

We have hosted many workshops at the Summit on a yearly basis, including a panel that examines the intersection between race, ethnicity, sexual orientation, and gender identity. One year, the panel was composed of executives who came from different racial and ethnic groups and were also gay. They discussed their experiences of coming out in the workplace in two ways — one as a person of color and the other as a gay person. The discussion was impactful, and I was pleased to have participated as the moderator.

> **We have hosted many workshops at the Summit on a yearly basis, including a panel that examines the intersection between race, ethnicity, sexual orientation, and gender identity.**

Citi's visible support for the lesbian, gay, bisexual, and transgender community is also aligned to the engagement of allies. Once people become involved and openly supportive, it creates an opportunity for others to be visible, either as allies or as lesbian, gay, bisexual, or transgender. There is also a great opportunity for straight allies of the LGBT community to bring a viewpoint that seems more objective, as they are not members of the community they are advocating for, yet still consider the issues to be very important. The same dynamic occurred when men supported the women's rights movement. People can open doors on behalf of others.

In order for progress to continue, straight allies need to stand up for what we know is right, even if it means that people may question our sexual orientation. A friend of mine, who is heterosexual, was invited to participate in a panel on allies. It wasn't billed as an ally panel, but instead as a Pride Month panel. She shared that when she first saw her name listed on the sheet, she was afraid that people would think that she is a lesbian. Then she thought about her reason for participating in the panel: her sister is gay, and my friend was going to talk about the importance of family support. In the end, she decided that she did not care what people thought, and she participated in the panel. She demonstrates an important point: it is critical for more people to step up and be supportive, even if it means that we may be perceived differently.

> **" Straight allies need to stand up for what we know is right, even if it means that people may question our sexual orientation. "**

I've been surprised and troubled by how many people are still in the closet at work. This is an indication that aspects of the culture across our workplaces need to change. I can only imagine how difficult it must be for people to come to work and have to hide an important part of their identities. It must cause a lot of stress. The idea that people have to cover up such a significant part of their lives has made LGBT diversity work so important to me. I hope that all of the work we've done at Citi to create concrete policies and foster mutual understanding will help more people feel safe to be out at work.

> *It takes strong allies to use their unique, objective voice to bridge the gap between cultures and overcome discrimination.*

At the end of the day, discriminatory behavior may be based on the color of our skin, because of whom we love or how we express our gender identity. Prejudices can be expressed in subtle ways, and it takes strong allies to use their unique, objective voice to bridge the gap between cultures and overcome discrimination. I've seen the power of this as a straight ally to the lesbian, gay, bisexual, and transgender community. As a woman and as a person of color, I have also experienced the strength allies provide when other people have advocated on my behalf.

Diversity is a field in which there is always something more we can do to help support employees. We only need to bring the conversation to the table for people to understand the importance of inclusion, because most people would agree that fairness really does matter.

Tom Johnson

Tom Johnson is Vice President of Finance, Global Business Services at The Clorox Company, where he operates an organization that provides shared services to the company's business units. Tom co-led efforts to bring domestic partner benefits and other equitable policies to Clorox, which eventually resulted in the company's perfect score of 100 on the Human Rights Campaign Corporate Equality Index. Tom was one of the founding members of Clorox Pride, the company's employee resource group for gay, lesbian, bisexual, and transgender employees and their advocates. He also serves as President of the Board of Directors for Out & Equal Workplace Advocates. Tom and his partner, Bruce, live in Northern California and enjoy spending time hiking, skiing and practicing yoga.

Never underestimate the ability for a person or organization to evolve. You can create opportunities for others to evolve and experience positive change. I have seen this evolution and powerful change in three dimensions: myself, my family and friends, and my employer.

Myself. I was the sixth of seven children raised in a working class family of devout Catholics in Rochester, Michigan. Similar to many families in the Detroit area, my father was a skilled tradesman who worked for one the automotive companies and my mother worked full time raising my siblings and me. With that many children living in a three-bedroom home, our household could be a little chaotic. But, my father ruled the house without debate, discussion or exception. At the end of the day, his word was the final say on any issue.

Growing up, our family never had conversations about sexual orientation. However, I understood at an early age that anyone who did not fit a conventional gender profile was not acceptable in my family or my community. I distinctly remember a teacher who was a little too stylish and effeminate for Rochester circa 1976. Although his wife was a school counselor, and people often saw them together, he was the subject of much suspicion and ridicule.

In a similar way, some people perceived that I was somehow different. Although I was a popular student and had a lot of friends, I was teased because people suspected that I might be gay. One particularly memorable incident occurred in high school. While walking into the gym for a school assembly, a large group of students in the bleachers started chanting, "Eat, drink and be merry! Tom Johnson's a fairy." I felt terrible — and, of course, humiliated.

For a long time, I was certain that I was destined to live my life as a charade and to hide my true self. I believed that revealing my sexual orientation would be devastating to relationships with my friends and family. Consequently, I dated women all through high school and college and felt like I was the only gay person in the whole state of Michigan. Shortly

> **" I felt like I was the only gay person in the whole state of Michigan. "**

> " I felt incredibly liberated and excited to live a life of integrity and authenticity — and I wanted to tell the world. "

after graduating from college, I headed to Boston and began the process of accepting myself and coming out. For me, it was a long process of undoing years of denial and internalized homophobia.

Then, I met my partner and, for the first time in my life, I felt the "real me" was loved and accepted. With the support of my partner and a few (thousand) sessions of therapy, I realized I had spent 32 years pretending to be something I wasn't. I finally accepted me. I felt incredibly liberated and excited to live a life of integrity and authenticity — and I wanted to tell the world.

My Family and Friends. For eight years, my family and friends thought Bruce was my roommate. I finally told my brother, sisters and a few friends, and they responded so positively that I decided it was time to tell my parents. I thought it was best to share the news in a letter to give them time and space to process the news.

My parents were less enthusiastic about my news. My mom acknowledged receiving the letter by leaving a message on my answering machine at home (knowing I'd be at work). It was one of those rare times that she said she loved me. But she also said they would need some time to digest the news.

We did not speak for almost three months and, after that, the annual trips my parents took to visit me and "my roommate" stopped. When we started talking again, it was clear that any discussion about Bruce and my sexual orientation was not welcome. I visited them for the next few years — without Bruce, of course.

Since my parents didn't discuss such personal matters, I wasn't aware they were working through their own coming out process — that is, coming out as parents with a gay son. Six years after I came out to them, I visited my parents in Florida where they and my brother and sisters had relocated. I was at lunch with my parents and two of my sisters when the conversation turned to my parents' upcoming 50th wedding anniversary. My father, who was very introverted, said perceptively, "I suspect you three are planning a party for our anniversary, and I don't want anything to do with that. What I would like to do is to go on a cruise to celebrate, and I want all of you to come with us." Then he turned to me deliberately and said, "And I want Bruce to come, too." We all nearly fell out of our chairs in surprise.

Many members of our extended family joined us on that cruise. A few of my aunts were quite conservative, and my father told them very clearly, "If you have a problem with Tom and his partner, then I do not want you to come." He became not only my protector, but also Bruce's protector. On one of the first nights of the cruise, we were enjoying cocktails under the stars on the ship's upper deck, when my father approached Bruce and told him in so many words, "Let me know if you have problems with any of my brothers or sisters, and I will take care of it for you."

After the cruise, my parents became very involved in our lives and welcomed Bruce into the family. I was fortunate to have an honest relationship with my father for a couple of years before he passed away in 2000. My mother is still a fervent LGBT advocate and supporter in her retirement community. She will not tolerate any disparaging remarks about LGBT people, and she has lost friends over it. I feel so fortunate to have this honest, caring relationship with my parents.

At an earlier point in my life, I could not have imagined my parents making such a magnificent transformation. The support of my family and friends has been empowering and instrumental to living a happy, fulfilling, and authentic life.

> " The support of my family and friends has been empowering and instrumental to living a happy, fulfilling, and authentic life. "

My Employer. Coming out as a gay man at work was the furthest thing from my mind when I joined Clorox in 1988. Despite its location in Oakland, California — right across the Bay from San Francisco — there was no indication that coming out would be good for my career. There were no domestic partner benefits, no policies signaling intolerance for discrimination, no LGBT employee resource group, and certainly no LGBT employee in a leadership role. I wanted to progress in my career, but I saw no one like me in the management or leadership ranks. I concluded that the safest option for my career was to stay in the closet.

In one of my early roles at Clorox, I worked on cross-functional teams responsible for bringing new products to market. We did a lot of brainstorming on these teams, which required us to reveal our personal habits and practices while thinking creatively about innovative new products. Each time I had an idea, I had to filter it, and ask myself, "If I say that, will that cause people to think that I'm gay?" Through my effort to protect myself, the company lost good ideas and I wasted an incredible amount of energy.

I was finally compelled to come out of the closet when Clorox offered me an expatriate assignment in London. I'm sure the company envisioned the low-cost transfer of a hard-working single guy. I surprised my boss by telling him that I wanted to accept the position, but my partner would have to come with me. Although there were no policies in place at the time to indicate how a domestic partner would be included in such an ex-pat assignment, my director worked with Human Resources to devise a package that would enable me and Bruce to relocate to London. We knew that Bruce could not join me on a spousal visa, because this was not yet legal for same-sex couples in the United Kingdom.

So, he entered the country on a tourist visa knowing he would be unable to work and would need to leave the country every six months to renew his tourist visa. When Bruce was detained by immigration officials shortly after our arrival and threatened with deportation, Clorox again rose to the occasion and hired an immigration attorney at the company's expense to resolve the matter.

That was the start of the journey that has led to Clorox becoming a visible champion of workplace equality around the world for LGBT people. The difficult and complicated experience with our international relocation was the impetus to work with Clorox Human Resources to implement more equitable policies and benefits, starting with equal health care benefits for employees and their domestic partners. The business case was relatively simple: technology companies were beginning to attract most of the top talent in the country.

As a consumer products company located in the Bay Area, we needed to attract and retain a diverse employee population reflective of our consumer base. Clorox could not afford to be at a competitive disadvantage in attracting talent. As a result, in 1998, Clorox was one of the first consumer products companies to implement domestic partner benefits. That is just one indication of the company's support for its LGBT employees and their advocates. Today there are many examples of the company's commitment to its LGBT consumers and employees including: CEO-level sponsorship of Out & Equal, domestic partner benefits and other inclusive policies, company support for the Employment Non-Discrimination

Coming out at work was one of the most positive actions I have taken to move my career forward.

Act, a perfect score on the LGBT Corporate Equality Index and several out LGBT leaders in many parts of the company.

Looking back on my career at Clorox, I believe that coming out at work was one of the most positive actions I have taken to move my career forward. Coming out allowed me to be authentic and bring my whole self to the workplace, and to channel my energies into driving business results rather than hiding part of who I am. After I came out, a close colleague admitted she had felt a level of distrust with me. She had a sense that I was holding something back, but didn't know what. It is not possible to be an effective leader without a foundation of trust among your team. For that reason, I believe being out of the closet at work has freed me to think more strategically and creatively about how to grow the business, to be a more candid and empathetic leader of people, and ultimately, to be a more successful employee.

Coming out to myself, my family and friends, and my employer has been incredibly liberating and allowed me the opportunity to live a happy, honest, authentic life. At an earlier point in my life, I could not have imagined being out, I could not foresee my parents making such a remarkable transformation, nor could I see having a career as an out gay man with the full support of my employer. There is nothing more powerful than living a life with integrity. People and companies can surprise you in positive ways… if you give them the chance.

> **" People and companies can surprise you in positive ways... if you give them the chance. "**

Rosalyn Taylor O'Neale

Rosalyn Taylor O'Neale, Vice President and Chief Diversity & Inclusion Officer at Campbell Soup Company, is one of the nation's preeminent speakers, educators and consultants on leadership, diversity and inclusion, race, and gender. O'Neale joined Campbell in 2008 after more than seventeen years of global diversity expertise across a range of industries and cultures. During her career, she has been a corporate executive, business leader, consultant and author. Rosalyn attended Indiana University and earned a master's degree in social work from the University of Louisville. She is the author of *7 Keys 2 Success: Unlocking the Passion for Diversity*. She currently serves on the Out & Equal People of Color Advisory Committee.

When I joined Campbell Soup as Chief Diversity Officer in 2008, the company had just received its first 100 percent score on the Human Rights Council's Corporate Equality Index. The health care benefits for domestic partners had been implemented years earlier. What has increased since 2008 is a deliberate effort to integrate training modules in our Campbell University offerings, which include information, case studies and role-plays that focus on sexual orientation and gender identity.

Treating people fairly is a cultural value at Campbell, and it includes all sexual orientations and gender identities. Recently, when we were preparing to ask employees for documentation of people listed as dependents on their health care policies, we carefully examined what we would need for domestic partners documentation that was sensitive to challenges faced by same-sex partners.

An important part of our diversity and inclusion evolution is our LGBT network, OPEN. This business resource network continues to grow with encouragement and investments of time and resources from my office and the senior leadership. Every year, OPEN helps people find safe ways to come out at work — whether that's by publicizing Coming Out At Work Day events or last year's LGBT Pride Month event, which asked all employees to share pictures of their families. This event allowed people to come out in pictures shared with colleagues, who talked about how wonderful it was to get to know one another.

Things have changed so much since I was a Black child in the South during the 1950s and '60s. My childhood experiences made me passionate about diversity. Back then, public bathrooms were still segregated. I witnessed the effects of racism on both Black and White people. Fighting injustice and addressing "isms" were the focus of conversations at the dinner table and in churches and schools.

However, living through the 1960s racism and the Civil Rights struggle did not prepare me for 1970, when I became aware of my sexual orientation and the ensuing challenges. I went to dinner one evening with two professors from my college. I knew one of the women, but it was the first time that I met the other, Lee. I remember that she had the most beautiful eyes I have ever seen — gold with flecks.

I was living with my parents. When I arrived home, my mother took one look at me and pronounced, "Something's very different about you, and it's not good." I became very intent on seeing Lee and spending time with her. Within a month, my mom surprised me with the question: "Is there something going on with you and *that woman?*" I said, "Yes." It did not seem worth lying, and it was clear she knew. The truth resulted in my having to move out, find a job, and face ten years of a very strained relationship with my family.

My best friend also reacted very badly when I told her. We had been inseparable since high school, and she freaked out. I think it was because we had always done everything together — finished high school, gotten pregnant at the same time — and I suspect she thought we would also have to be lesbians together. It took us about five years of being apart to see that we were and would always be best friends — never lovers. Only one of us would be a lesbian.

I have always been out at work. I had a Black aunt who "passed for white." Being in the closet about her race caused her to be isolated from family and required her to make up her life story and present false versions over and over. I vowed I would never be in the closet about anything.

Whenever I meet people and any personal detail that involves my sexual orientation comes up, I come out of the closet. For example, I may get asked, "What did you do over Christmas?" My answer always begins, "My wife and I…" As a consultant for most of my career, I have found coming out in a work setting to be somewhat risky, ranging from slightly uncomfortable to downright scary, because I know that homophobia and/or heterosexism could cause me to lose a contract.

> **Being an African American, a woman, and a lesbian has made my work life complicated.**

Being an African American, a woman, and a lesbian has made my work life complicated, because each group has rules that exclude a part of me. African American employees expect me to be heterosexual and are often uncomfortable when I talk about my wife — and even more so when they find out that she is White. Men are surprised that I am a lesbian; I often hear, "You don't look like a lesbian." I frequently have to address covertly sexual issues. Since I am the Chief Diversity Officer, these issues are rarely overt. The LGBT groups at work have always been primarily White and male. As an openly lesbian African American, I am often seeking peers and relationships from an increasingly diminishing pool.

Advocacy for all groups of marginalized individuals has been a part of my work for most of my career. However, two events brought the need to ensure LGBT equality in the workplace front and center. In one instance, I was hired by an African American woman. I was sure she knew that I was a lesbian, because I interviewed for the job in a three-piece, navy blue pantsuit with a man's tie and a short Afro. I was sure that my sexual orientation would not be an issue, because I work in Human Resources. But within the first six months, it became clear that my boss was not comfortable with an "out" lesbian working for her.

> " It is never enough to have laws and policies in place. There have to be people willing to guide the organization to be more inclusive. "

The second moment of truth happened when I was carrying out a large consulting contract that required an extensive cultural assessment of the organization that hired me. I reported back to the CEO in front of his HR executive and senior team that his gay employees were uncomfortable bringing their orientation and identity to work. He responded, "Well, tell me who they are, so I can fire them." Both events helped me to personally understand the need for advocates in the workplace. It is never enough to have laws and policies in place. There have to be people willing to guide the organization to be more inclusive and to identify and rectify the subtle and not-so-subtle ways that LGBT people are excluded, whether through language that managers and colleagues use or through worksite behavior and actions.

Coming out and being out at work continues to be part of my life — like being Black and a woman. "Isms" are a part of my life. Being an African American lesbian is complicated. White lesbians do not want to deal with their racism any more than Blacks (and all other races) want to deal with their heterosexism. The advantage I have over many other Black lesbians is that I am a Chief Diversity Officer (CDO). My work is to create ways for people to learn about the impact of biases and stereotypes on minority and majority members. It is my job to change behaviors and help companies become more aware and inclusive. I am sure that life would be much more difficult if I were in a job with less power to address prejudice.

I often say, "There are more people who don't care that you are lesbian or gay than people who do care." Of course, it is important to acknowledge that it is much scarier if the person who does care has the ability to use negative and coercive power over you. I found myself in that predicament early in my career. My response was to change jobs, because I knew that I could not change the bigot. Bigots are a loud and obnoxious minority, but they are definitely not the majority. Most people want coworkers who are helpful, respectful and contribute to the success of the team or group. For this majority, whom you sleep with, snuggle with, or have sex with is not important.

I am convinced that leaders' behaviors can quickly create inclusion or exclusion. I remember counseling a CEO to ask his lesbian executive about her spouse with the same ease and frequency he used when asking his heterosexual

> " I am convinced that leaders' behaviors can quickly create inclusion or exclusion. "

executives about their partners and spouses. Everyone knew that she was a lesbian, but no one talked about it. His behavior change made it possible for her to come out and for the company to become one of the best places for LGBT employees to work.

When I came to Campbell, I brought my passion for Out & Equal's work to create equal policies, opportunities, practices, and benefits in the workplace. As the CDO, I support our OPEN network. I am involved in creating an inclusive workplace in every Campbell Soup Company facility — in Europe, Asia, Canada, Mexico, and the United States. We recognize that employees from diverse cultures bring diverse views about sexual orientation and gender identity into the workplace. In a previous consulting assignment for a large multinational company, we collected legal mandates regarding sexual orientation. We discovered that Campbell Soup operates in surprisingly few countries where it is illegal to be LGBT. Of course, it is still *difficult* to be LGBT in many of these countries. As the Chief Diversity Officer, I help leaders and managers understand their role as advocates for all employees. When we encounter cultures that traditionally shy away from acknowledging LGBT issues and challenges, we bring the topic to our management training courses. We also make sure to include LGBT topics in our diversity calendars of events, as well as our policies and practices.

> " Employees from diverse cultures bring diverse views about sexual orientation and gender identity into the workplace. "

I think that being out, being open and allowing people to become comfortable at their own rate has allowed me to impact workplace equality. I come to work every day hoping that because of who I am or what I do, LGBT employees working at Campbell — or any of the many organizations I have worked for — will understand the power of authenticity. I hope that someone will see me and say, "If she can do it, so can I." It is not always smooth; it is a challenge when I encounter a negative response. I am not asking anyone to marry me, but I am demanding to be treated with dignity and respect as an African American, a woman and a lesbian.

Sander van't Noordende

As group chief executive of Accenture's Management Consulting Growth Platform, Sander van't Noordende is responsible for the company's capabilities and services across seven service lines. He oversees several company-wide initiatives, including Analytics, Sustainability Services, and Business Process Management. He is also a member of Accenture's Global Management Committee. Sander holds a degree in industrial engineering from the Eindhoven University of Technology in the Netherlands, with a specialty in finance and marketing. He was a keynote speaker at the 2011 Out & Equal Workplace Summit.

I must have been twelve when I realized I was gay. I felt a bit nervous, a little special, lonely every now and then, and of course a bit excited. I never hid who I am. Sexual orientation was not much of a subject in my family. I have two gay uncles and two lesbian aunts who were so completely accepted that I did not realize they were gay until I was a teenager. This is liberal even in the Netherlands, and I feel very lucky that my family was always relaxed about these issues.

As a college student, I lived in a fraternity house and played on the field hockey team. My fraternity brothers talked a lot about women, and I told them that I was gay because I did not feel like pretending or playing games. They completely accepted me. It has always been simple: if people do not like who I am, I will find other people to be around. I realize that this can be harder for people who do not come from accepting families.

Two weeks after I joined Accenture in 1987, I brought my partner along with me to an office party. No eyebrows were raised, and the whole experience was very positive. It was the most natural thing to do, and I thank my family upbringing for the fact that I felt quite normal in doing this. From the first day, it was all of me who joined Accenture. I never considered the option of hiding my sexual orientation, and I never advertised it either. I just lived my life, and it was okay.

Sexual orientation should never be a factor in your work product or success. If you are considering coming out at work, keep in mind that timing and tone are extremely important. I remember meeting with a client for the first time who told me within a few minutes that he was gay. It had nothing to do with our conversation, and it felt uncomfortable. I think this reflects the importance of treating the issue of sexual orientation at work in a normal, relaxed way that will make other people comfortable.

> **" Sexual orientation should never be a factor in your work product or success. "**

Being gay is an important part of who we are, but it is not our only defining characteristic. There are many other, more important things that define each of us: our talents, our nature, and how we relate to other people. These are some of the qualities that help drive success at work.

In my opinion, being out at work is a two-directional phenomenon. On one hand, employers have the obligation to make everybody feel accepted at work regardless of their backgrounds. On the other hand, each employee has a responsibility to make their colleagues feel comfortable with them. What might seem completely normal to one person may not seem normal to other people. It is important to find the right tone and common ground.

You should be judged by the job you do and the results you produce. Nobody should ever be judged by their sexual orientation. If you are working for the right organization, you will feel accepted and confident to do your best work. Fit is about comfort. It gives the confidence you need to be successful and productive. If you are in an environment where your sexual orientation is an issue for your employer and this cannot be changed, then it may be better to focus your energies on finding a new job where you can concentrate on becoming successful and delivering a solid work product. There have been significant advances for the lesbian, gay, bisexual, and transgender community at Accenture since I joined the firm in 1987. Back then, Accenture only offered domestic partner benefits in a few countries and any discussion of gay employees made people blush.

> **" Fit is about comfort. It gives the confidence you need to be successful and productive. "**

Over the years, lesbian, gay, bisexual, and transgender individuals have become a visible and integral part of Accenture's inclusion and diversity agenda. Accenture now has a Global LGBT Network, which brings our LGBT community and allies together for networking and mentoring. Accenture now offers domestic partner benefits in thirty-nine countries.

Our Global LGBT Network has chapters that are essential in driving change at local levels across many of the geographies in which Accenture operates. These groups help increase awareness and work to prevent discrimination based on sexual orientation. They also identify how Accenture's policies may affect same-sex couples around the world. Accenture's Global LGBT Network also works closely with our Inclusion & Diversity teams to help craft inclusive recruitment and retention policies. For example, in some countries, the Network helped create policies offering domestic partner benefits and assisted in shaping Accenture's recruiting efforts for lesbian, gay, bisexual, and transgender employees.

In 2002, Accenture established a Supplier Diversity Program in the United States to develop and expand relationships with diverse businesses, creating opportunities for these enterprises to grow their businesses while strengthening our supply chain. Reinforcing our commitment to the LGBT community, we provide support and mentoring to LGBT-owned businesses that participate in the program. We also routinely assess our larger suppliers to ensure that they support and promote LGBT equality in their own companies. We are in the process of expanding this program to the United Kingdom and the Netherlands by inviting LGBT-owned businesses to participate in procurement opportunities, and by providing them with mentoring and access to business knowledge and skills through our LGBT Network.

I am proud to serve on the Accenture Diversity Council at the executive level, where we address the widest possible view of inclusion and diversity, going beyond gender, race, religion, ethnicity, sexual orientation, and gender identity and expression to create a work environment that welcomes all forms of differences. As a team, we assess the global inclusion and

> **"Create a work environment that welcomes all forms of differences."**

diversity challenges Accenture is facing, set strategic direction, and prioritize our actions. Why all the focus on diversity? The answer is simple: diversity is not just about helping people. The world is diverse, and Accenture has to be diverse in order to interact with our clients and our business partners.

I am also absolutely convinced that diverse teams generate better answers. If a team does not have the capacity to consider different points of view, they will always come to the same conclusion rather than finding the best solution. Diversity has to be part of our DNA as a company in order for us to be successful.

> ❝ Diverse teams generate better answers. Diversity has to be part of our DNA as a company in order for us to be successful. ❞

In conclusion, there is still a lot of work to be done to make workplace equality a reality. I have seen so much change and positive progress during my twenty-five years at Accenture. I see first-hand the hard work that Accenture's Global LGBT Network is doing to make workplace equality a reality across the globe, and I fully support their efforts. We must keep moving towards fully inclusive workplaces. Equality is crucial to success.

Deborah Dagit

Deborah Dagit is the Vice President and Chief Diversity Officer for Merck. Ms. Dagit was born with osteogenesis imperfecta (brittle bone disease). She is four feet tall and uses a wheelchair. Ms. Dagit played a key role in the passage of the Americans with Disabilities Act through lobbying efforts.

She has been a strong, tireless, and visible advocate to the lesbian, gay, bisexual, and transgender community throughout her career as a diversity leader and has implemented domestic partner benefits in three companies. Ms. Dagit also served as the Co-Chair on the Board of Directors for GLSEN.

Under her leadership, Merck has been on the DiversityInc Top 50 Companies for Diversity for the past 10 years and in 2012 was ranked by *Diversity Inc Magazine* as number 16 in the 50 top firms to work for as a result of their diversity policies and company culture. Ms. Dagit has also won an array of awards, including the 2010 Winds of Change Multicultural Forum on Workplace Diversity Award; 2006 Champion of the Year Award from Out & Equal; and the 2000 Exemplary Leader Award from Silicon Graphics.

Prior to joining Merck in 2001, I interviewed with many Fortune 250 companies, most of them on the East Coast. I was surprised and dismayed that, despite my strong resume and ten years of experience as a successful and well-regarded diversity leader, I was repeatedly rejected as a candidate and explicitly told it was because of my disability. In one particularly memorable situation, after several phone interviews, I was flown to New York City for an interview. After seeing me in person, the recruiter canceled all of my other interviews. He explained that the firm was not comfortable considering someone like me for the job. However, given my subject matter expertise, they wondered if I would be open to working "behind the scenes" if they hired someone with strong media and government contacts who did not have diversity experience. I declined to consider this "opportunity."

Shortly thereafter, I became Vice President and Chief Diversity Officer for Merck, where I have the good fortune to be part of a company that values the many dimensions of diversity. As a person with a visible disability, I have felt valued, respected and supported to do my best work with all of the accommodations I need to be safe and fully productive, whether I am in the office or traveling on business. As an ally, I have been able to be part of fostering an environment where it is safe for my lesbian, gay, bisexual, and transgender colleagues to be out at work, receive access to terrific benefits and celebrate our pride in our community.

> " I became a strong advocate for the LGBT community early on, when I learned that two important people in my life were gay. "

I became a strong advocate for the LGBT community early on, when I learned that two important people in my life were gay. Living with osteogenesis imperfecta has meant a lot of broken bones in my life; I broke my leg just as I was preparing to head off to college in 1977. As a result, my plans changed, and I commuted to a local community college for the next 18 months while my leg healed. One of my high school friends, Andy, drove me back and forth every day to my college classes. At one point, a mutual friend mentioned to me that Andy was gay. But, at the time, I did not really understand what that meant. I sought guidance from a counselor at the college, but my initial questions came out so inarticulately that the counselor assumed instead that I was questioning my own sexual orientation.

During the same time period, I learned that my youngest cousin, Kurt, was gay. He and I were inseparable as children. Kurt came out when he was only sixteen, and our family, his friends, and his school reacted very negatively. My friend Andy helped me understand what Kurt was going through, and we offered Kurt as much support as we could, but we were both still students. Kurt ended up having to move out of the house and live with friends to avoid being on the street. He contracted HIV and died when he was only twenty-eight.

Finding out about Andy and Kurt led me on my own journey to understand more about sexual orientation and LGBT people. I was very fortunate during those "disco years" of the 1970s to develop a rich network of friends in the LGBT community. They gave me the opportunity to learn what it means to be an ally, skills I still value to this day. Kurt's memory inspires me in my work to help LGBT young people; I served for seven years on the board of directors of GLSEN: Gay, Lesbian, Straight Education Network and have long been a supporter of PFLAG: Parents, Families and Friends of Lesbians and Gays.

By the time I became a diversity leader in the corporate world in 1991, I had become an advocate for LGBT rights, and I considered

> **" I considered myself part of the LGBT community as an ally. "**

myself part of the LGBT community as an ally. Early in my career, I was working for Silicon Graphics, and we had hired a business consulting company to provide leadership training. One of the consulting company's leaders, who was also a well-known author, spoke out publicly at that time about his opposition to the movement for same-sex marriage rights in Hawaii. I felt it was so important to stress that we could not do business with another firm that did not provide a safe environment — both for their LGBT employees and their clients. Working with our LGBT leaders, I went to speak to the head of our human resources and procurement departments, and I requested a meeting between the leadership teams at Silicon Graphics and the consulting company.

The leadership at Silicon Graphics supported this initiative, and we held a series of very intense meetings. In the end, the leader from the consulting company agreed to refrain from expressing his opinions against LGBT people in public in the future, and his organization took concrete steps to ensure that their environment was a safer one in which to come out. They created new diversity policies, which applied to their full-time employees and contractors.

> **" We can create powerful change when we demonstrate courage, candor, and tenacity. "**

Through this process, I discovered that we can create powerful change when we demonstrate courage, candor, and tenacity. The Silicon Graphics team stood up on principle in this situation, and it made a difference for many employees in both companies. The discussions also served as a good lesson. Sometimes, companies are not willing to provide a safe working environment for all of their employees simply because it is the right thing to do. In these cases, the best response is to show a solid business case for that company to address diversity issues.

These rich and fruitful discussions also revealed the many challenges that arise in navigating issues of sexual orientation and faith. Many people around the world still believe that a child is born with a disability as some kind of punishment for the child and his or her family. Others believe that having a disability puts you in some kind of saintly sphere, living with a divine challenge and overcoming the obstacles. Some people believe that being gay is a punishment or a sin. Stigmas associated with LGBT people tend to be based on arguments of values or faith, while the stigma around disabilities tends to be around people's discomfort and fear of having a disability themselves, as in "there but for the grace of god..." — and that they would never be able to fire someone with a disability.

The great progress that has been made around work-related issues in the LGBT space could be really helpful in addressing the lack of progress that we have seen with regard to people with disabilities. Homosexuality is no longer defined as a mental illness and has become, instead, a social issue. In many cases, the movement for change has altered the way that the LGBT community is viewed. The result of this change is that someone who identifies as LGBT is viewed as a whole person who is different from others in one aspect — sexual orientation or gender identity. In the workplace, this progress translates to seeing, hiring, recruiting and developing lesbian, gay, bisexual, and transgender individuals as whole, authentic people. There is greater acceptance and awareness than in the past. Opportunities

> "Opportunities in many companies are no longer limited by the perception of someone as LGBT."

in many companies are no longer limited by the perception of someone as LGBT.

Similar progress still needs to occur for people who are differently abled. It's still too often the case that when someone views a person in a wheelchair, the disability is the only thing that they see; the wheelchair and the disability become that person's defining characteristic.

Some of the initiatives that have created equitable work environments for lesbian, gay, bisexual, and transgender employees are the same steps needed to create change for people who are differently abled. We need to create employee resource groups for differently abled employees, provide resources and support, expand benefits and articulate the business case for having employees who represent this customer population.

We also need to be vocal in addressing issues of sexual orientation and disabilities. Remaining silent on the issues will never bring change. In the space of creating inclusion for the lesbian, gay, bisexual, and transgender community, I have found that language choices are very powerful. For example, when I am speaking publicly, and I refer to my husband as my male partner, everyone who is LGBT in the room will understand that I'm an ally. Spelling out the words "lesbian, gay, bisexual, and transgender" also fosters inclusion and greater understanding.

> **"Be vocal in addressing issues of sexual orientation and disabilities."**

I addressed the issue of language choices at the Senate Health, Education, Labor and Pensions (HELP) Committee hearing in 2011 by offering a set of recommendations, including reframing the way we talk about people with disabilities. Like many who identify with the community of people with disabilities, from a young age I was told that I was "special." This included the special school I attended for the first few years, the reason why the local newspaper featured me in the Sunday living section, the wheelchair I used after a broken bone or surgery, the place where I received health care, and the various adapted activities I engaged in. By the time I was in first grade, I knew that if you have a disability, "special" had a different connotation: different from your peers; worthy of prayer or divine intervention; and, unfortunately, capable of less than what is expected of others.

Fifty years later, we still use "special" to describe the ways our society views people with disabilities. While the intent was and is to depict these things in a positive light, I suggest that we avoid the word "special" when referring to things related to disability. For firms that have a global footprint, you may want to consider adopting Differently Abled, which translates better in many languages.

For both the differently abled and LGBT communities, it is so important for allies to create a safe space where people can be their true selves — whether they are coming out as LGBT, or being open about having a disability. I have mentored people through their coming out process and do my best to support them so that they will feel safe in coming out to others. The most enjoyable thing about being a member of this community at work is helping people to not only be openly lesbian, gay, bisexual, or transgender, but also to be whole and feel affirmed. No one should ever feel that being LGBT is something that other people might not respect — or an aspect of identity that might negatively impact their work if others knew. At the end of the day, I will always be proud of the fact that I had the opportunity to play a part in helping many people

> " For both the differently abled and LGBT communities, it is so important for allies to create a safe space where people can be their true selves. "

integrate their personal lives with their work so that they can be even greater as leaders and happier as people.

Coming out is not an easy decision. I could never generalize by saying that everyone should come out at work and that staying in the closet means that they aren't courageous. It's very situational: sometimes it's safe to be out and staying in the closet is a missed opportunity. At other times, the person in the closet has accurately judged the climate and coming out would be really risky. In the latter case, it would be good to look for another place to work where you can be out. If that's not possible for financial or practical reasons, it's important to really find a way to take care of yourself because it really does create a lot of stress and burden. It's always a good idea to go to someone else in your organization to think the matter through. Find an ally or another LGBT person who has a good sense of the politics, and also has the organizational savvy and understanding to help you profile the potential consequences.

> **"** When I mentor people who are thinking of coming out at work, I help them decide how to navigate the risks and the rewards. **"**

When I mentor people who are thinking of coming out at work, I help them decide how to navigate the risks and the rewards. I have seen some of this great change during my career with Merck. One of our biggest accomplishments so far has been the creation of ten global constituency groups that represent populations that would otherwise remain underrepresented. Every one of these groups fully includes our LGBT colleagues as equal partners and object if they sense in any way that the LGBT group is being left out. A great example of the support that Merck employees show for the LGBT constituency occurred in 2008, when the ten global groups were given an opportunity to make only a handful of recommendations to our executive committee. They made a total of four internal recommendations, including a request to implement same-sex domestic partner benefits in all of our markets across the globe. This demonstrated that the nine other constituency groups who were not LGBT were willing to prioritize LGBT rights and equal benefits as one of only four issues to address that year.

Merck has been acknowledged as a leader in LGBT inclusion, and yet we continue to strive to make our resources more globally available, further enhance the visibility of our LGBT colleagues and help enhance health care outcomes with our LGBT customers. An example of this is our "Living Positively" campaign, which is an innovative outreach effort to help people in the LGBT community who are HIV positive to live full lives. Our CEO has been a strong and vocal champion for LGBT colleagues as a straight ally. It's nonnegotiable at Merck that LGBT people be treated with the same dignity and respect as other employees.

> **It's nonnegotiable at Merck that LGBT people be treated with the same dignity and respect as other employees.**

Of course, we still have many opportunities to create a more equal work environment. Merck is one of the world's largest pharmaceutical companies, with 85,000 employees in more than 140 countries. I know that there are colleagues who don't feel safe being out at work. Merck does not yet have enough out and proud role models at the executive levels.

Creating an inclusive and equal environment in a diverse group of people is always a hero's journey. There are many situations that require you to visualize yourself as a powerful ally willing to stand up and be recognized in order to protect underrepresented people. When people are able to be courageous and candid with each other in service of the broader community, then they are truly able to effect change and become heroes.

Claudia Brind-Woody

Claudia Brind-Woody is the Vice President and Managing Director for IBM Global Intellectual Property and Technology Licensing. She received the IBM Chairman's Award for her work on the Global Y2K team and also has two IBM patents pending. Claudia co-chairs the IBM Executive LGBT Taskforce. She has been the keynote speaker at diverse global forums including: the 2008 European Commission on LGBT Rights in Brussels; the 2009 International Conference on LGBT Human Rights in Copenhagen; the 2009 and 2010 Europride Business Forums in Zurich and Warsaw; The Danish Industry Council Diversity Symposium in 2010; the 2010 Company Pride Platform and the 2011 L-Women at Work conference in Amsterdam; and the 2012 Out & Equal Executive Forum in San Francisco. Claudia serves on the Board of Directors of Out & Equal and co-chairs their Global Advisory Committee. In 2011, she received the Out & Equal Trailblazer Award for her work in LGBT diversity and was listed in *GO Magazine*'s "100 Women We Love: Class of 2011." In 2012, she received the

Emily Wirsing Kelly Leadership Award from Mary Baldwin College. She lives with her wife, Tracie, in Oxfordshire, England.

In 1956, when I was still a toddler in Southern Virginia, Frank Kameny marched on the U.S. capital in protest after he was fired from his job with the federal government for being gay. Sixty years later, the United States still has no nationwide nondiscrimination policy protecting lesbian, gay, bisexual, and transgender individuals in the workplace. Homosexuality is still criminalized in a number of countries and in some locations is punishable by death. Equality is still a dream.

Some things have evolved. Even in the small factory town where I grew up, anyone who owns a television knows the meaning of the words "lesbian" and "gay." Many businesses have surpassed local law in providing protection for LGBT employees through the creation and enforcement of nondiscrimination policies.

Other things have yet to change, and some of the existing inequalities have greatly affected my life. The United States Defense of Marriage Act still denies visas to same-sex couples. I recently moved to the United Kingdom to join my wife, Tracie, because she is a citizen of the U.K. and did not have the right to a U.S. visa based on our partnership. The laws in the United Kingdom recognize me as her partner and therefore afford me the ability to live in the U.K. with Tracie as her partner. Even though our relationship is only called a civil partnership, we receive all of the same rights and benefits as any British married couple.

> **" Change takes time. "**

Change takes time. I have seen some great progress made for women in the workplace since I began my career in women's athletics as the Assistant Athletic Director at the University of Tennessee and then at the University of Texas in Austin. I was not out of the closet, because we were trying to establish opportunities for female athletes, and people at that time called all women playing sports "dykes," whether the women involved were gay or not. As a result, those of us who were lesbians were very closeted.

I came out at work when I was the Assistant Dean of the Graduate School of Business at the University of Texas. I was fortunate to be in Austin, which is a liberal city with an open-minded university community. The Associate Dean was in a mixed-race marriage, and the Dean was in a heterosexual marriage. We were all good friends and professional colleagues.

I have experienced more discrimination as a woman than as a lesbian because being female is my most visible characteristic. People do not make assumptions about my sexual orientation based on my appearance, but they have placed limits on me for being a woman. I saw this firsthand when I worked for a company where the senior management was composed solely of bearded white men, all graduates from one of two Louisiana universities and all members of the Church of Christ. I did not attend either of those universities; I did not belong to that church; and I cannot grow a beard. I quickly saw that in that company, the glass ceiling was triple-glazed. Part of creating change is to understand when a barrier exists that cannot be removed. At such times, you have to remove yourself from the situation and take the opportunity to move on, make a difference, and educate people.

> **"I have experienced more discrimination as a woman than as a lesbian because being female is my most visible characteristic."**

I left that company to work for the Atlanta Committee for the Olympic Games and then took a job with IBM in 1996. Working for IBM has been an amazing experience. IBM has a long history of taking corporate social responsibility very seriously. IBM offered women equal pay for equal work back in the 1930s, long before the federal nondiscrimination act of 1963.

Back in the 1950s, IBM was beginning to build plants in the southern United States and was considering sites in North Carolina and Kentucky. However, these states still had segregation laws separating Whites and Blacks in housing and in public and private accommodations, including bathrooms and drinking fountains. The IBM leadership team said they would not build plants in locations where all IBM employees were not going to be treated equally. As a result, North Carolina and Kentucky changed their laws within three years, because the states wanted the economic benefits of having huge IBM plants.

Since the 1980s, lesbian and gay employees have been protected at IBM and enjoy domestic partner benefits. The executive leadership at the top of the company supports the global LGBT task force. We also try to go a step further by engaging people's hearts, not just obtaining their acquiescence to corporate rules. Each employee's direct manager creates a lot of the workplace climate. If a direct manager subtly discriminates against an employee because of the individual's gender identity or sexual orientation, then that creates an uncomfortable work environment.

We work to educate our managers so that a comfortable workplace climate is established at the top and cascades down. At times, we have encountered first-line managers whose culture or religion has instilled certain prejudices in them that go against IBM's diversity policies and workplace culture We try to educate them on what is appropriate for managers in our workplace. If this effort does not work, we ask them not to be managers; if there is still an issue with the workplace climate they are creating, they are likely to be asked to leave the company. We have also fired clients who could not deal with people of color or women working on their accounts.

We prefer not to walk away from employees or clients, and we always try to educate first. A great example of this occurred when we first opened our offices in the Middle East. We refused to alter our corporate nondiscrimination policy and insisted on having the whole policy available on the Internet internally and externally, including the sexual orientation and gender identity provisions. In one country, we had to take a stand to allow men and women to work at the same conference table without a glass wall separating them. We made it clear: we respect your culture, but within IBM walls, our male and female employees need to be able to work together.

We share best practices with other companies and collaborate with our traditional competitors because we believe that the message of diversity is essential. We are sure that we can make a difference in the world, and sometimes we do that by holding hands with our competitors to make a statement about diversity, equality, and corporate social responsibility.

> **" We share best practices with other companies and collaborate with our traditional competitors because we believe that the message of diversity is essential. "**

Diversity is important for IBM's talent recruitment and retention. It is essential for creating an innovative workplace culture, which benefits our clients and customers as well. Consider the high-tech areas of the United States that have an immense amount of success. This innovation correlates directly with the fact that these places have a high tolerance for difference and welcome gays and lesbians. When a company embraces differences, it opens itself up to innovation and success.

In my case, I have found exactly what I need in my role with IBM. The company supported my marriage by allowing me to transfer my position to the United Kingdom. They have also given me the time to be able to hold my line of business role as a senior leader in the company and still do my "night job" in the diversity space. I have been very fortunate to have the opportunity to lead our international diversity initiatives as one of the co-chairs of the Global IBM LGBT Diversity Task Force. I have helped IBM understand that we still have a lot of work to do in the United States and globally.

IBM encourages its employees to serve on the Board of Directors for nonprofit organizations because we feel we have a duty to invest not only money, but also our time. By doing this, we are able to offer nonprofits our insight, expertise, and experience. I chose to serve on the Board of Out & Equal because I believe that it is the leading nonprofit for workplace equality for LGBT individuals. I want to see the same change Out & Equal has influenced in the United States extended globally. Bringing together corporations on a global level has real potential to make a difference in the world. By joining corporate brands together, we can influence governments and countries to change the experience of lesbian, gay, bisexual, and transgender people across the globe.

> **By joining corporate brands together, we can influence governments and countries to change the experience of lesbian, gay, bisexual, and transgender people across the globe.**

LGBT equality is still in the making. Although it is empowering to consider all of the things we have accomplished, we are only scratching the surface. It is concerning to consider the state of the world today. No one should ever have to worry, "Will I lose my job if my employer discovers that I'm gay?" Worse yet, there are still places where people genuinely fear being stoned to death or hung simply for being themselves.

Each country has its own laws and cultures, and the degree of discrimination varies. In certain states in the United States, gay couples can adopt children, yet only a few states support marriage equality. Spain and Italy are both predominantly Catholic countries, but Spain has legalized same-sex marriage while Italian culture widely perceives gay people as pedophiles. Even with all the variations, it is possible to make positive change. We have to build diversity within the cultural boundaries of each country and slowly start to create a better work environment. I hope that sixty years from now, we will find that LGBT, gender and racial equality is more than just a dream. By bringing the power of our brands together, we can change hearts, minds and laws. We can influence cultural change and improve the workplace for people throughout the world.

Louise Young

Dr. Louise Young is a Senior Software Engineer at Raytheon in Plano, Texas. She is the founder of Raytheon's Gay, Lesbian, Bisexual, Transgender, and Allies (GLBTA) employee resource group. Louise has been a lesbian activist since 1971 and has received numerous awards and honors, including Out & Equal's 2002 Trailblazer Award. She is a former co-chair of the Human Rights Campaign's Business Council and appeared in a March 2005 issue of *The Advocate* in the article, "Gay Corporate Leaders." The Raytheon Global GLBTA Employee Resource Group has named Louise their "President Emeritus for Life." In 2003, she was commended by Raytheon CEO Bill Swanson as one of six Raytheon Diversity Heroes at the annual Raytheon Diversity Forum. Louise lives in Dallas with Vivienne Armstrong, her partner of forty-one years.

Photo courtesy of Dallas Voice
Photographer Terry Thompson

When I was a girl growing up in the small town of Ada, Oklahoma, I often rode my bicycle around the East Central State College campus near our home and dreamed of the day that I would go to college there. I finally enrolled in 1965 and envisioned that I would one day teach at the college in my beloved hometown.

I graduated from East Central with a B.A. in geography and went to graduate school at the University of Colorado in Boulder. In 1971, I had finished all of my Ph.D. coursework and received a job offer to teach at East Central. This was my dream! The month before I returned to Oklahoma to start teaching, I fell in love with my one and only partner, Vivienne Armstrong. We met at the University of Colorado campus through their new Gay Liberation Front organization. I told my parents about Vivienne. They were wonderful and excitedly welcomed her into the family. Vivienne and I moved to Ada, where I started teaching, and she enrolled at East Central in their new four-year nursing program. Vivienne was already a registered nurse but wanted to get a Bachelor of Science degree. I felt things were perfect.

In May 1974, I took a one-year sabbatical, and Vivienne and I moved back to Colorado, where I finished my dissertation. Just before we left Oklahoma, Vivienne graduated at the top of her class with a B.S. in Nursing. In Colorado, she worked so that I could devote myself full time to writing my dissertation.

Things suddenly changed. East Central wrote me that I should not return to my teaching job, because the enrollment would not support my position on the faculty. I knew this was not true, so I made some off-the-record inquiries. I discovered that the real reason that I was not allowed to return was because I was a lesbian. During my time on the faculty at East Central, Vivienne and I had visited some gay bars in Oklahoma City, ninety miles from the town of Ada, to dance and have fun. Unfortunately, a student from East Central saw us there and reported me to the administration. This was a career-ending event in the early 1970s.

My world was shattered. It was August 1975. I now had a Ph.D. but no job. We were in Denver, not back home in Oklahoma. I was a year away from tenure, so there was no process by which

I could appeal. This was a devastating blow, because I liked my job, and I was good at it. In fact, I was one of the most popular instructors in the school. Also, my parents who lived in Ada were in declining health. We really needed to be there. We were in a tight situation.

After I finished my doctorate, I was unemployed for a year. Vivienne was the school nurse at the Cerebral Palsy Center in Denver. She was an extremely popular and valued member of the staff. I received a job offer to teach at Southern Illinois University. I traveled there to make arrangements but eventually declined the job.

Meanwhile, Vivienne had given her notice at the Cerebral Palsy Center. The head of the center asked why she was leaving, and she said, "I guess you know that Louise and I are together. We're moving to Edwardsville, Illinois for her teaching job." He wished Vivienne good luck.

A week later, after I turned down the teaching job in Illinois, Vivienne returned to the Cerebral Palsy Center to ask for her job back. Although the Center had not hired another school nurse, they refused to rehire her. Vivienne asked why they would not rehire her, and the head of the organization very clearly said, "Because you are a lesbian."

"Well, I was a lesbian last week, and you cried when I left," Vivienne replied, in shock.

"Yes, but now we *know* that you're a lesbian, and you cannot work here," he responded. Vivienne and I contacted the American Civil Liberties Union in Denver. They were willing to take the case, but in the meantime I was offered a job with Texas Instruments in Dallas. We really

By that time, both of us had lost our jobs because of our sexual orientation. This propelled us even further into activism.

needed to move nearer to my parents, and Dallas was relatively close. There was no reason to pursue reinstatement in the Denver job if we were moving elsewhere.

So, off we went to Texas in September 1976. By that time, both of us had lost our jobs because of our sexual orientation. This propelled us even further into activism. We felt a burning need to do something to change the world so that people would not continue to lose jobs the way that we had lost ours.

Soon after we arrived in Dallas, we looked for an LGBT organization. The Dallas Gay Political Caucus, which has since become The Dallas Gay and Lesbian Alliance, was the perfect fit.

> " We felt a burning need to do something to change the world so that people would not continue to lose jobs the way that we had lost ours. "

Vivienne and I proposed a plan to organize the Dallas LGBT community to become involved in politics by registering our voters, questioning candidates and publicizing their responses regarding LGBT rights. The Dallas Gay Political Caucus adopted the plan, and we moved forward with it. Another of our organization's goals was the elimination of Section 21.06 of the Texas Penal Code, which criminalized same-sex intimacy in private. That statute was being used to discriminate against people even in their jobs. Only in June 2003 did the U.S. Supreme Court strike down this section of the Texas Penal Code, in the landmark case of *Lawrence versus Texas*.[1] It took twenty-six years for the law to be repealed. As Martin Luther King, Jr. said so eloquently, "The arc of the moral universe is long, but it bends toward justice."

---

[1] The case involved two men in the Houston area who were jailed after the police entered their home and arrested them for allegedly violating state sodomy laws.

When I began working for Texas Instruments, I did not try to hide my sexual orientation. I really felt like I had nothing to lose, and I knew that I would rather sweep floors than hide who I am. Vivienne and I were very public about our role with the Dallas Gay Political Caucus, and that put us in the newspaper and on television. My employer knew about me, and I felt free.

In 1993, another Texas Instruments employee and I decided to form an employee resource group for LGBT employees. We knew that other companies were adopting LGBT-friendly policies. We also believed that inclusive policies for all employees would benefit the company and the employees. Our newly formed employee resource group worked with upper management to add sexual orientation provisions to the nondiscrimination policy at Texas Instruments in 1996.

In 1997, Raytheon bought the defense sector of Texas Instruments, and my job area was part of that purchase. Half of our LGBT employee resource group's members went to Raytheon. At the time, Raytheon did not have a nondiscrimination policy protecting LGBT employees. "I just don't want to climb that mountain again," I groaned, but it had to be done.

We felt that Raytheon would respond to us. To our delight, Raytheon added a nondiscrimination policy covering sexual orientation. In 2002, Raytheon added domestic partner benefits. In 2005, Raytheon became the first company in the entire defense and electronics industry sector to score 100 percent on the HRC Foundation's Corporate Equality Index. Even with the 2012 CEI's more stringent criteria, Raytheon continues to score 100 percent.

GLBTA formed a sound partnership with Raytheon's upper management, the corporate diversity and inclusion office and the other Raytheon employee resource groups.

> " Diversity is a win-win for the company and its employees. "

We feel that we are valued. That is what is really at the heart of it all: diversity is a win-win for the company and its employees. Raytheon's President and CEO, Bill Swanson, is a big supporter of diversity and inclusion. He truly walks the talk. I hold him in the highest esteem. He is my corporate hero. I am lucky to work for a company that I admire so very much.

In 2008, Vivienne and I were contacted by the head of financial development for the college where I had lost my job in the early 1970s. The college had been renamed East Central University. She contacted Vivienne and me during a visit to alumnae in the Dallas area. We agreed to meet, and she asked us to make a generous donation. I related the story of losing my job in 1974. She looked at me and said, "Don't you think maybe it's time to bury the hatchet?" Vivienne and I looked at each other, and I said, "I think it is."

We established the "Louise Young Diversity Lecture Series," an endowed lectureship. In 2009, I was invited to deliver the first lecture at East Central. My topic was "Homosexuality: Why Talk About It?" I was back on the campus for the first time in thirty-five years, but as I walked through the doors, I felt the years roll back. I was a young, enthusiastic instructor in my twenties again. However, this time, the walls of the campus buildings were lined with posters carrying my image and announcing my lecture.

There was a good-sized crowd at the lecture. Four of my Ada High School classmates were there, along with a current faculty member who had been my colleague in the early 1970s. I had not seen him in thirty-five years. It was a poignant moment of recognition: if I had not been let go, I, too, would have been a faculty member nearing retirement.

The president of the university introduced and welcomed me. A student read my biography, which included the fact that I was not allowed to continue to teach in 1975 because of my sexual orientation. You could have heard a pin drop. The feedback on my lecture was tremendous! One student told her professor that it was simply the best lecture she had heard during her entire college career. When the lecture ended and the hall began to empty, many audience members stopped to shake my hand. I tried to freeze the moment in my mind, for I knew I had just experienced one of the best days of my life.

Before I left town the next day, I drove by the house where I grew up. My parents had both passed away in the early 1980s, and strangers now lived there. I paused in front of the small house. To my amazement, I saw that the basketball hoop was still where my father had nailed it on the garage back in the late 1950s so that I could shoot baskets. I closed my eyes and pictured my father — my hero — standing on the ladder, carefully attaching the goal for his beloved daughter and only child.

I remembered as I grew up how many hours I spent in our driveway shooting baskets and dreaming of life — imagining who I would become and what I would do. My parents drilled a special bit of advice into my head: "Above all, make a difference in the world." On that day so many years later, I smiled to myself, with tears in my eyes, knowing that I had been true to their counsel.

> "Above all, make a difference in the world."

Patrick O'Donnell

Patrick, a principal at Deloitte & Touche LLP, provides professional services to large, multinational clients. A member of Out & Equal's Board of Directors, Patrick holds several leadership roles at Deloitte. Specifically, he serves on Deloitte's national lesbian, gay, bisexual and transgender (LGBT) advisory team and he is the national advisory partner champion for inclusion and recruiting. Patrick is also a sponsor of Deloitte's employee resource group, Gay, Lesbian, Or Bisexual Employees & Allies, which focuses on workplace equality and community issues. Through these leadership positions, he is directly involved in several talent initiatives focused on recruitment, development and retention of people from diverse backgrounds. Outside of Deloitte, in addition to serving on the board of Out & Equal, Patrick also serves as a regional trustee of the Point Foundation, which provides college scholarships, mentoring, and leadership training to students who may face obstacles in relation to their LGBT identity or expression. Patrick lives in New York City with his partner, John.

I'm from a small town on the Jersey Shore. Neither of my parents went to college. My mom was an administrative assistant, and my father was a carpenter and manual laborer for most of my life. I went to a Catholic high school during the mid-1980s, right when the AIDS epidemic began, and there were frightening messages circulating about homosexuality. I dated women throughout college and had some serious relationships, but, in my early twenties I began to realize that I had to be realistic with myself if I was going to build a lasting relationship. I finally came out to myself and began to interact more openly with other LGBT people.

After a while, I decided to come out to my parents. I showed up at their house just before Thanksgiving. I remember standing in the stairwell of the basement, nervously whispering on the phone to a friend, "I'm not sure I can do this." My friend told me to just enjoy being home and not worry about it. I hung up and went back to the kitchen.

"Do you have something you want to tell me?" my mother asked. "Yes," I responded. She said, "Come into the living room with your father." I finally told them, "I am gay." My parents were accepting, and my mother was even a little indignant: "What did you think we were going to tell you? That we don't love you?" They went through a period of adjustment after that. I told my brother not long afterwards, and he was unfazed by it. I later introduced my parents and brother to my partner, John, and he eventually became part of the family.

I like to think that I was never really in the closet at work. At Deloitte, the work environment focuses on performance, and for the most part it seemed to me that people did not discuss their personal lives to any great extent. I joined Deloitte in 1997. While I was still in a junior position, one of my coworkers and I came out to each other. That conversation made a big difference. Over time, I came out to other people, and they often revealed that my sexual orientation was something they already knew about me. I realized that perhaps I just was not actively engaged in discussing those aspects of myself with others and may have been missing out.

I still distinctly remember the first time I cautiously entered the LGBT business resource group meeting at Deloitte. I was afraid that I might be judged for being gay or held back professionally, because others might then have negative views or misperceptions of me due to my sexual orientation. In reality, being "out of the closet" was a very positive experience. I remained involved with the employee resource group and eventually became the Partner Advisor for the New York region's chapter of Deloitte's LGBT Business Resource Group. I have also served on the Executive Leadership team for the portion of the organization in which I work, and I'm the Partner Champion for inclusion and recruiting efforts.

My colleagues support me when I walk in the AIDS Walk, and many attend LGBT-related events as allies because I have asked them to come. This kind of support means the world to me. I feel entirely comfortable at the organization and bring my partner to many Deloitte events.

> **"As a leader, I am confident and comfortable voicing views that more junior associates may not be willing or able to express."**

I have never actively worked for a nonprofit related to LGBT rights, advancing the political agenda or influencing media images. However, the success I have been able to achieve personally and professionally enables me to give back to the community in ways that I had not envisioned. I mentor and connect LGBT people professionally with others who are willing to help or with whom they can identify as LGBT professionals. As a leader, I am confident and comfortable voicing views that more junior associates may not be willing or able to express. I have a professional track record at Deloitte that allows me to represent my LGBT colleagues with senior leaders.

Deloitte has also been very supportive of my serving on Out & Equal's Board of Directors. I have had a phenomenal experience from a personal and professional development stand-point every year at the Workplace Summit. Deloitte is a significant sponsor of Out & Equal, and I wanted to take that relationship a step further by becoming more directly involved. I remember the first time I walked into the Summit: I was amazed by the two-thousand plus people, all in one place, who were either LGBT or allies. I was blown away by the sheer scale of the gathering and the diversity of the people there. I was also struck that there were so many people representing so many companies and regions. It was a true turning point for me.

> **"** I remember the first time I walked into the Summit: I was amazed by the two-thousand plus people, all in one place, who were either LGBT or allies. **"**

I had dinner not long ago with a former colleague who told me that I had been one of his first gay men-tors, over a decade ago. This conversation, so many years later, was incredibly gratifying, because I realized I had made an impact simply by talking to this person about what he could do profes-sionally and how I had handled being out at work. At the time, I thought it just a casual conversation; I didn't expect it to have an enduring impact.

I had another discussion in a different setting with another male colleague. I told him that I am out at work and do not have any problems as a result. That opened a whole dialogue, during which he asked me questions about who knows and how it works. I hadn't realized he still wasn't out at work, but found his caution understandable. After our conversation, he felt safe to come out at work and did so. I knew this time that our conversation would have a lasting impact.

The workplace is becoming a safer place to be open and authentic. There has been great progress in the last fifteen years. Yet, there is still a significant amount of progress to be made in parts of the U.S., both geographically and within certain organizations. We have not achieved as much as I might hope, but corporate America is a much better place to be lesbian, gay, bisexual, or transgender than it was when I started my career nearly twenty years ago. Many companies, including Deloitte, view diversity as a business imperative because clients expect it.

Here at Deloitte, the environment has changed a lot over the last several years. Our LGBT business resource group has been active for more than ten years. The group has experienced peaks and valleys along the way but, overall, people generally feel more comfortable becoming involved than they might have felt five or ten years ago. I think the environment has improved, and an increasing number of LGBT employees and allies have become involved. These people set examples and demonstrate that it is acceptable and even beneficial for people to be themselves at work. Merely being out at work creates a positive environment. I continue to hope that the world's attitudes on this social issue will continue to progress, so that one day people can state who they are, bring their whole selves to work, and there will be no issues with it.

> " Every LGBT individual who is out of the closet helps every other LGBT person who is not. "

We need more people who currently lack the confidence to come out of the closet to conquer their fears, so they too can serve openly and proudly as leaders who can mentor others. Every LGBT individual who is out of the closet helps every other LGBT person who is not. Sometimes the impact of being out can be measured and sometimes it cannot be, but, there is no question that when LGBT people are comfortable with their whole selves in all aspects of their lives, a personal and professional world of opportunities can open up for them.

As used in this document, "Deloitte" means Deloitte LLP and its subsidiaries. Please see www.deloitte.com/us/about for a detailed description of the legal structure of Deloitte LLP and its subsidiaries. Certain services may not be available to attest clients under the rules and regulations of public accounting.

Julie Hogan is Vice President of Strategic Client Operations at Xerox. During her twenty-five years at Xerox, Julie's roles have spanned the services business across the country. Originally from Chicago, she served in the United States Navy, providing tech support for classified defense computer systems and intelligence projects. Julie serves on the Out & Equal Board of Directors. She resides in San Ramon, California, with her wife, Allison.

My time in the Navy helped me discover my authentic self while also teaching me to hide it. I had no idea that I was a lesbian when I joined the military, but that all changed when I met a great group of women who I was stationed with in Florida. We spent time together on duty and played sports in the evenings, but they disappeared on the weekends, and I was never invited along. After a few months, they finally admitted that they were going to lesbian bars, the beach, and parties and did not want to tell me for fear of being outed. So I asked them to take me along, and that is where it all began. After some time, I met a civilian woman and had my first lesbian relationship.

I had to be very secretive, because at the time, being outed or identified as gay meant getting kicked out of the military. The Uniform Code of Military Justice clearly stated that being gay was not tolerated. This was before "Don't Ask, Don't Tell," and new recruits were required to disclose their sexual orientation when signing up with the military. The military believed that if you were gay and working in intelligence, you could be blackmailed into giving up secrets.

After leaving the Navy, I was hired at Xerox Corporation in 1987, and being out of the closet at work was nowhere in my vocabulary. The company had a wonderful culture of diversity; however, I did not know any openly gay employees. Over time, I selectively disclosed my personal life to coworkers, and coming out became a daily decision as people inquired about my personal life.

The biggest challenge I faced as a lesbian occurred when I was hired for a position in Charlotte, North Carolina, in 1998. I became more reserved about my sexual orientation because of the conservative culture and environment in the Carolinas. I found out much later through my boss that one of the local managers who had also interviewed for my job had approached the Vice President in charge of the hiring decision and told him, "You should not hire Julie Hogan. She is a lesbian, and that will not go over well with employees, customers or the leadership team here in the Carolinas." Fortunately, the hiring VP was a straight ally and fully supported the diversity culture at Xerox.

When I got the job and arrived in the Carolinas, I didn't walk in the door announcing that I was gay. Some of the local team assumed or had heard through the grapevine about my sexual orientation, but no one explicitly asked me, and I did not immediately offer this information. As time progressed, I developed great relationships with the organization, except for a small group of men who really didn't want to work with me. They never said anything that would violate the company's diversity policy, but they did everything they could to keep our team from growing and moving forward. To improve productivity, I sat each one of them down and set expectations, so that I could hold each accountable for his performance. It became pretty ugly in some cases, because the issue was really me against them.

As hard as it was at times, my goal was to do my job well and always exceed expectations. I knew that if my sexual orientation were really the issue, I had Xerox behind me, backing me up. Over time, seven out of the original thirteen members on my team retired, and Xerox's corporate culture and diversity values prevailed.

By the end of my stay in the Carolinas, I started to come out publicly to my direct staff and my senior staff, and then to more and more people. I hosted events at my home and invited everyone, and my sexual orientation became a non-issue.

In 2004, I transferred to the San Francisco Bay Area, where I moved into a very senior role with many employees and a lot of responsibility. By that time, most of the leadership team that I worked with already knew about my being a lesbian. I decided that it was time to be completely out of the closet. Where better to let my gay flag fly than in San Francisco?

> " Seeing other openly LGBT leaders bringing so many great changes to their work environments inspired me. "

My boss was an ally and the corporate sponsor of GALAXe, Xerox's LGBT employee resource group. He invited me to attend the Out & Equal Workplace Summit in Chicago. Seeing other openly LGBT leaders bringing so many great changes to their work environments inspired me to step up as a leader and a role model at Xerox as an open lesbian. I received so much inspiration from the three-day conference that I called Selisse Berry and set up a lunch appointment to find out how I could get more involved with Out & Equal. I attended the first Executive Forum as a part of the "San Francisco 24" and eventually joined the Out & Equal Board of Directors. I felt that I had become part of something bigger, and I saw that I had the opportunity to make a difference at Xerox. Ultimately, it made me a better leader, which translated to better business for Xerox and more success for me.

Becoming an out executive has opened up conversations with other executives who feel comfortable enough to discuss diversity issues with me. When I go to senior meetings, executives ask questions and want to share that they have a family member who is gay. Other times, they want to test their own cultural competence of the LGBT community. By being so out and open, I have opened the door for others to be more out and open with me about their lives.

> **Becoming an out executive has opened up conversations with other executives who feel comfortable enough to discuss diversity issues with me.**

In 2008, I was the vice president of the Pacific Region, where I led an organization of twenty-four hundred people, and we had a recognition event to which employees and their significant others were invited. I announced ahead of time on the sign-up sheet that I would be attending with my partner, Allison. Other gay employees discovered that I was bringing my partner and decided to also bring their partners to a company function for the first time. The night of the event, there was a dance party after dinner, and Allison and I made sure we were the first ones on the dance floor. Little by little, other lesbian and gay couples started to feel comfortable joining us on the floor. For the first time in all of the Xerox events I have been to, I counted ten same-sex couples on the floor. It was amazing. The fact that so many people felt comfortable bringing their partners to a company event made me so happy. I know it was their own courage that brought them there, but I know I had some small part in opening a door to that as well.

I have several LGBT people working for me now, and those employees feel very comfortable discussing their lives with me. One employee was out to his family and his friends, but at work he did not mention his husband of twenty-five years. I asked him, "Why haven't you brought your partner to any of our events?" He replied, "Because I've just always kept my work and personal lives separate." After twenty-five years together, he finally brought his partner to a company event. It is never too late to make change.

I encourage people to step up. Be true to yourself. I think a huge burden lifts from your shoulders when you stop exerting so much effort to hide. You cannot imagine the positive impact you will have on the people around you. Xerox has a twenty-plus year history of milestones in creating a diverse work environment. We have scored 100 percent on the Human Rights Campaign's Corporate Equality Index since it began. Every time the bar was raised with new requirements, we met and discussed it with the company, and they always rose to the challenge. The CEI is only one index, and we reach beyond that and strive to have the highest standards and excellence around diversity. Over time, Xerox added domestic partnership benefits. We developed fully inclusive language in our nondiscrimination policy. Xerox supported the amicus brief against the Defense of Marriage Act, and we supported marriage equality in New York.

> **"Whether or not you are in a leadership role, one person can really make a difference."**

Through my process of coming out at work and facing personal challenges, I have realized the power that each of us has to make a difference. If we have the courage to step up and become out leaders, we can effect real change. My colleagues and employees have told me that I have made a real difference with my willingness to be out, share my story and support GALAXe. Whether or not you are in a leadership role, one person can really make a difference. You may not even be aware of the impact of your actions, but you can give others courage and strength by being open and willing to give back a little of your time.

Mike Feldman

Mike Feldman is Hewlett-Packard's Vice President and General Manager of the enterprise business for the Printing and Personal Systems Group at HP with responsibility for sales in the Americas. Mike leads a team shaping driving sales and services for the HP personal computer and printing portfolio to business and public sector customers in the U.S., Canada, and Latin America. He lives in Los Angeles with his partner, Art Jalandoni. Mike serves on the Out & Equal Board of Directors and co-chaired the O & E Executive Forum in 2012.

When I was five years old, I knew that something was different about me. I had an attraction to boys but tried to fight it. There weren't any public gay role models at that time — it was before *Ellen* and *Will and Grace*. I wanted to like girls so that I could fit in. I wanted to be "normal" like my parents and my brother. I hoped these feelings for other boys would just go away. But, of course, they didn't. By the age of twelve, I came to realize that this is who I am. I promised myself to hide it from everyone forever.

I didn't want to disappoint my parents and family. My parents are incredibly loving, supportive, selfless people. They did everything for my brother and me. They always put us first. I wanted them to always be proud of me and never to have to worry about me or my life choices. I was a conformist for the most part: I didn't have tattoos or piercings or wear edgy clothes. I wanted to always fit in and never stand out. Being gay seemed to jeopardize all of that. What would people think about me? How would they treat me? It was too overwhelming.

With time, the burden of hiding who I really was became too much. I was constantly lying about everything in my personal life, and I couldn't keep the lies straight. When I finally did come out to my family, I was thirty years old. I felt liberated. I became a lot closer to my family and friends. I was free to live my life authentically.

Coming out at work took a bit longer. I was actually in the closet for the first fifteen years that I worked at Hewlett-Packard (HP). I rationalized this by thinking that my sexual orientation had nothing to do with my work. This was really an excuse. The truth is that I was really afraid of how my colleagues would react if they found out, and how they would view me. Ironically, a lot of people had gotten a false impression of who I really was. They thought I was too focused on work and didn't have any kind of a social life. Of course, this wasn't true, but I wasn't sharing that part of myself with them. I was guarded and tried to avoid building personal relationships with colleagues.

> **All of these barriers were limiting my work abilities, and I finally decided that I didn't want to live that way anymore.**

All of these barriers were limiting my work abilities, and I finally decided that I didn't want to live that way anymore. The burden of keeping such a big part of me a secret was no longer tenable. I wanted to be my full, authentic self at work. I realized it was safe for me to come out at work in 2004, after seeing that HP was a premier sponsor of the Out & Equal Workplace Summit and that HP was also celebrating our participation in LGBT Pride in several cities across the U.S.

Coming out at work was a process. Once I made the decision, it took me about a year to do it. I planned to start by coming out to my boss, though I could not seem to drum up the courage to do it in person. I tried several times, but each time I was unable to say it to him. I finally decided to write him an email one Sunday afternoon. The moment I hit the send button, I feared that I had made a mistake. I waited for his response for an agonizing four hours. When he did reply, his supportive and caring words made my eyes fill with tears of joy. He reinforced our friendship and his belief in my work and personal abilities. He also made it very clear that my being open about my sexual orientation would change none of the positive things in our relationship or my status with the company. I wondered why it had taken me so long to take this step. He asked me that as well and said, "Mike, I've known you for fifteen years, and I'd love some feedback. Did I do anything to make you uncomfortable? Why did it take you so long to tell me? I can't wait to meet your partner." What a great guy. He and his wife are still close friends.

After this, I began to tell my staff in a more casual way — by just mentioning "my partner" in conversation. I think everyone was relieved that I was finally being upfront about it. The feedback I got from people was, "Mike, we thought all you had was HP." They didn't necessarily think I was gay, just a workaholic, very one-dimensional and only focused on my career. And the people who worked for me, I think, had felt very intimidated. When I told them that I was gay and I have a full life and a partner, now of nine years, and we have two dogs and a cat, and we love to hike and travel, people responded with, "Not only is this guy authentic and has a lot of credibility, but he's also got a full life and is very similar to us." I think it's helped tremendously, and I have now been promoted three times at HP since coming out. So it certainly hasn't hurt me, and I think it's made me a much better contributor to Hewlett-Packard.

I was still guarded in some situations and especially with customers. Eventually, I realized that being in the closet with anyone was wrong for me. I've yet to have a bad experience at HP or with customers. I've been lucky, but I have had colleagues who have faced discrimination or experienced bigoted comments, and there are still broad issues that affect us in the workplace.

> **" Coming out was a very positive journey. "**

Coming out was a very positive journey. I am grateful for all of this and feel lucky to have had nothing but great experiences. HP has proven to be a great place to come out, and my colleagues have all been supportive. I've also been very involved with Out & Equal, which has given me the confidence and tools I need to be comfortable being out and authentic in the workplace. I am forever grateful to this wonderful organization.

Part of what's positive in my personal experience stems from the broad advances that workplace equality has made over the last fifteen years. HP has evolved in that time from a very conservative company to a diverse organization. When I joined HP in 1988, the company's nondiscrimination policy did not explicitly prohibit discrimination based on sexual orientation. When Carly Fiorina came on board as CEO, she made a positive impact for the LGBT community at HP by helping to institute the proper protections for our community. We added sexual orientation as a provision to the nondiscrimination policy in 2002. Since then, we have improved same-sex partner benefits, including adding tax-equity, and we now include gender reassignment benefits.

I try to help effect change by serving on HP's Pride executive council. This gives me the opportunity to discuss these issues with our human resources and diversity and inclusion leadership, as well as our business leaders. Many people have told me I am a role model for them at HP as one of the few executives at the company. Some of my LGBT colleagues have told me that they felt comfortable to come out of the closet at work because I have been visible and demonstrated that you can have a successful career and be out.

I truly enjoy serving on HP's Pride executive council. In that forum, we discuss the issues our community faces at HP and we handle any matters that come up. As an example, we had our Pride group put up posters celebrating LGBT Pride Month, and some employees didn't care for that. We stepped in and had discussions with employees and managers to explain why this was important and in line with HP's values. I've also had the opportunity to personally discuss LGBT issues with our former CEO. Through ongoing communication and education, HP has adopted policies I am very proud of and has scored 100 percent on the HRC corporate index.

I think the best policy in any circumstance is to be honest, true to yourself and authentic. Hiding in the closet is not helpful in most situations. It puts up barriers and creates distrust. I know that it's still hard for people to come out at work, even at HP. It's painful to see, but I understand it. In the end, to be the best you can be, you have to show up at work as your full self — you have to be authentic and let people know who you are. It's part of work and part of being a creative and effective team player. I look forward to a time when this is a complete non-issue for everyone.

> **" You have to be authentic and let people know who you are. "**

Charles Lickel

Charles Lickel, retired Executive Vice President of IBM's Global Research Software Strategy, was one of the company's first openly gay executives. He was appointed co-chair of the IBM Gay, Lesbian, Bisexual, and Transgender Diversity Task Force by then-Chairman Lou Gerstner. Recognized as a diversity leader during his IBM career, Charles has received many awards, including the Computing Research Association's 2011 Nico Habermann Award for outstanding contributions in increasing the number and successes of underrepresented groups in the computing research community. He also received the 2009 Harvey Milk Alumni Award from the University of New York at Albany. He was honored in 2001 as one of the Gay Financial Network 25 for his effectiveness in shaping a diversity-friendly climate at work, as well as for service as a role model in business leadership. Charles was instrumental in creating the LGBT Leadership program in the Anderson School of Management at the University of California Los Angeles. He is a Senior Fellow of the American Leadership Forum and serves on the Board of Directors for Out & Equal Workplace Advocates and The Guidance Center in New York.

Some people would say that engineering Watson[1] was the highlight of my career with IBM, but the truth is that the most impactful and meaningful experience for me was working with the company's Global Gay, Lesbian, Bisexual, and Transgender (GLBT) Task Force. Created in 1995, the mission of the Task Force was to increase IBM's success in the marketplace by focusing on LGBT constituencies as customers. The Task Force developed a set of recommendations for IBM to build a more inclusive, diverse work environment. Gays and lesbians were already included in the nondiscrimination policy in our United States offices. We recommended that IBM take its policies a step further by offering domestic partner benefits.

That same year, my partner and I relocated to California so that I could accept a major new role leading a software lab. Many of my new colleagues did not know that I was gay. At the first executive meeting, another team member said, "It's ridiculous that IBM is starting to consider providing moving benefits for gays and lesbians. The next thing you know, they'll be offering benefits for our pets, too." Another executive stepped in and said, "Charles, you must have a strong opinion about that, since you're leading the GLBT Task Force." I responded, "I just relocated from the East Coast for this position. IBM paid for my dog to move, because we *do* have benefits for animals." The discussion ended there. Domestic partner benefits were implemented shortly after that, and it was the first great success of the GLBT Task Force.

---

[1] Watson was credited by the *New York Times* as being a type of technological Holy Grail. Not only did the computing system store information and provide answers, but it also proved able to select a correct answer in milliseconds. Watson's capacity was demonstrated on live TV on the *Jeopardy* show.

Lou Gerstner drove the formation of the diversity task forces, which resulted in domestic partner benefits, diversity network groups, and our gay and lesbian sales efforts. In 2000, Samuel Palmisano took these efforts a step further when he came on board as president and chief executive officer of IBM. He immediately set up a meeting with all of the co-chairs of the GLBT Task Force, and we discussed how to include transgender and bisexual individuals in our global policies. IBM had already started offering transgender benefits but did not include gender identity in its nondiscrimination policy.

One of Sam's first initiatives was to enforce a single nondiscrimination policy around the globe. Before that, each regional office could have a different discrimination policy than the other offices. Once we had a global diversity policy, we were able to insist that all offices post and enforce the same policy. Sadly, there are still many countries where LGBT people are not safe. We are always careful not to "out" people in those offices. It is very important that there always be one person in each country who is willing to stand up and be willing to drive change. Luckily, more and more countries have diversity chapters for LGBT individuals. We have made good progress in Latin America and Asia, implementing benefits and building communities to provide LGBT employees with the support that they need. Today, IBM's nondiscrimination policy includes sexual orientation and gender identity and provides a single standard for our offices around the world.

> **"** It is very important that there always be one person in each country who is willing to stand up and be willing to drive change. **"**

When we started to implement global diversity issues, I chose to work on Latin America, because I thought it would be one of the more challenging regions for LGBT inclusion. I worked with the Latin American executive team to create leadership seminars for employees who were out at work in Latin America. We also brought in their local leaders to discuss diversity issues. This initiative helped people come out and also made local executives' LGBT support very visible. The initiative proved to be quite powerful and transforming. I was amazed at how quickly they were able to implement all of the benefits and policies across each of the Latin American countries in which we did business.

Coming out is truly a never-ending process. The journey began for me in 1994, when I had already been working with IBM for sixteen years. I had always maintained a private, closeted life. For much of that time, being in the closet did not seem to matter because I did not have a partner. My coworkers mostly assumed that I had never married because I was shy or introverted. The truth was that I avoided personal conversations with them, because I never wanted to be dishonest with my team members, and I did not feel comfortable coming out at work.

> **" Coming out is truly a never-ending process. "**

This all began to change when Lou Gerstner joined the company and began focusing on diversity initiatives. I started to realize that it might be safe for me to come out of the closet. I reached out to a few of my gay coworkers and asked about the potential consequences and impact. I also discussed it privately with Linda Sanford, one of my key bosses. She encouraged me to come out, because she was sure that it would be a groundbreaking move that would allow me to play a larger leadership role at IBM.

After much deliberation, I wrote a letter to Lou Gerstner telling him that I was gay. I explained that my sexual orientation helped me better understand people, which in turn had helped me be successful at IBM. I also told him that as a high-level vice president, I thought I could help shape the LGBT agenda for the company.

Lou was very supportive, and he appointed me as co-chair of the GLBT Task Force. I was the first person in such a high position in the company to come out, and I received a lot of support for it.

Coming out is always a journey. People often ask me for advice on this big decision. I think that one of the most important things to do is to find a peer mentor and ask this person to nudge you if it seems like you are going too far. It is critical not to lose focus on doing the best work possible in your job; that is the best way to change people's views. People come out in different ways, and it is important to have someone to help you gauge whether you are being professional, to help others around you become more accepting.

Developing a support system at work is important, because you need people to be there for you if you ever face discrimination because of your sexual orientation. Despite all of the progress that has been made in creating safe work environments for LGBT individuals, there will still be a few staff members who will try to discriminate. You will probably never be able to prove discrimination very easily, but a support system can help you either rectify the situation or get out of it completely.

Everyone who champions diversity at IBM tries to make the effort to have an open door policy and mentor people. I have always been available to anyone who wants guidance about diversity issues, and it has never been an overwhelming responsibility. An innate filter exists, because people will often talk to their coworkers instead of approaching the leadership team. It takes a lot of courage to reach out to an executive, and it could be crushing to an individual who does so — and very detrimental — if we did not make ourselves available.

Because I believe that being visibly out and open is a powerful agent for change, I never hesitate to be out around customers, and I

> **Being visibly out and open is a powerful agent for change.**

address issues of diversity whenever I have the opportunity. For example, I have always talked about LGBT issues with my global teams. I tried to make progress without being offensive by asking questions, listening to concerns and trying to create bridges.

> **People can completely change their negative opinions about the LGBT community as a result of knowing someone who is lesbian, gay, bisexual, or transgender in the workplace.**

People can completely change their negative opinions about the LGBT community as a result of knowing someone who is lesbian, gay, bisexual, or transgender in the workplace. It is possible to help this process. A great example of this happened during one of our first diversity classes at IBM. The trainer was talking about a gay sales representative, and a few of my peers made some very homophobic comments. I spoke up and explained why their comments were hurtful and inaccurate. Each person who had made a comment approached me later and profusely apologized. They explained that they were wrong and said that they hoped I would not hold it against them, because they respected me a lot.

When leaders take a stance on diversity issues, it sends a message to every employee in the organization about what matters and sets an extremely positive level of expectation. If company leaders do not discuss these types of issues, or are not visible in front of audiences and employees, it sends a strong message that diversity is not important.

As we implemented changes in IBM, one of the most powerful things we asked executives to do was to actually say the words "lesbian, gay, bisexual, and transgender" while talking to their employees. A lot of people would leave the LGBT group off the list when talking about IBM's diversity groups. We made a large effort in reverse mentoring by asking senior executives to mention the LGBT group and spell out "lesbian, gay, bisexual and transgender." We successfully managed to engage senior vice presidents in using these terms, and it helped us drive the changes we wanted to make. We also spent time with lower and middle management talking about diversity issues and trying to raise awareness around each minority group represented at IBM.

We also made sure to offer training and career development to LGBT individuals. An excellent example is the training we created for our LGBT employees. We began to hold some of our leadership and GLBT Task Force efforts in concert with the Out & Equal Workplace Summit. The Summit has been a very useful tool for developing interpersonal and leadership skills, which in turn allowed employees to become much more successful in their careers. The energy level people gained from the Summit and the IBM LGBT leadership training events has been enormous, and almost all of the participants have said it was a life-transforming experience that improved their sense of self and self-worth. The Summit has also sparked their desire to step out as leaders at IBM to help drive change.

Like any other corporation, IBM experienced some pushback when we first started to implement diversity initiatives in the United States. Some employees were opposed to workplace equality for lesbian, gay, bisexual and transgender people. We had to allow time for them to vet their religious concerns and for us to explain that IBM was making these decisions because it was important to value and respect all employees. We were patient at first in trying to educate and explain. After eight years, we started to take a firmer stance: this is who we are as a company. If you do not like it, IBM is not right for you. Everyone has the right to his or her own views outside of work, but nobody has the right to make someone feel unwelcome in the workplace.

Some people who oppose equal rights for LGBT employees say that we should keep sexual orientation out of the office. This stance overlooks the fact that straight people talk to their coworkers about their husbands or wives without giving it a second thought. Why should it be any different for someone with a same-sex partner? In the corporate environment, where people put in so many hours at work, it is natural to talk about aspects of our personal lives in the office.

In fact, coming out improved my relationships with my coworkers and direct reports, because it was the first time that I began having open, natural conversations with my colleagues. Almost everyone who worked for me over the previous five years approached me after I came out and said, "Charles, we always knew you cared about us, and we loved working for you. But it always bugged us that you never talked to us about our families.

> **"Coming out improved my relationships with my coworkers and direct reports."**

We felt the need to do that, and it was the one thing you never ventured into. You stayed focused on business all the time." In retrospect, I realized that before coming out, I had avoided these conversations so that I would not have to either keep secrets or lie to my colleagues.

Building a diverse and inclusive work environment is not just about making people comfortable at work. The business case is clear and undeniable. One of the best examples I know of came from another executive's direct experience and his sharing his story with me. IBM had submitted a bid to a client for a lucrative project. The executive managing the project put together a team of his best people. Despite the hard work, the client chose another supplier. The client explained, "IBM had the best proposal, but we were going to have to transfer large numbers of our people to IBM, and the people you put in front of us did not reflect the people working for us. In the end, we took the other bid, because we were very uneasy about giving you the business." As a result, IBM lost a big contract. It is tough to do business if your company does not reflect your customers.

Internally, diverse teams are critical in this world of constant change. Business is evolving so quickly compared to thirty years ago. Companies need to be able to bring together diverse ideas to keep up with the progress happening all around us. Over the years, I have been part of teams that were blinded because they all came from the same background. When the world changed, they were not able to respond. For example, there was a very important group in IBM that had been successful for over twenty years with great growth and profits. When the PC era emerged, the group was slow to change and

> " *Diverse teams are critical in this world of constant change.* "

that put IBM at risk. We brought together a leadership team with people from diverse backgrounds and experiences, and the blend of talents and perspectives paid off. The new leadership team turned the group around so completely that it is still a vital and thriving part of IBM today.

Sometimes people make the mistake of thinking that having a diverse set of leaders creates complexity that could slow down the decision-making process. I have seen the opposite result at IBM: groups with diverse leaders are able to quickly determine the best course of action, because they are able to analyze the wide range of options more rapidly. As a result, having diverse perspectives actually speeds up the team and makes the group more accepting of any changes that need to take place.

Hiring the best talent is another important issue. A new generation has entered the workforce. Even with unemployment rates rising, there is still a war for talent. There is a very real competition to attract young leaders who will be able to sustain the organization for years and years to come. The younger generations coming to the workforce do not want to join a company that does not embrace people of all colors, backgrounds, experiences, and sexual orientations. I am always amazed at the number of young people at IBM who come up to me and say, "Charles, your diversity efforts are why I'm here. I hear that IBM made a lot of strides towards creating a diverse and inclusive work environment, and I heard you're one of the people who drove that."

> **"The younger generations coming to the workforce do not want to join a company that does not embrace people of all colors, backgrounds, experiences, and sexual orientations."**

By creating a diverse workplace that values all employees, companies are able to create an environment where people really believe that they are part of something special and want to contribute to the success of the organization. This helps retain and motivate employees, because they feel that they are personally making a difference. It gives employees something to be proud of when they leave for the day.

In conclusion, I have had a lot of great opportunities at IBM as a result of coming out of the closet. The diversity task force made a better work environment for a lot of people. Coming out was monumental for me. It helped my career and also allowed me to truly effect change at IBM.

Policies are not enough. They do not count for anything if the actions of the leaders and individuals in the company do not follow them. Ultimately, any company that does not create an inclusive and diverse workforce will have difficulty attracting and retaining employees and customers.

Renee Brown

Renee Brown is a Senior Vice President and the Director of Enterprise Social Media at Wells Fargo. She served as the Executive Sponsor of Wells Fargo's PRIDE team member network for three years and, pre-merger, of Wachovia's LGBT resource group, GALEA. As an out lesbian executive and trailblazer, Renee has served on many diversity teams and committees to develop and support greater equality in the workplace. Raised in Louisiana Cajun country, she now makes her home near Charlotte, North Carolina, with her partner, Kelly, and their nine-year-old daughter.

I was twenty years old, sitting in my dorm room at Louisiana State University when my phone rang. It was my mother calling, and I could tell she was mildly hysterical. "Your sister is a lesbian!" she said. "I always knew about *you*, but your sister, *too?!*" And that is how my coming out with my mom happened: a surprising accident. In that coming out, I learned it is possible to live under the same roof with someone for sixteen years and have whole worlds of emotion left unspoken.

Fast forward twelve years to a transition through merger from the old Wachovia out of Winston-Salem, NC, to the new Wachovia through an acquisition by First Union. At the announcement, I poured over the First Union diversity information online and was pleased to see a much better company policy in place. My partner, Kelly, and I had been considering starting a family, but we knew the old Wachovia diversity stance was far from welcoming. When we moved to Charlotte, I quickly made an appointment with a gay doctor to talk about the area's options for us to start a family. We moved in the early summer, and by August we found ourselves standing in our master bathroom staring in utter shock at the pregnancy test showing a very clear "positive." What happened to the proverbial, "Plan to try for a year before you become pregnant?" Like most great things in my life, the speed of that change was not planned, but, on reflection, it was a blessing.

My coming out at work story starts with that positive pregnancy test in August of 2002. I had never overtly lied in the workplace about being a lesbian, but I did not freely offer that data point to just anyone. However, when you are a pregnant lesbian, you have little choice but to come out in every single meeting and gathering. By winter, I was obviously pregnant, visibly so when I walked into a room. Because of that, I evolved from being mortified by having to come out multiple times a day to having fun with it. I was in a brand leadership role that required me to work across the enterprise, meeting with teams from across the company each day.

> **" When you are a pregnant lesbian, you have little choice but to come out in every single meeting and gathering. "**

Here is the flow of the typical conversation that unfolded pretty much every time I walked into a conference room: "Oh

Renee, congratulations on your pregnancy. I did not know you were married!" And my response was, "I am not." Then I would wait and watch the thought bubble rise above their heads and the panic appear in their eyes. Once I felt they had suffered enough, I would jump in, saying, "I have a partner. We have been together for eight years, and she plans to be the stay-at-home mom when our daughter is born in May." I would continue speaking until I could see that they had calmed down. It was amazing how one of two paths would emerge: we would either move into the business meeting very quickly, or if my reply had piqued my colleagues' curiosity, I would go on to explain how a household with two women can get pregnant. That was always a fun "teaching moment."

Those months of practicing coming out over and over again were a great way to experience many reactions and become comfortable with hearing myself saying the words. Coming out is still not easy in all situations. When I am in a thoughtful work mode, the task of sharing that I love differently requires shifting to a more vulnerable, emotional state. It's not a productive shift for me, but necessary. If I were to offer advice to someone considering coming out at work, it would be to practice in a safe place and actually hear the words come out of your mouth; that will make it easier to say them at the office.

In the realm of corporate diversity policies, I feel that I have been blessed to have been part of many mergers. With every change has come opportunity. With each bank merger, I have enjoyed improvements in diversity policies and practices. Wells Fargo has solid diversity practices in place, and being based in San Francisco offers a terrific backdrop to have positive conversations about LGBT equality. Wells Fargo has a history dating back more than twenty-five years of support for our community, and it is great to be a part of the next chapter. No company is perfect, and there are many areas where we still need improvement. I plan to continue to be a voice of change that is needed on a variety of issues, including tax benefit equalization and Wells Fargo's need to take a public stand in support of marriage equality. We have an open leadership team, and dialogue will continue.

I feel my role as a high-performing leader, a mom, long-term partner and a lesbian has been to bridge similarities and differences daily with straight and LGBT colleagues. Being a high-performing leader has been my ticket in to have a seat at the table. I feel my impact has often been of unspoken strength — knowing when to state the obvious inequity, and knowing when to offer a meaningful look instead and communicate nonverbally.

In addition to working to shift my straight colleagues' perspectives, I have also helped more than one LGBT colleague come out of closet — sometimes after many years there. By standing out and speaking up, I have served as a role model for several folks who are a generation my senior. In just being myself, I can make it plain that the positive impact outweighs the potential negative conflict.

> **" The generations before us suffered in silence, while my generation has a voice. "**

Among my fellow employees, the generational differences are very clear. Aside from a few trailblazers, the generations before us suffered in silence, while my generation has a voice. I feel the work of the next generation of LGBT leaders will be to continue our fight in the U.S. and to also give voice to those struggling in other countries for women's rights and LGBT rights. In addition, I feel LGBT folks can benefit by reaching beyond our family and direct concerns to add our voices to support other Americans facing discrimination in the continuing fight for racial equality or on behalf of those who are being discriminated against because of their social class, body size or religion. It is by helping others that we can help ourselves.

In the workplace, I have always enjoyed serving on diversity councils and with the employee groups. In each of these roles, I have learned much as well as been able to contribute. My experience with one person in particular, my first transgender colleague, forever changed me, and for the better. I was serving on a diversity council with a fellow I knew professionally, and one day he asked to have coffee and talk. Over coffee, he confided his struggle with gender identity and shared his plan to transition to a woman the next year. He was, at the time, a married man with a child. I stood by him through his transition and saw his family torn apart, and I watched as his job was eliminated. I invited him to our church, where he found an open and affirming community of support to help him when he felt he had no family. As she emerged in the transition, she landed a job in another state, and, based on our online exchange, seems to have started anew. This experience proved a steep learning curve for me. Observing the transition process was heart wrenching and taught me the power of friendship and the need for unconditional love.

> **"** My experience with one person in particular, my first transgender colleague, forever changed me, and for the better. **"**

I feel my largest impact in the workplace was to advance dialogue on LGBT rights at Wachovia, to be a voice and shoulder for my LGBT colleagues, and to advance a proposal in the Wells Fargo environment that I feel will soon be approved to proceed and will help balance the scales of equality. While I have often taken the microphone to represent our company, my best work has been done behind the scenes, and that is where my pride resides.

Over the last fifteen years or more, the largest obstacle to workplace equality that I have encountered has been the "protecting" of the most senior leaders who would prefer LGBT employees remain silent and stop seeking "special rights." I have encountered well-intentioned straight allies who have shielded those in the C-suite by having work slow-walked or issues simply left unaddressed. I am hopeful that those enablers will realize their role in maintaining inequality and will shift their behavior over time.

Out & Equal has been a breath of fresh air. I was new to the organization and attended my first Summit in 2010. It was an amazing experience. I had never been in a room of more than a thousand LGBT folks and allies. It brought tears to my eyes. After that experience, I attended the Out & Equal Executive Forum and found it a safe environment that offered amazing networking. I have remained in touch with many from the Executive Forum in meaningful ways. In a recent job transition, I tapped into that network to help connect me to their leaders in the social media space. Having contacts at other Fortune 500 companies with access to senior leadership is an invaluable gift; the fact that these contacts are LGBT is a terrific advantage! We are blessed to have Out & Equal at our side in our march towards full equality.

> " Out & Equal has been a breath of fresh air. I had never been in a room of more than a thousand LGBT folks and allies. It brought tears to my eyes. "

Christie Hardwick

Christie has more than thirty years of experience with Fortune 500 companies, nonprofit organizations and grassroots organizing efforts. She holds a master's degree in Organizational Development, is an American Leadership Forum Senior Fellow and served five years as an executive member of the Women's Leadership Board for the Kennedy School of Government at Harvard University and as past president of the National Board of Directors for GLSEN: Gay, Lesbian, & Straight Education Network. She provides strategic thinking and personal guidance services to clients across the United States. Christie has facilitated the Out & Equal Executive Forum since 2008. She lives in Provincetown, Massachusetts, with her wife, Jane Harper, and their four children.

If someone had told me in 1990, when I was running for my local school board, married to my Italian husband, raising three children and working on the presidential campaign, that by 2001 I'd be the president of the board for the Gay, Lesbian, & Straight, Education Network, I wouldn't have believed it. And now working within the LGBT equality movement nearly full time, I can't imagine it any other way.

My eight-year, second marriage to my lovely husband was ending. We could not agree on anything about how our lives should work, and we found ourselves in therapy. The savvy counselor separated us upon finding out I had "no desire" for my partner. My husband went to another therapist, and I stayed with mine until she grilled me with so many tough questions that I had to admit to myself that things were not as they had seemed with me.

People have asked me if she came right out and said, "Do you think you're gay?" But she didn't. She was a pro. She asked me how I felt about men, and then she asked me how I felt about women, and then she noticed all the light in the room. At first, I was literally outraged. I was mad at God — as I understood the divine then. I was shaking my fist and my head saying, "Come on, really? I need to be a woman, black, *and* a lesbian? What are you thinking?"

> **"** *Come on, really? I need to be a woman, black,* and *a lesbian?* **"**

Once I got over being mad, peace began to descend on me, because I was starting to feel like I belonged in my skin. Like many people, I started out thinking maybe I was bisexual, because I had married men and had children with them, and I had enjoyed some of the time with them. But then I thought about both weddings, and if you had been outside the churches where I was married, you would have seen me moments before my weddings with tears rolling down my young face.

With the first marriage, I was eighteen, and my "mother-in-law-to-be" saw me crying on the steps and asked, "What's wrong? Don't you want to marry my son?" I only thought for a moment and looked into her sweet face and knew I would go through with it. There was no one there for me. My mother's religion kept her from attending my wedding, and I didn't see her again until I nearly died in childbirth a year later.

At nineteen, I became a mother of twins, and I was divorced from my blonde surfer husband by the time I was twenty-one. On my own for five years, I began a career in high tech, hiring engineers for a semiconductor firm. My best friend at the time worked at a language school and was always bringing her sometimes interesting and other times goofy students out with us. I married one of the interesting ones and had a third child with him before our marriage crumbled. The marriage was completely over with my words, "I'm attracted to women." I was thirty-four years old, and when I had married him at twenty-six, I had stood outside the little chapel, frozen in my steps, crying when our minister found me and gently said, "You don't have to do this." But I imagined the crowd inside waiting for me and my sweet husband-to-be, and I couldn't think of any reason for my tears, and I loved him.

In retrospect, I can see that my soul was crying out for attention. Marrying was not what I needed to be doing. I had no idea who I was or why I was making these choices. In spite of myself, I became the mother of four amazing, beautiful people who turned out spectacularly.

Once I accepted my true self, I was on a mission. I went to a local bookstore where I'd been told lesbians hung out, and they had a little backroom where they held a "coming out" workshop. I went to the workshop and left there sure I must not be gay, because every woman looked similar and liked folk music, and I loved Motown and wore skirts with flowers. I got over that idea as soon as I attended my first Women's Weekend. I was so happy and joyful and decided there couldn't be anything more beautiful than women lying naked on their bellies around a pool in the summer sun, up in the mountains, far from everything I knew.

I had my first lesbian kiss, and I finally understood what all the poets, singers, and romantics had been blabbering about. Finally.

After a year of acting the teenager, I connected with a woman who would be my partner for eight years.

Telling my ex-husband and my children that this was all real for me went better than I'd thought it would. At least it went better with the children. To this day, I feel sorry that I didn't know myself better. My dear second husband loved me and was a dedicated father and a good man. He was hurt and took my coming out personally for some time. I'm glad to say he remarried soon after and lives happily with his wife and three beautiful daughters, who enjoy my son as their big brother. Initially, his wife was uncomfortable with our friendly relationship as exes, but then at age nine, my son told her, "Stop worrying about my mom. She's gay!" For him, I hand-wrote a storybook about how you love differently, whether it's people or flowers or anything else, and it makes you who you are uniquely. He was fine with it at his age. The fifteen-year-old twins responded in their own ways, perfectly suited to their personalities.

I came out on a Mother's Day, feeling peaceful and healthy and good about myself. I had remained in therapy for a few years and had worked out all the layers of feeling about homosexuality that I had inherited. When I told my eldest daughter and son about my sexual orientation, my daughter said, "I knew that!" and my son was troubled. He asked, "Does it mean you won't run for mayor, or that you'll be marching in parades now? I wish you hadn't said it out loud; it makes it true."

> " I came out on a Mother's Day, feeling peaceful and healthy and good about myself. "

We continued to talk, and I was receptive to their questions, and I lived my life openly. Over time, all three children came to accept and love my partner. When the youngest became a teenager, he yelled one day, "I wish you could just be normal like the other moms!" I was surprised to find out he was referring to my having a meditation room and not to my sexual orientation. He and I did have a few tough discussions in which I tried to convince him that my love for women was not a rejection of all men in all ways. He felt that if I couldn't love his father, perhaps I couldn't love him.

When I was divorced from my second husband, I went back to work full time. I'd been working from home as a training and development consultant while my youngest was in preschool. I remember standing in the hallway of my new office, noticing it was the time of day I would usually have picked him up from school, and tears began streaming down my face. I knew someone else would see his smiling face every day, and that clock went off in my heart for weeks. Since I was back in the workforce in 1993 after having been at home for five years, I decided I would re-enter as an out lesbian and try my luck. I joined a very progressive company that was considered the "cool" place to work back then. I was not only accepted, but they went out of their way to provide a supportive atmosphere.

> **There were reprints of an article on everyone's desk, "How to Work with Your Gay Coworker."**

This was a global technology company, and my immediate manager was a woman from England. The day I arrived in the office, there were reprints of an article on everyone's desk, including mine. The title of the article was "How to Work with Your Gay Coworker." I was actually embarrassed. I thought, "Does it really take instructions to work with me?" Her intention was good, but a little over-the-top. It was one of those companies that did all the right things. In the early nineties, they had policies for fair treatment, same-gender partners were invited to social events, there was an employee group, and gay pride was celebrated every year.

All that said, there was little sensitivity to anyone who wasn't comfortable being out. It was common to hear straight allies bemoan,

"What's the problem with him? Everyone knows he's gay." At a team-building event, one of the top execs in the company put out the question, "If you could kiss anyone you wanted in life, who would it be?" I had transferred out of my original workgroup and was new to this one. I went up to the microphone, paused and said, "Jodie Foster?" People giggled, but I realized I felt put on the spot, and I was the only one that day who answered with someone of the same gender.

Compared to what I heard from friends and colleagues about other companies and communities, I was living and working in a paradise of acceptance. There were a few awkward moments when I first came out and several friends chose to maintain relationships with my husband instead of me, or when men at work asked me for dates and I had to explain about my girlfriend. But all in all, living and working in Silicon Valley and being out were not difficult for me.

I was promoted regularly and ended my tech career in 2004 as a Vice President, after being an executive for several years. My authenticity was often cited in my reviews and in several awards I received for leadership. I believe that my authenticity started with being my full self and not pretending to be a heterosexual woman.

> " I believe that my authenticity started with being my full self. "

The culture of this company was conducive to my being fully included, because it was a creative, innovative company that wanted everyone to bring everything they had to keep pushing the envelope of what was possible. It was a lot like a college campus or an artists' center. No one was expected to conform, and everyone was expected to make a unique contribution.

The company ran into some trouble in 2000 when they decided to hire the firm that taught The Seven Habits of Highly Successful

Leaders. The firm's founder openly shared his religious view that gay, lesbian, bisexual and transgender leaders were not acceptable in his definition of healthy, equal people. During this controversy, I met Selisse Berry. She showed up on our doorstep and invited us to join her in making our workplace truly safe and inclusive for LGBT people. In those days, she was a force of one, but her clarity, determination and ability to show us where we were not hitting the mark of a truly equal workplace got our attention. Seven years later we met again. She was holding a Summit for two thousand people and managing a brand that meant workplace equality for hundreds of premiere companies.

Today, I find myself called upon by organizations that aspire to be more inclusive of all aspects of diversity. My identity — which includes black, woman, lesbian, mother, minister and social activist — plays a role in my guidance to corporations.

I recall the first conversation I had with a CEO of a Fortune 500 software company. Even though his company was consistently rated as a great place to work and found itself high on the *Fortune* magazine list, it was lagging in the area of LGBT equality. I gave him a briefing on the complexity and breadth of the LGBT equality movement and was privileged to conduct focus group sessions with a mixed-level group of LGBT employees. He listened and learned. He learned about the gay man who was among his highest-ranking leaders and who feared coming out could harm his career. He heard from a female employee who felt free to tell coworkers about two of her three children, but often left out her transgender son because of her own fear of rejection. He learned about the intersection of race and sexual orientation from a lesbian mother who had adopted a child of Mexican heritage with her partner and attends the Latino employee group in affinity with their adopted son.

The CEO was struck by the complexity of his LGBT employees' and allies' lives. He was surprised that even in the company's award-winning culture, individuals who support the freedom of

> **" The CEO was struck by the complexity of his LGBT employees' and allies' lives. "**

LGBT people, *"allies,"* were constantly having to educate their peers about inappropriate comments or presumptions. After a year of exposure and connection with his LGBT employees, including executive leaders, the company changed two of its long-standing policies. The company took a position supporting ENDA and extended full health benefits to transgender employees.

Another client, a global banking institution, was lagging behind its competitors and had no currency with those who look for and value diversity, outreach and inclusion. I had the opportunity to interview twelve of the company's top executives from around the world and learn about their attitudes and ideas related to diversity and inclusion. In my report, I showed how their thinking was neither consistent nor tied to any central philosophy of the company. Each executive had a different reason why he or she thought the company should care about diversity. Each had a different view on how assertive the company should be in recruitment, promotion and retention of diverse employees. Their attitudes ranged from, "We don't have problem here," to "The culture is cutthroat and there is no commitment to bringing in diverse voices." Some felt that having a diverse workforce was a good marketing decision but not important to the functioning of the business. Few recognized the value of bringing in the unique perspectives of those from different cultures, ethnicities, gender, sexual orientation, and even worldview.

As a result of my white paper describing their thoughts, the executives committed to a series of meetings in order to hash out together what they wanted the company to be and what its culture would look like. They had to decide together how to become welcoming and inclusive of all employees and what practices they were willing to engage in to ensure that all levels of the workforce reflected their constituency.

> **"I was struck by how important the corporations were as change agents for equality."**

When I originally started working in high tech, I had given up on my plans to be a teacher, because as a single mother I didn't believe I could afford to be a teacher. So I spent many years on the board of GLSEN and served equality in the area of kindergarten through high school education. Meeting Selisse again, I was struck by how important the corporations were as change agents for equality and was deeply impressed by the inroads made by Out & Equal. I joined her as a consultant in 2007 to create informative and motivating experiences for lesbian, gay, bisexual and transgender executives as a means to help usher in the age of workplace equality. I became a teacher after all but in a way that I couldn't have envisioned. Nor could I envision this *out and equal* life with all of its unexpected challenges, new opportunities and many blessings.

Ivan Scalfarotto

Ivan Scalfarotto is Founding Executive Director of "Parks — *Liberi e Uguali*." The nonprofit organization supports Italian companies and Italian branches of multinationals in developing and implementing comprehensive diversity policies and practices that include and protect lesbian, gay, bisexual, and transgender employees. Ivan has twenty years' experience as a Human Resources executive and as a strategic Human Resources advisor. He has worked for Italian and international companies in Milan, London and Moscow. He served as Co-Chair of CitiPride, Citigroup's LGBT network in London. Ivan lives in Milan with his partner, Federico, and their two cats.

I am a full-blooded Italian, raised in Southern Italy during the 1980s. Italian stereotypes related to gender expression have not evolved much over the years. Perceptions have evolved somewhat over the years, but when I was a teenager, gay men were still viewed as people who did not behave like men. As a manly boy who was attracted to other men, I did not understand where I fit into the equation. I felt like an alien. I was a very social, outgoing guy, and it was difficult to keep such a big secret. I ignored my feelings until after I had finished college with top marks and landed a great job with a prestigious bank.

I began to come to terms with my sexual orientation once I was on my own and able to adequately support myself. I knew that I would be able to take care of myself even if my family rejected me. In reality, my entire family was extremely accepting, and my father was quite offended that he was the last to know. I explained that I told him last because he was the person whom I was most afraid of losing.

When I joined Citi as the Head of Human Resources for Italy, I was working for a very diversity-friendly company. Despite this, I did not feel safe coming out in Milan because the climate is openly homophobic: people would not come out at work and most people would tell you that they don't have any gay or lesbian colleagues. Also, Milan's business community is very small, and I was a young, bright guy with potential. I thought, "If I tell Citi that I'm gay, everyone in Milan will know, because gossip spreads like wildfire here. Will a big, domestic bank in Milan hire me in the future if they know that I am gay?"

Of course, I knew that Citi would have no problem with my sexual orientation. When I took a position in London, I came out to my new boss. I also asked for the opportunity to do some diversity work. Diversity was a different department from Human Resources, and so my boss introduced me to the Head of Diversity, who reported directly to the CEO of Europe, the Middle East, and Africa. I still remember our first conversation, when the Head of Diversity asked me, "You are an Italian man. Why are you interested in diversity?" I replied, "Because I'm gay." A few months after I moved to London, she called on me to serve as the HR liaison to the new gay and lesbian employee resource group (ERG) being created by the London team.

A year after I came out, I attended my first Out & Equal Workplace Summit in Minneapolis. It was a life-changing experience. I had never before seen such a huge number of LGBT professionals gathering together. It was a huge jump for me: I had thought that being "out and equal" at work was a contradiction in terms. Seeing so many successful and openly gay, lesbian, bisexual, and transgender people was an emotional shock for me. The Summit gave me the boost to become even more involved with CitiPride and the bank's diversity effort. I became more involved with the employee resource group and eventually became the group's co-chair.

As a Human Resources professional and a gay man, I saw the importance of diversity and inclusion firsthand. As soon as I was out at work, I became more relaxed and focused, and I felt a lot of gratitude to Citi for letting me be myself. This increased my motivation and made me more confident at work. I saw the benefits of a diverse work environment again when I was offered a position as the Head of Human Resources in Moscow. The bank was investing heavily in Russia, but the post in Moscow was not an easy sell to Citi's high-performers. I was happy to embark on this new adventure as long as my partner could come. We both needed visas and a work permit. I told Citi that I would only take the position if Federico could come with me. Citi agreed, and it was a win-win situation. Citi was able to put an experienced person into the Moscow office to run Human Resources during a time when the bank was growing very quickly, from three hundred to six thousand staff members. I also benefited greatly from the opportunity and received a lot of important professional and personal experience.

When I first arrived in Moscow, I was interviewed for the local bank newsletter; the article was a means to introduce me to the employees. The first question in the interview was about my family. I answered, "I moved to Moscow with my partner and my cat." A few days later, my deputy — a very knowledgeable and expert Russian woman — knocked on my door and sat in the chair across from my desk with an embarrassed smile. She whispered, "The Internal Communication Department is willing to change one of the answers in your interview." I asked which question she was referring to, and she replied, "The one about your family does not sound right in Russian. The Communications Department would prefer to say, 'I am not married, and I have a cat.'"

"No way," I said firmly. "I want to say who I am. I do not care if it doesn't sound right in Russian. It sounds right to me." After the interview was published, I received an email from an employee I had never even met. He wrote, "Thank you for your courage. I am proud to have an HR Director like you. Please don't tell anybody I wrote this email to you." That email is still on the list of things I am most proud of from my stay in Russia. During my tenure there, we conducted diversity training for hundreds of employees in Russia, the Ukraine, and Kazakhstan. Mark Robinson, the charismatic and visionary CEO of Citi at that time, supported me in these efforts.

> " We conducted diversity training for hundreds of employees in Russia, the Ukraine, and Kazakhstan. "

During those years, my relationship with Selisse Berry, the Founding Executive Director of Out & Equal, developed. We started to envision Out & Equal doing some work in Europe. It was in 2009 at the Workplace Summit in Austin that I realized that I wanted to devote my life to creating workplace equality for LGBT people in Italy. I called my partner, Federico, from Austin and told him I was going to leave Citi and start a nonprofit group. A few days later, I began conversations with Citi about leaving the bank.

I left my role as Citi's Head of Human Resources of Banking for Western Europe in 2009 to form Parks, an Italian nonprofit employers' organization working under the patronage of the Italian Ministry of Equal Opportunities. I felt that it was essential for me to do something to bring change to Italy. Italian culture is still very homophobic, and being openly gay in Milan is still a huge career risk.

We officially launched Parks in January 2011. The main goal of Parks is to support member companies in the process of fully appreciating business opportunities related to having a comprehensive diversity strategy in place. Parks' mission is to focus on what may be the most culturally challenging, overlooked areas of diversity in Italy: sexual orientation and gender identity.

Addressing LGBT issues in Italy is very important. Even left-wing politicians oppose marriage for same-sex couples. Homophobia and heterosexism are the norm. Italians do not understand that homophobia extends beyond violence and includes hateful words. Because of my social standing as someone who has worked abroad in high-level positions with international corporations, no one says inappropriate things to me personally. When I am representing Parks, though, I have a different experience. Many people say that their companies are not interested in joining Parks because LGBT issues are not important in the workplace. Some say that sexual orientation has nothing to do with work. Others make homophobic comments without even considering that these remarks are hurtful to me.

Some companies have responded that they do not have any LGBT employees. Others acknowledged that they must have a few gay or lesbian employees but said that these individuals were invisible and had not requested anything from the firm. We began to break the wall of silence around homosexuality in the workplace in Italy by simply having companies acknowledge the existence of gay employees.

One big challenge is the perception of diversity in Italy. Many companies view diversity as a list that continues to grow longer. These companies address diversity issues one at a time, starting with women and then expanding to people of color, then employees with disabilities. Having adopted this model, they are not willing to address sexual orientation for another five years, until they feel they are "ready." I always explain to them that diversity is not a line — it is a point that continues to expand. You cannot start with women first, and then Black, and then disabled people, and then foreigners and gay people many years later. You have to create an inclusive workplace for everyone from the beginning, because diversity issues are not credible otherwise. If you support women, but at the same time you are racist, women will not trust the effort you are making.

> " *Diversity is not a line — it is a point that continues to expand.* "

You have to make it clear that you are investing in every employee's talent and the human capital of the firm.

A lot of companies approach Parks and do not allow us to discuss LGBT issues at first. We use a holistic approach by conducting general diversity training and introducing the concept of diversity as a whole. Once the organization has developed an understanding of the benefits of diversity in the workplace, we are able to integrate LGBT issues as part of a holistic diversity strategy. Using this method, homosexuality becomes a reasonable subject even in a place like Italy.

Citi was incredibly supportive when I left to form Parks. In fact, it was the first business to join the organization. Paolo Arnaldi, the Chair of Parks' Board of Directors, is also Citi's Head of Human Resources for Western Europe, based in Milan. We currently have thirteen other member firms, including IKEA, Johnson & Johnson, Lilly, Roche, Linklaters, IBM, Clifford Chance, and Telecom Italia. The Italian Association of Human Resources Directors was our most recent addition. Their membership signifies an important step for Parks because it has helped strengthen our reputation within Italy's Human Resources Community. We helped IKEA extend benefits to lesbian and gay employees and their families. We are now beginning the same process with Johnson & Johnson. We also ran the first survey on the perception of LGBT issues in the workplace at three IKEA stores, covering nearly one thousand employees. We have done dozens of diversity sessions for our member companies, and we help them with their internal communications. We were also recently granted a mandate from the Italian Ministry of Equal Opportunities to run a three hundred sixty-degree diversity project in the southern part of Italy.

In May 2012, we organized the first "GLBT People at Work" forum, which was sponsored by the U.S. and Dutch embassies and held in Rome. More than one hundred and fifty people attended the event. We presented Selisse Berry with the first ever "Parks Award," and the Board of Directors voted to make her an honorary member, because she has been instrumental in changing the lives of a multitude of lesbian, gay, bisexual, and transgender people at work. I am very thankful that she inspired me.

> **" I hope that by inspiring change in Italy, I will make it safer for people to be true to themselves. "**

I am amazed at the many ways that life has changed since I was a child, afraid to admit my own sexual orientation. I hope that by inspiring change in Italy, I will make it safer for people to be true to themselves. Milan has become my home, and I am grateful for the opportunity I have to continue changing the environment for lesbian, gay, bisexual, and transgender people at work.

Donna Griffin

A twenty-seven-year employee of Chubb, Donna Griffin served as Chief Diversity Officer and for fourteen years as Director of Worldwide Operations. Donna spearheaded Chubb's minority talent management strategy and diversity education efforts across the organization and was an influential advocate for Chubb's diversity efforts and accomplishments externally. As an ally, Donna is the  founding corporate sponsor of Chubb's Black Employee Network, and she has also served on Chubb's Women's Development Council and the Gay and Lesbian Employee Network. She served on the Strategic Planning Committee for Executive Women of New Jersey and the Advisory Board for the Rutgers Institute for Women's Leadership. Donna has won many awards for leadership. In 2011, the National Gay & Lesbian Chamber of Commerce named her Outstanding Corporate Leader of the Year for Diversity and Leadership. *New Jersey Business Magazine* honored Donna as one of 2010's "Best 50" women in New Jersey business, as well as one of 2003's "25 Women of Influence;" she was also named one of the 10 Most Powerful Women in New Jersey Business in 2006 by the *New Jersey Star Ledger*. She serves on the Out & Equal Board of Directors.

I kept my personal life out of the work environment for many years. This changed in 1996, when my partner was dying of ovarian cancer. She took a terrible turn for the worse six months before she passed away. I was working as the head of global operations, which was a high profile job that required me to travel all over the world. I needed to be home with my partner and could not fulfill all of my job commitments. I finally went to lunch with my boss and told him. He asked all of the right questions, and I received an immense amount of support from him. The president of the company also took me aside at one point and said, "Donna, I know you've chosen to be private about your personal life. I respect that, and I also know you're going through a difficult time. If there's anything I can do, or that the company can do, all you need to do is ask."

The support I received during this terrible time in my life was incredible. It really spoke to the quality of the people at Chubb. Coming out to the management team was very freeing. It was nice that they knew and that coming out did not have an impact on my work.

> **" I had a responsibility as the most senior gay person in my company to be a role model. "**

Three years later, the Chief Diversity Officer invited me to speak to the Gay and Lesbian Employee Network. They were hosting a leadership conference in conjunction with the Out & Equal Workplace Summit. The conference completely changed my perspective, because I heard many stories about the issues people were dealing with in the workplace. I was so touched that I stayed and went to the Summit for the very first time. It was a life-changing event, because I finally understood: I had a responsibility as the most senior gay person in my company to be a role model. The Summit filled me with a sense of pride in who I am and in other people who are successful and out within their organizations. It instilled a sense of activism in me, and I was inspired to create change for others in my organization and other companies.

Shortly thereafter, the Chief Diversity Officer decided to retire, which opened up the perfect opportunity for me to devote myself full time to diversity work, which had become a passion for me. I applied for the newly open position and became the Chief Diversity Officer, a role I held for two years until I retired. Being in that role meant that I was the standard bearer for the company and needed to be very public about my life. Someone asked me once in an interview if people in the company thought it was odd that I was a white woman working as the Chief Diversity Officer. I responded, "I'm not your standard fare white woman, because I'm a lesbian."

"As Chief Diversity Officer, I focused on obtaining full transgender benefits and medical coverage for Chubb employees."

During my tenure as Chief Diversity Officer, I focused on obtaining full transgender benefits and medical coverage for Chubb employees. I had a strong relationship with the senior manager who was the corporate sponsor for the LGBT network, and we worked together to push this initiative forward.

I also developed a program for women of color within the organization. We put together a senior mentorship program by selecting nine women at vice president levels and hiring outside consultants to develop these women's leadership skill sets so that they could move into senior vice president positions. This was so successful that we followed up with a mentorship program for fifteen assistant vice presidents. I was a leading advocate for the women of color initiative partly because I was not a member of the group, and I think it is important to do things that are not self-serving.

Chubb's lesbian, gay, bisexual, and transgender resource group, GLEN, has been successful, and I have seen positive changes in the workplace climate as a result of people being out and open. Chubb has an incredibly supportive work environment for its diverse employees. Once, a brand-new employee complained to human resources about the huge rainbow flag we were displaying for Gay Pride. The HR representative told him, "If you have that much of an issue with it, perhaps this isn't the best place for you to be working." That kind of LGBT support is so important.

After I came out at work and realized the importance of serving as a leader, I began to use the power of my position to influence other people. Since Chubb is a leader in diversity initiatives, other financial companies have reached out to us for advice. I helped other companies create LGBT employee resource groups. I have also lobbied for the Employment Nondiscrimination Act in Washington, D.C., as well as tax equity and medical benefits.

I met with state senators from New Jersey to discuss the value of diversity to large companies like Chubb. I explained that we have locations across the country, and it is a priority for us to be able to treat all of our employees equitably. It is very cumbersome for a company's accounting system to implement the technology changes needed to keep track of states with civil unions, same-sex marriage and domestic partnerships. The company wants to treat LGBT individuals the same as its other staff members, and yet LGBT employees are taxed for their partners' medical benefits. Looking

> " It is very cumbersome to keep track of states with civil unions, same-sex marriage and domestic partnerships. "

to the future, I hope that Chubb moves forward with tax equity. More importantly, I hope that the Defense of Marriage Act is repealed so that companies will not have to independently address this issue, and people can truly receive fair and equal treatment.

Interestingly enough, I came out at work years before I came out to my mother. I lived away for so many years that it never seemed important. When I became the Chief Diversity Officer, I realized that my being lesbian would become very public knowledge. One Thanksgiving morning, my mother and I were having coffee and reading the paper. I told her, "There's something about me that is important for you to know. I'm gay." She looked at me and said, "I didn't know that." I responded, "I'm approaching retirement, and I want to be able to spend more time with you. But I can't leave out such a large part of my life. I've met someone, and I'm really happy." She replied, "That's great. Why don't you bring her down?"

We continued the conversation, and she said, "A lot of Irish families have a maiden aunt. I thought you were just a career girl." I explained to her, "No, I'm really happy. I have a great life, and Mary Ann is an important part of it." Once she knew about Mary Ann, my mother completely embraced her. The only thing I regret is that I did not tell her earlier. We've always been a close family, and now my family has totally embraced my life, my partner, and me.

Steve Sears

Steve Sears was Vice President of Marketing and a twenty-one-year veteran of PepsiCo, Inc., where he served in a wide variety of roles, including national oversight of such brands as Pepsi-Cola, Mountain Dew, Aquafina, Lay's, and Fritos. From 1998 through 2001, he was chief marketing officer for Frito-Lay's business unit in Australia. Now based in Kansas City, where he lives with his partner, John Lavryssen, Mr. Sears previously served as Treasurer and Vice President on the Out & Equal Board of Directors.

As a child growing up in the suburbs of Kansas City, Missouri, it was obvious to me there was something about my personality and mannerisms that gave me away. In the 1960s, gay people were unheard of in our community, but I was teased and bullied through grade school and junior high for being effeminate. I hated being picked on. I would do anything I could to avoid that, and the last thing I wanted to do was exacerbate the bullying by affirming that I was gay, which was what I was being teased about in the first place. I thought to myself, "I will outgrow this feeling of intimidation and grow into my own personality and my own skin." I did not talk to anyone about the bullying, and my parents had no idea that I was being harassed.

It got better when I went to high school. My peer group started to mature to the point where people could appreciate one another's differences. All of a sudden, being creative and smart were no longer deficits that made me weird, but instead were recognized as talents. My junior and senior years in high school were two of the happiest years of my life. The bullying and teasing stopped, and I became celebrated for my skills and talents.

> " *The bullying and teasing stopped, and I became celebrated for my skills and talents.* "

I was very closeted and even homophobic in college. I had plenty of female friends who came to our college fraternity parties, and I let my fraternity brothers think I had girlfriends. For most of my twenties, I enjoyed the fact that I was doing well socially and academically, and my career was starting to blossom. Why would I want to start publicly dealing with my sexual orientation and potentially put all I'd accomplished and overcome at risk? I certainly did not want to return to those terrible feelings and experiences I'd had as a child.

The turning point for me came as I was approaching thirty. I started to realize that my social circle had become a bunch of married couples and me. I was the oddball who never dated and always went alone to social events. I had to ask myself if I wanted to be single for the rest of my life and deny what has clearly been a part of me since my earliest memory, which is that I am attracted to men and not women. I realized that I would have to stop worrying about what other people might think of me.

When I was thirty, I started to take tentative steps to discreetly meet men. I slowly learned what it means to have gay friendships and relationships. I began to learn the culture of the LGBT community. At first, I was afraid that I would be spotted in gay places by people I had not yet come out to. After a while, I stopped being afraid. It took several years to go through this process. Every little baby step I took towards coming out to myself and others was well thought through in advance. Planning was very important to me, because I didn't ever want to have regrets or wish that I could put the genie back in the bottle. I wanted to make sure that I was emotionally prepared for the outcome. It was painfully slow, but it felt right for me.

Along the way, I met a gay couple who encouraged me to attend a weekend coming out seminar. It was an amazing three-day workshop that gave me some great tools to consider ways in which I could tell my family. After the seminar, I decided to write a full disclosure letter to my family about my sexual orientation and the bullying I'd experienced as a child. After three months of writing and rewriting, I was happy with my letter and shipped it overnight.

I watched the clock nervously the next day, wondering when my parents would receive the package. When I came back from lunch that day, there was a note on my desk from my assistant, saying that my father had left a message, "Everything is ok." My parents were fantastic and later told me that they considered my letter a gift. My mother started making copies of it and giving it to friends and extended members of the family. She explained that she was not ashamed at all, and she wanted people to know what we were going through as a family. She felt that the best way to express that was through my own written words. I was a little shocked at first, but then I understood.

> " My parents were fantastic and later told me that they considered my letter a gift. "

In much the same way that I took my time to come out in my personal life, I waited for the right moment to come out at work. I joined PepsiCo in Dallas in 1987, right out of graduate school. Being in the closet was awkward, because my career was the top priority for me at that time in my life. It became increasingly challenging and frustrating to keep my work and social lives separate, particularly when I met my life partner, John, in 1997.

I decided to come out of the closet when I was offered an international assignment to help form the executive team in Sydney, Australia. I was excited to have such an incredible opportunity, but I had to deal with the fact that the company thought I was single. I decided I would only take the assignment if John could come with me. I knew that meant that I would have to come out to PepsiCo's most senior executives. The executive team responded in a very positive way, and all of the policies that existed for married employees were extended to me. It was uncharted territory for the company, because at that point there were certainly no openly gay senior executives in the company, much less gay expatriates being sent overseas. There were no policies in place for PepsiCo to refer to in this situation. The executives who were personally involved in this new assignment were senior enough to make the decisions that they felt were right. John received health care, his moving costs were covered, and we were granted the housing and travel allowance allotted to married couples. Everything was handled beautifully, and I was so thankful that it was all so easy.

It was uncharted territory for the company, because at that point there were certainly no openly gay senior executives in the company.

At the same time, I thought it was unfair that no one else in the company had access to the same benefits. My post in Australia was far away from any in-house discussions about policy changes. I vowed to myself that I would try to make some policy changes when I returned to the United States.

In 2002, I had my chance when I moved to PepsiCo's global headquarters in New York to become the Vice President of Marketing. I was the first openly gay executive. I started to become very involved in the cause of creating LGBT inclusion policies. I consulted directly with the Senior Vice President of Human Resources to implement domestic partner benefits. A small LGBT employee resource group (ERG) was already active in New York. I became the liaison between the policy makers and the ERG members.

My most visible act of coming out occurred when I was invited to Puerto Rico to take part in a PepsiCo meeting that brought together the company's executives from around the world. The event invitation included spouses. A handful of people knew I was gay, but I had not come out to all my colleagues. I decided that bringing John to the event with me was the right thing to do. It was really exciting, because we were the first and only gay couple to ever attend something like this within the company. We were completely accepted. In fact, the Chairman of PepsiCo went out of his way to introduce himself to John and patted me on the back for bringing him.

> **"** We were the first and only gay couple to ever attend something like this within the company. We were completely accepted. **"**

I was promoted to Vice President of Pepsi-Cola Marketing shortly after a TV commercial featuring Carson Kressley was created.

In the commercial, a handsome man is shown walking down the street drinking Diet Pepsi. As he passes, a dozen beautiful women gather behind him, including

Cindy Crawford, who lowers her sunglasses to take a better look. Then Carson walks past the man and does a double take, lowering his glasses to check him out too.

The ad was so entertaining that my boss and I decided that we would like to feature it as our Super Bowl commercial for the year. We felt so strongly about it that we sought approval from the Chairman of the company, who was a very conservative, religious man. Eventually, he gave us approval to air the commercial. It became one of the most talked about Super Bowl advertisements, because it was the very first in that timeslot to feature an openly gay person. The company received a GLAAD award for the ad.

Another year, Pepsi's LGBT employee resource group wanted to have a PepsiCo float in the New York City Gay Pride Parade for the first time ever. I was happy to fund that as a marketing expenditure, but I had to gain approval from the most senior leaders. Some top executives were concerned that conservative groups might target PepsiCo for supporting LGBT causes. Obtaining approval required several challenging discussions with people across the company. In one particular conversation, a Senior Vice President told me, "I will hold you personally responsible if anything bad happens as a result of this." I agreed to take full responsibility. We created a fabulous float, and it proved to be a big success, particularly in the eyes of our LGBT employees. In fact, PepsiCo has had a float in the parade every year since.

I truly believe that coming out of the closet improved my work life. Within PepsiCo, we were all working in a very ambitious environment, and no one wanted to take risks that might in any way affect our careers. Considering the potential risks, people really appreciated

> **"The fact that I was so comfortable being openly gay gave me added credibility, both on the topic of crafting policies and in all of the other work I did."**

the fact that I had the courage to be honest about this aspect of my life. The fact that I was so comfortable being openly gay gave me added credibility, both on the topic of crafting policies and in all of the other work I did.

During my time at PepsiCo, the LGBT rights movement was starting to reach a point where smart, educated people were coming out of the closet, and allies were beginning to better understand and speak up for their gay colleagues and friends. I became involved with Out & Equal during my last years at PepsiCo. At that time, PepsiCo was on a trajectory towards becoming a fully inclusive and diverse work environment. Our involvement with Out & Equal provided a lot of great support and guidance in developing even better policies.

> **Our involvement with Out & Equal provided a lot of great support and guidance in developing even better policies.**

My last trip to Dallas for PepsiCo took place in June, during Pride Month. The main entrance of our office building featured a magnificent four-story atrium. As I walked in, I saw a massive rainbow flag, spanning one hundred feet, hanging from the top railing all the way to the floor. It took my breath away to see this symbol of inclusion in a building where I had been closeted for so many years. It was a beautiful way to end my tenure with PepsiCo.

Tara Bunch

Tara Bunch previously served as Senior Vice President of Global Customer Support Operations with Hewlett-Packard. She was responsible for delivering customer support services across all of HP's consumer products, as well as directing HP's commercial and enterprise printing services and support portfolio. As President Emeritus of the Out & Equal Board of Directors, Tara also chaired the organization's national development committee and co-chaired the Executive Forum and Leadership Celebration. She lives with her family in California.

As a mother of three young children, I feel a great responsibility to be a positive role model and create a better future for my kids. I strive to inspire them and others by being a visible role model for advancing social change and workplace equality. We each have the power to influence the environment in which our children will grow up. At the same time, we set an example for our children so that they can be proud and confident as they navigate through life's challenges.

Children and families may face some biases and prejudice in their lives when they have same-sex parents. I have been so proud of my children for facing those challenges confidently and with self-assurance. I try to set an example for my children by being secure and positive, so that they will also respond in a confident way when asked about our family. We have experienced many types of reactions from others and my kids have flourished in all of these settings and have never been embarrassed by the fact that they have two moms. As a parent, it is great to see my children thrive and be so resilient in a wide variety of circumstances.

> **" We each have the power to influence the environment in which our children will grow up. "**

In the workplace, managing secrets, feeling threatened and not being able to be your whole self consumes more energy than people realize. When you don't feel safe and at ease as an employee, you spend a lot of time worrying about what you say and whom you say it to. Under these circumstances, it is impossible to devote all of yourself to innovation and creativity.

I experienced this when I first transferred to a small town in Colorado with HP many years ago. I was coming from the San Francisco Bay Area. Colorado was more conservative, and I was moving into a new position with a new group of people. I was concerned about being accepted as a lesbian. It took about a year for me to build relationships and feel comfortable enough to open up. I was doing a good job at work, but I did not take a lot of risks. I spent a lot of time thinking about returning to California because I felt uncomfortable and stifled. When I finally came out to a few people, they were far more accepting than I had ever imagined they would be. I realized in retrospect that I should have given them a chance earlier and much of the issue was with how I was approaching the situation.

The tipping point for me was when I became involved with Out & Equal. Seeing other lesbian, gay, bisexual, and transgender people who were out in senior executive positions gave me the courage and confidence to be out and open with my coworkers. I decided to step forward and be a much more visible and active role model, both as a female executive and as an out lesbian. Once I became open and unreserved, I felt more confident taking risks at work and knew I achieved much more than I had ever been able to when I was hiding part of myself. Coming out allowed me to bring more of myself to the office and be more approachable and really share more of myself and my personal values with people. My career accelerated when I was open and took risks, personally and professionally.

> **" My career accelerated when I was open and took risks, personally and professionally. "**

A great example of this happened when I assumed the customer services function at HP. The group was facing numerous challenges, and I was taking on a highly visible leadership role where any failure would have been very visible. At the same time, there was a need for more executives to step forward and be openly GLBT role models. I became a much more visible and active executive sponsor of Out & Equal and HP PRIDE and also began serving on the Executive Diversity Council at HP, representing the LGBT community in global diversity. The personal satisfaction I received from these efforts infused my work with a lot of energy, drive, and confidence. As a result, I felt more comfortable than ever in taking risks at work. The outcome was amazing. There was a lot of innovation and improvement on all levels, and our team knocked all of the metrics out of the park — from customer satisfaction to cost. This role constituted my biggest career success to date. Everyone benefits when we bring our whole selves to work.

The business case for diversity is undeniable. In order to attract and retain the world's best talent, organizations have to create an environment where employees want to be involved and feel proud of where they work. Employees are diverse, and so are customers. When a company excludes one group, they narrow their market, whether it's in terms of the talent they attract or the customers they serve. People want to buy from companies and brands that they identify with and respect. Brands that really flourish are created by organizations that embrace change and diversity.

> **" To attract and retain the world's best talent, organizations have to create an environment where employees want to be involved and feel proud of where they work. "**

Success should be based on individual drive and determination. Imagine how the world would benefit from everyone having the opportunity to reach their full potential. No one should ever be limited because of their ethnicity or religious background, or have fewer opportunities because they have same-sex parents or because of who they love.

When we consider this from a global perspective, it is clear that we have a long way to go. Many people make the mistake of considering LGBT diversity from a U.S. or U.K. perspective, which can lead to a sense of "mission accomplished." However, considering diversity at a global level, or even in the more conservative areas in the United States, we're far from being able to guarantee workplace equality. There are people today living in India, China, and the Middle East who cannot reach their full potential because they are being persecuted or ostracized for being LGBT — or limited in their career or educational options because they are female. In some countries, citizens are being stoned or hung because they are lesbian, gay, bisexual or transgender.

At the same time, consumer power, job growth, and company investment are increasing in locations where LGBT diversity is not accepted or supported. Highly evolved companies with great diversity policies face huge challenges in bringing LGBT diversity to the work environment in these regions. Corporations need to continue pushing for progress while remaining culturally sensitive and aware. We need to respect and understand local laws and cultures while influencing them in ways that support a more open workplace for all employees.

Organizations can make an immense difference by having visible role models at executive levels who are willing to be open, transparent, and outspoken in their support of workplace equality. I saw the impact of this with our team in India. Over a three-year period, we saw significant increases in the number of female managers and female employees. We hosted a women's forum with an all-female executive panel with vice presidents and senior vice presidents from HP's worldwide locations. We each spoke about our experiences and answered questions about the intersection of career and family and the unique challenges we have overcome.

> **"** *I talked openly about my experience of being a parent in a same-sex relationship and the unique challenges of being an "out" lesbian at work.* **"**

During the forum, people asked me questions about my family. I talked openly about my experience of being a parent in a same-sex relationship and the unique challenges of being an "out" lesbian at work. I think there were a few people who were taken aback a little, but I felt that it was important to be open about my life, and I knew there was probably at least one LGBT person in the room who felt relieved by my speaking frankly and openly. By presenting diverse women in leadership roles who are strong and confident and open, HP demonstrated to our employees in India the commitment the company had to diversity and that they have the same opportunities for advancement. It set a tone in the organization.

All of these experiences have taught me that one person cannot change the entire world, but each of us can influence and educate others and over time this can indeed change the world and influence change in a really positive way. By being visible role models, we can set the tone within our organizations. Little by little, we can make a difference in a positive way and benefit ourselves, our families, and our communities.

Lori Fox

President and Founder of Lori Fox Diversity/Business Consulting, Lori works as a diversity/business consultant and personal coach, consulting with individuals and corporations on workplace issues, especially LGBT personal and professional development. A transgender woman, she lives her life with a passion for authenticity and excellence. Lori served as a Director of Human Resources and a Business Partner of a Fortune 100 company for two decades in U.S. and international assignments. Lori works in leadership, training and coaching roles for local and national organizations, including Out & Equal, where she serves as National Chairperson of the Transgender Workplace Advisory Board. She is a frequent speaker on LGBT diversity issues at university campuses, churches and business organizations throughout the U.S.

"No one can make you feel inferior without your consent." Eleanor Roosevelt's words speak volumes for members of the lesbian, gay, bisexual, and transgender community. Teaching and coaching people to embrace and accept their authentic selves and guiding employers in creating supportive and inclusive workplaces is my passion and my profession. I use my voice and actions to help other people so that they do not have to face the same difficult decision I did: I chose to end my twenty-year career in Human Resources with a major corporation because the company could not accept me for who I am: a transgender woman.

> **" No one had to tell me that transitioning at my former company would put my job at risk. "**

No one had to tell me that transitioning at my former company would put my job at risk. The company's nondiscrimination policy included sexual orientation, but provided no protections for gender identity and expression. In fact, I knew of at least one employee who was fired for gender expression. I discovered this during a conversation during the company Christmas party with a regional operations leader. The regional leader said that he had fired someone earlier that day, and explained, "The employee was just too effeminate looking, and our customers would not want that. Besides, 'he' wanted to come in wearing women's clothes, and our customers would totally disapprove." I asked him why he did not simply move the person to another job so that s/he would not interact with customers. He responded, "We cannot have that in our company. It is unacceptable." Being very closeted at the time, I felt powerless to do anything. I also felt that if I advocated too strongly, I too would be implicated.

This is what the power of fear and shame can do in a non-inclusive LGBT workplace culture. Not standing up for what I believe in was one of the most painful consequences of living a lie by being in the closet. It was unconscionable for someone to be fired simply for being their authentic self, which had absolutely nothing to do with the individual's job performance.

I finally came out to one of my colleagues who worked in the corporate diversity department. He identified as a gay man. He shared his experience of struggling through his own coming out process at work and told me that, as a result of coming out, he felt happier in his personal and professional life than ever before. I shared my personal dilemma with him, and he cautioned me, "Lori, when you come out, everything about you is going to change: physically, emotionally and even legally; everything, from your physical appearance to changing every legal document that identifies you as who you are, from male to female."

I knew and accepted this, and I understood that I had no choice. I realized that my transition was truly about embracing and accepting change in my life. I was tired of living a lie and hiding my authentic self for so long. I also understood and accepted that this dramatic personal change would affect everyone around me including my family, friends and work colleagues. I also knew that there might be negative consequences.

> **" Successful and progressive companies that value and care about their employees do not resist change. "**

My friend and colleague told me, "Before you make this decision, you have to ask yourself if you are ready for a fight." I was confused by his remark; I believe that successful and progressive companies that value and care about their employees do not resist change. They embrace the uniqueness and subtle differences that each employee brings to the workplace; they do whatever they can to make it work.

Moving forward, I was extremely conflicted. I enjoyed my challenging work and the interaction with my colleagues and friends, yet there were no inclusive transgender policies or benefits in place, and there would not be in the foreseeable future. I finally came to the agonizing conclusion that I did not want to work in an environment where I could not feel safe living and working as my authentic self. Through much introspective personal work with a therapist, I made the difficult and courageous decision to leave my job. I realized that I could no longer hide who I was. I could no longer live and work in a culture of shame and repression, where some employees were deemed acceptable and others were not.

> " I did not want to work in an environment where I could not feel safe living and working as my authentic self. "

I felt deep inside, however, that I would have other great professional opportunities in my life, living and working as my authentic self, using my skills, talent, experience, and networking resources to truly make a difference in the world. I would choose to live my life on my terms, in concert with one of my favorite quotations, by Mary Manin Morrissey: "Courage manifests itself only in the presence of fear. Taking a step in a new direction where we've never been before can be uncomfortable, sometimes frightening. Our other option is to stand still and never move at all!"

For anyone who identifies as LGBT, coming out to family can be intense and even painful. Fear, rejection and scorn haunt so many of us as we travel through our life's journey to find peace, acceptance, and authenticity. This journey can often take years as we struggle to stay emotionally and physically connected with family and close friends, sometimes losing those once closest to us.

My mother, in particular, really struggled with my announcement that I was a transgender woman in the process of transitioning my life from male to female. After many long discussions, I reminded my mother of a story she used to tell about her own difficult experience as a girl in Catholic grade school. She was born left-handed, and the nuns would periodically slap her wrist with a ruler for writing with her left hand.

"How did it make you feel to be demeaned and punished just because you were left-handed?" I asked her.

"I felt terrible about it," she replied.

"So why didn't you change, then?" I asked. "Why didn't you start writing with your right hand, like they insisted you do?"

"Because that's not who I am," she responded.

"Did God create you as a healthy baby girl who just happened to be left-handed?" I continued.

She responded affirmatively, and I concluded my point, "Mom, it is the same case with me.

"There is nothing wrong with me. I have struggled most of my life with the incongruent feelings that I was born in the wrong body. God created me this way: as a healthy, loving person who identifies as a woman.

"The same way that being born left-handed does not make you inferior, being born a transgender woman is who I am; it's who I have always been."

> **" God created me this way: as a healthy, loving person who identifies as a woman. "**

My mother finally connected, at a much deeper, emotional level, with my comments and observations, and my family began to understand that I truly had no choice if I were to live my life in an authentic and healthy way.

Dealing with my family and leaving my job were two huge milestones for me. These challenges have inspired me to reach out and assist other women and men who struggle with gender identity and sexual orientation issues. I now passionately devote my professional time to working with others navigating the challenges of their own personal and professional transition. I work with a fascinating variety of companies and nonprofit organizations, assisting management and Human Resources as they create and implement cultures of inclusion within the workplace to ensure that all employees are truly valued and treated with dignity and respect.

Organizations that genuinely support and value difference and inclusion at all levels of their employee ranks will proactively establish workplace policies, practices, and benefits that positively impact recruitment, staffing, and retention of all individuals, including transgender women and men. I love the work that I do, and I feel so proud to be an inclusive member of our incredibly diverse LGBT family.

> " I feel so proud to be an inclusive member of our incredibly diverse LGBT family. "

As the very proud Chairperson of Out & Equal's Transgender Advisory Board, I want to sincerely and lovingly thank Out & Equal Founding Executive Director Selisse Berry for her inspiring vision in founding and growing the world's largest nonprofit organization specifically dedicated to creating safe and equitable workplaces for lesbian, gay, bisexual, and transgender people. I attended my first Out & Equal Workplace Summit twelve years ago in Cincinnati, Ohio. Even though my employer would not pay for me to travel and take part, I knew that I had to be there — to actively participate and connect, at a deeper level, with so many other individuals who shared Selisse's vision and work.

The great singer Joni Mitchell once said, "In order to strike the nerves of people's lives, you have to strike the nerves of yourself at the very deepest level possible!" After living and struggling in a deep closet for so many years, denying a life and a voice for my true self, I realized that I, too, had to find the courage to reach out and make a difference, and I finally found my authentic family at that very first Summit.

When I first heard Selisse speak, I felt so many conflicting emotions rising within me. I felt safe; I felt joy, I felt inspired, and I felt connected with her and so many other wonderful LGBT business professionals, friends and activists. Selisse's vision and leadership have truly been an inspiration. As Out & Equal continues to evolve and grow, I believe that each of us has an obligation to support and be a role model for the next generation of the diverse LGBT family. I believe that we all possess courageous spirits and powerful voices capable of "striking the nerves of ourselves and others at the very deepest level possible!"

> " Each of us has an obligation to support and be a role model for the next generation of the diverse LGBT family. "

Adrian Balaci

Adrian Balaci has been working across Europe as an environmental business leader since 2003 with several organizations including the World Bank. He is an advisory board member for Budapest Pride and a board member for Amnesty International Hungary. Mr. Balaci was instrumental in forming the Hungarian LGBT Business and Human Rights Forum, a volunteer initiative advocating workplace equality and working to create new awareness among employers. Born in Romania, Adrian now lives and works in Budapest, Hungary.

There have been many advances in workplace equality for lesbian, gay, bisexual, and transgender individuals in the United States and the United Kingdom. However, the same companies that campaign under the flag of diversity in the West shy away from creating equal work environments in their global locations. With the exception of a few major corporations, most companies do not apply their diversity policies globally. In order to support basic human rights in the workplace, it is very important for corporations to start implementing global anti-discrimination policies.

Failing to provide protections to all employees creates unsafe work environments. Unequal treatment in the workplace fosters intimidating and unproductive environments. When lesbian, gay, bisexual, and transgender people suffer unfair treatment and discrimination in the workplace, they are often forced to hide their personal lives at work. Doing so can increase stress and make employees who seem to be "hiding something" appear untrustworthy, thereby diminishing their professional reputation and performance.

Companies have the opportunity to make powerful changes by explicitly including sexual orientation and gender identity in their policies in every location and by providing LGBT support groups for their employees. Leadership teams can make an immense difference by bringing LGBT employees to the table with human resources and diversity managers. By ending workplace discrimination, companies are able to attract and retain the best talent. Enabling employees to be themselves at work allows employees to be productive and successful — benefiting both the employee and the company for which they work.

> " *Companies have the opportunity to make powerful changes by explicitly including sexual orientation and gender identity in their policies in every location.* "

The lack of global equality is in part due to the fact that the standards used to rate workplace equality in companies located in the U.S. and the U.K. do not take into account diversity policies in employers' global locations. Some companies presume that they would lose money through local boycotts and other types of resistance if they were to support diversity policies abroad that are

LGBT inclusive. The business case becomes crystal clear when the entire corporation is responsible for the actions it takes across the globe. Creating one standard to review companies based on their global diversity policies and inclusion initiatives would make a difference, because that measurement would hold corporations accountable for their actions worldwide.

It always surprises me to see companies in Hungary resisting change. Hungary has progressive legal rights for gay people. These include civil partnerships for same-sex couples and a federal anti-discrimination law that covers all sectors, including employment, and stipulates nondiscrimination based on sexual orientation and gender identity. These laws apply to all companies operating in Hungary. If a person has been the target of discrimination, there is a fairly simple process to file a complaint, and this action almost always results in a fine against the company — an outcome that is costly and generates negative media coverage. However, the legal groundwork is not enough. The implementation of these laws needs to be improved, because their application varies drastically from one case to the next. Workplace equality is a complex issue that is difficult to measure. Gauging lesbian, gay, bisexual, and transgender issues in company policies and discourse can be a challenge.

> " Creating one standard to review companies based on their global diversity policies and inclusion initiatives would make a difference. "

We created the Hungarian LGBT Business and Human Rights Forum to urge companies to start implementing their diversity policies in Hungary. So far, we have managed to assist three companies, including Morgan Stanley, in creating LGBT employee resource groups. We recently worked with the Hungarian National Police Force, which employs over forty thousand people, and their labor union. As a result, both the police union and the force changed their nondiscrimination policies to include sexual orientation and gender identity. The police force will also begin doing diversity training.

My interest in this work stems from my professional passion for human rights, as well as my personal experiences as a gay person. I must have been three years old when I realized I was gay. I told my mother that I did not want to kiss the princess in the school play because I liked the prince. She did not take it seriously. I came out officially at the age of eighteen. It was difficult for my evangelical Christian parents, but I insisted that they accept me for who I am. My other family members and friends were not surprised, and most of them were very happy about it. When I came out, it just meant that we started talking about the subject in normal conversation.

> **I told my mother that I did not want to kiss the princess in the school play because I liked the prince.**

I have never been in the closet at work. I work with various financial institutions, including the World Bank and commercial banks. People do not know what to expect when I show up to business meetings with my pink laptop and colorful, informal outfits; they usually just assume that I must be very creative. In Hungary, family and relationships are common discussion topics in the workplace. Even if I were not openly gay, it would be challenging not to discuss my sexual orientation in a professional environment.

I can only think of two uncomfortable encounters that happened as a result of a colleague discovering my sexual orientation. One such experience occurred with a work acquaintance. We had a comfortable relationship and were always discussing our mutual interests. One day, she asked if I had a girlfriend. "Of course not," I replied. "I thought you knew that." She said, "Oh, Adrian, that's such a shame. You deserve a pretty girl." I responded, "That is not a very nice thing to say. I find women pretty as human beings, but I am not attracted to them."

Another incident occurred at a work conference in Brussels when a conservative French woman in her sixties attending the conference said that gay marriage is immoral. I argued that she believes this because the issue does not affect her personally. We agreed to disagree, and the conversation ended there.

These two encounters made me even more appreciative of the straight allies who advocate for LGBT rights. Heterosexual individuals who support the LGBT community play an essential role in effecting change. As the majority, allies have the potential to strongly influence issues with their voting power. Greg Dorey, the former British Ambassador to Hungary, is an excellent example. He has been a huge supporter of LGBT rights and endorsed the Hungarian LGBT Business and Human Rights Forum. During his 2011 speech at the Forum, he stated that supporting diversity was "not only morally right, but could also create competitive advantages for companies and even entire societies." Allies like Ambassador Dorey are essential, and we cannot make change without them.

> **"Allies have the potential to strongly influence issues with their voting power."**

There are still over seventy countries where people are fined or imprisoned for being lesbian, gay, bisexual, or transgender. Serving on the Board of Amnesty International Hungary has provided me with the opportunity to advocate for human rights and equality for lesbian, gay, bisexual, and transgender individuals. Amnesty International and several other organizations have been campaigning for many years for a change at the United Nations level vis-à-vis rights for LGBT individuals.

The first major improvements occurred in July 2011, when the United Nations Human Rights Council passed a resolution supporting equal rights for all, regardless of sexual orientation or gender identity. Another huge step forward was the report conducted by the United Nations about discrimination against LGBT people across the globe. U.S. Secretary of State Hillary Clinton contributed to the global change with her simple, beautiful words to the United Nations General Assembly in 2011: "Gay rights are human rights."

> **"** *U.S. Secretary of State Hillary Clinton contributed to the global change with her simple, beautiful words to the United Nations General Assembly in 2011: "Gay rights are human rights."* **"**

The big question is whether corporations are going to keep up with the changes that are happening around the world. The fact that many corporations do not have LGBT employee resource groups in Hungary and do not create safe and equitable environments for their LGBT employees in Hungary is an indication that these corporations are not keeping up with the legal advances. Corporate social responsibility should not only exist in the West. Corporations have the opportunity to effect change in a very real way across the globe simply by applying one standard for all of their field offices, regardless of the location.

Cynthia Martin

Cynthia was the first "out" executive at Eastman Kodak Company, and one of the few openly LGBT executives in the country during the '90s. Formerly Kodak's President of Global Services and Vice President of Brand and Marketing at Blue Shield of California, Cynthia's career recognitions include being honored by the Gay Financial Network in their first list of the 25 most influential LGBT leaders. She is the Board Chair for Openhouse, an organization providing LGBT seniors with housing and services. Former Co-Chair of the National Business Council at the Human Rights Campaign, Cynthia's board service has included organizations focused on a wide range of issues including the economically disadvantaged, drug and alcohol recovery, and girl's empowerment. Cynthia served as Co-Chair of the first Out & Equal Executive Forum in 2008. Cynthia and her partner, Out & Equal's Founding Executive Director Selisse Berry, were married in July 2007. She and Selisse share a home in Berkeley, California, with their four-legged children, Avalon and Mr. M.

I feel blessed. My life is rich, I'm healthy, and I'm surrounded by loving family and friends. But things weren't always so rosy.

As a student at Ursinus College, a small school in Pennsylvania. I played three sports and had high hopes of following in the footsteps of my grandmother, a semi-professional basketball player. She was also the head of a labor union for a pharmaceutical company — a nearly unimaginable feat for a Jewish woman in the 1940s. However, my own dream of becoming an elite athlete came to an end when I damaged my knee, an injury that kept me on crutches for much of my time in college.

While at Ursinus and dealing with the loss of my identity as an athlete, I also realized that I am a lesbian. All the pride I'd felt in being a talented athlete was replaced with shame for being a lesbian. I did not know anyone who I could talk to. Homosexuality was a subject largely absent in the media and forbidden among family and friends. At the time, my friends and I, many of whom later also came out, would publicly ridicule people who were "gay," "dykes," or "queer," while I withered inside.

As my college situation became increasingly miserable, I made a feeble attempt to take my life one night. Thankfully, it was half-hearted and a complete failure. Over time, and after a lot of ups and downs, life became easier as I developed a stable relationship and started a great job. I began to reestablish confidence in myself and to understand my own capabilities.

I came out to my sister and parents in the early 1980s. My sister was tremendously supportive, but my parents' initial response was: "We love you very much… and we'll find a doctor for you." That was a really hard conversation. We were all in unfamiliar territory. My parents eventually accepted me — and my partner at the time. I think they realized how hard it is to not have family support. When they were first married, they had experienced something along those lines from their own families: my mother was a middle class girl from New York and of Jewish heritage, while my father grew up in the Midwest in a Mormon family of modest means. I'm very thankful they were willing to learn and have supported me over many years since. They were so happy for me at my wedding to my wife, Selisse Berry, the Founding Executive Director of Out & Equal. My mom took our wedding album and showed it to her coffee klatch in North Carolina, and my dad told his siblings all about the ceremony. I'm so proud of them!

I was in the closet for more than a decade of my career with Eastman Kodak. I was openly lesbian among my friends in the community, but I didn't appreciate the value of being out at work. I used all the usual avoidance tactics, such as telling my coworkers that my partner was "a friend." As my career progressed, I ran into more and more people from Kodak in local stores and settings that made it obvious she was more than a friend. Even grocery shopping became uncomfortable because of the mask I was wearing.

> **" Even grocery shopping became uncomfortable because of the mask I was wearing. "**

In 1995, Kodak's new CEO, George Fisher, reinforced his commitment to diversity by establishing some core values for the company that specifically included lesbian, gay, bisexual, and transgender employees. I was asked to be his chief of staff, a big promotion with a lot of visibility. In an ironic twist of fate, the first assignment he gave me was to work with the LGBT employee resource group, Lambda, on the planning for their first management dinner. I had never heard of Lambda before, and here was my new boss, the CEO of the company, supporting their efforts to make Kodak a more diverse, inclusive, and respectful place!

After attending the event, and still officially in the closet, I knew it was time for a big change. The members of the Lambda Network were taking real risks. Many of them worked in the lower levels of the company — some on the shop floor. Yet they had the courage to stand up for their rights as LGBT employees. They were true role models, and I realized I had to stand with them and, in my new, very visible position, help lead the change in culture that George Fisher envisioned for the company.

So after giving a heads-up to the previous chief of staff and the head of Human Resources, I decided it was time to come out to my boss. Oh, and let me say again: he was the CEO of the company! I still remember that day. We were walking back to our offices after our first lunch meeting. I was carrying a yellow pad with a list of about twenty items to discuss with George. Number twenty was "Come out." I had decided in advance that whether I got to item nineteen or not, I had to get to number twenty. In the middle of the hallway and mid-stride, I finally said, "George, there's one other thing that I need to share with you. I'm a lesbian, and I'm going to come out and publicly support the Lambda Network." I'll never forget the moment. He stopped on a dime and then turned to me with a huge smile and said: "I am so happy that you shared this with me. I will do whatever I can to support you." It was a beautiful moment.

> **" I decided it was time to come out to my boss, the CEO of the company! "**

Just a few days later, I sent an email to the Lambda Network telling them that I was a lesbian and that I wanted to support them. It was a big deal in 1995 for this to take place at a global manufacturing company headquartered in upstate New York. The initial email to twenty-five people probably reached fifty thousand inboxes as my coming out went viral.

There was some negative reaction to my very public moment of truth. One employee sent George an email saying, "Homosexuality is morally wrong — it is against my religion. I cannot work in a close environment with homosexuals." George responded: "If that's the way you feel, then you should probably look for another place to work." His support was unwavering, and together with his wife, Ann, they changed the world within Kodak for LGBT employees.

One of George's first actions at Kodak was to create a set of core values, including "respect for the dignity of the individual." These values and George's deep belief in diversity led to the creation of a global diversity policy, which included a specific reference to lesbian, gay, bisexual and transgender employees. We also obtained Kodak's endorsement of the Employee Non-Discrimination Act [ENDA]. Kodak's head of Human Resources and I went to Washington to testify in support of the law.

The Kodak Lambda employee network was instrumental in executing the vision of cultural change within the company. They hosted educational programs for management at all levels and in various parts of the company, including some very tough manufacturing plants. Lambda's professionalism, focus on education, and desire to work with management was an extremely powerful formula for success.

> **"Lambda's professionalism, focus on education, and desire to work with management was an extremely powerful formula for success."**

While I was the chief of staff, the Lambda Network helped me put together the business case for domestic partner benefits. After working with human resources and the executive team at Kodak, the domestic partner benefits case went before Kodak's Policy Council, comprised of eight or so senior executives who met periodically to make major policy decisions. I was quite nervous the day before the Policy Council was to make a decision. The council members were all white, straight males over age fifty. I knew that there were some pretty conservative and possibly homophobic people in the group. The night before they made their decision, I left George an anxious voicemail, because I wanted to alert him that I was not sure I could stay impassive and emotionless during the meeting if the council voted "no." His reply opened my eyes to the challenging journey our allies face. He said that he was also nervous and wasn't sure how *he* would react. His reply lifted the weight I'd been carrying, and I felt real support as I walked into the room the next day. The Policy Council approved domestic partner benefits. Later, George shared with me that the fact I was openly lesbian and present in the room when the council made its decision had a huge impact, because it had made the issue more personal. That was another reminder of why it's so important for us to be out.

> **"** *The fact I was openly lesbian and present in the room had a huge impact.* **"**

When I was asked to be the President of Global Services, I became one of two women on the senior executive team of about thirty people. My own team included fifteen direct reports, with a global team of about thirty-five hundred. While I had worked for years in the Services organization with many on my direct team, most of that time I'd been in the closet. When I returned as President, I teamed up with the Lambda Network for an educational event called "the fishbowl." It allowed LGBT employees, including me, to talk about experiences in a way that made it safe for my management team to listen and learn. My team expressed that they were affected in a lasting way by that program, and it helped deepen our relationships and strengthen our team.

In 1997 I was asked to be a keynote speaker at an *Out & Equal in the '90s* event in my hometown of Rochester, New York. The talk was publicized in the local newspaper, and the article included my picture. When I saw that photo, I stopped breathing for a moment.

I realized that I'd just come out to everyone I knew outside of Kodak: my high school teachers, coaches, and friends, as well as my neighbors and acquaintances in my nearby hometown. I was a little concerned that I might receive some hate mail or that my home might be vandalized, but none of that happened. Instead, I developed greater awareness, confidence and motivation to continue working for equality in the workplace.

This gave me the courage to go back to Ursinus College, where I spoke to the president of the university about my difficult experience as a student coming to terms with my sexual orientation and being completely isolated. He was incredibly kind, thoughtful, and grateful for our discussion, and I can confidently say that no student there will ever have to experience what I did.

One other university experience holds a special memory for me. I was asked to participate on a panel of women executives at a Smith College leadership development program. In the audience were early to mid-career professionals from a number of large corporations: Chubb Insurance, Johnson & Johnson, and Kodak, to name a few. We were each asked to talk about one accomplishment that we were particularly proud of. My immediate thought was of two accomplishments: the redesign of Global Services to reflect a digital world and coming out. My thoughts raced as I considered the platform and my desire to make the Kodak employees in the room proud. I wondered if my coming out would embarrass them and tarnish Kodak's image. All the old fears surfaced. But as I searched the faces of the fifty women in the audience and realized that some of them had to be lesbians, I had my answer: I talked about both accomplishments. Afterwards, many attendees and fellow panelists thanked me. I'd done the right thing for everyone there — including myself.

Selisse and I met while on a National Business Council, and our paths crossed a number of times over the years. Just before I left Kodak in 2001, we ran into each other at the UCLA Leadership

Institute and a Reaching Out Conference. I knew she was a visionary leader, and then I had the chance to see what a fun and interesting gal she is, too. After several months of dating, I decided that San Francisco would be my next home. I packed up my dog, Mr. M, and with Selisse's cat, Avalon, our family joined together, and the four of us continue to enjoy life in the Bay Area.

> " *Like many, I assumed we were doing well on the diversity front, and so no one talked about it.* "

I was thrilled to find a great position in the health care industry with Blue Shield of California. There I was faced with some very different diversity issues. We were located in the middle of San Francisco with many LGBT employees. Like many, I assumed we were doing well on the diversity front, and so no one talked about it. It's true there wasn't blatant discrimination, but over time I discovered that there was a need for greater awareness.

For example, another lesbian on the executive team discouraged me from bringing Selisse to the board dinner. My colleague expressed concern that the Board of Directors was too conservative and would react negatively. Well, I brought Selisse to the dinner, and our presence was entirely welcome. I was also able to broaden Blue Shield's nondiscrimination policy to include gender identity and expression, but the backstory reveals the underlying challenge I encountered. When I first made the request, the head of Human Resources asked, "Now, what is gender identity? Isn't that the same as saying sexual orientation?" I had to explain the difference. Because the change had become a best practice, she agreed to update the company policy, but I came to see that full understanding or appreciation of what the provision meant hadn't set in. For instance, when the employee handbook was about to be approved, I had a chance to review it and found a

> **" Policies are necessary but not sufficient to create safe, inclusive work places. "**

dress code section that could have been disastrous for an employee whose coworkers considered the individual's attire too masculine or too feminine. Thankfully, the text was changed, but it demonstrated a lack of real understanding — and a need for education and commitment. Policies are necessary but not sufficient to create safe, inclusive work places.

When I look back on my personal and work experiences, I am struck by the change that one person can bring about and grateful

> **" I am struck by the change that one person can bring about and grateful for the opportunities I have had to make a difference as an out and open lesbian. "**

for the opportunities I have had to make a difference as an out and open lesbian. I've learned not to make assumptions, to value education and to appreciate that everyone is on a journey. Each of us has the ability to create change by simply being our true and authentic selves. By being visibly out and expecting equality, we can live our lives with freedom and joy and inspire others to do the same.

Scott Beth

Scott Beth joined Intuit in March of 2003 and is the Vice President of Finance Operations. In this role, Scott is responsible for company-wide sourcing and purchasing, including strategic supplier relationship management, cost and quality management, negotiations and contracting. Scott is also responsible for Intuit's Supply Chain and Order-to-Cash processes, which include order management, physical and digital fulfillment, accounts receivable and credit/collections. In 2011, Scott expanded his role to include real estate and workplace services for Intuit's global campuses. Scott held prior leadership positions at Agilent and Hewlett-Packard, earned his B.A. in economics from Stanford University, and serves on a number of boards and advisory committees, including the University of San Diego Supply Chain Management Institute. He serves on the Out & Equal Board of Directors.

When I was sixteen, I started working as a summer intern for Hewlett-Packard in 1977 doing cost accounting. The team there liked my work and asked if I could come by after school to continue to help out the finance department. I thrived in that environment. I loved HP, and I worked my way through college, spending twenty to thirty hours per week at HP. They paid half my tuition at Stanford, and I was able to earn enough money to pay the balance. As a result, my growing up really occurred at HP, where I learned about a culture of management by objectives and the importance of trusting that employees want to do the right thing. I learned the power of an open door policy. Many of the leadership attributes innovated and practiced by HP became the foundation for my own leadership skills.

In my senior year of college, I discovered I was gay, and it was an epiphany. I drove myself to the student health center and told the receptionist, "I'm gay, and I need to talk to someone." She directed me to a gay therapist, who did three powerful things: first, he allowed me to give voice to my sexual orientation; second, he advised me to meet other gay people and understand my community; and third, he urged me to connect with the LGBT group at Stanford. That's where I met my life partner, Keith, and we have been together for almost thirty years.

After I met Keith, I knew that I needed to come out to my family. I was tired of avoiding who I am and deflecting conversations. The feeling of coming out to my family was both freeing and terrifying. I didn't know anyone who was openly gay and proud of it. No one talked about the importance of authenticity and living your life with honesty. One of the few people I knew who was attracted to other men was a high school teacher who had married a woman. He told me he was gay and had lost a lover, and after that he had decided to marry a woman. I thought, "Is this how people live their lives?" This was during the early 1980s, and the political climate was so different from today.

During that same time period, I took a diversity course at HP. The outside facilitator had a word association game, and people were supposed to blurt out the first thing that came to mind. He said, "lesbian," and a senior leader, who was Mormon and explicit about his religious beliefs, shouted out the word "fear." It demonstrated the terror that people had of lesbian, gay, bisexual, and transgender people. They did not even want to have a word to acknowledge us, out of concern for what it might do to our society. I thought, "Okay, I guess I can't come out."

When I was twenty, I did come out at work to my best friend, who was a manager at HP and had a gay brother. I also brought a picture of Keith into the office and put it at my desk. People would come by and ask, "Who's that?" I would respond, "This is my partner, Keith." They would either ask questions or say nothing at all. Once, a Vice President I worked for called me "cupcake." It was so ridiculous that I burst out laughing and responded, "You've got to be kidding!" My spontaneous reaction set him back on his heels. His remark was not cutting or hateful; it was thoughtless. He called me to his office the following day and said that my reaction and his reflection on his behavior caused him to be embarrassed and regret having made the remark.

I also had some extremely positive experiences at HP ten years later. I was working as a director, and a vice president two levels above me really liked working with me. Bill often asked me to help solve issues, and I became his thought partner. He saw the fragmentation of ideas across the company and a lack of cooperation between businesses.

> **You never know where you will find allies.**

He engaged a senior manufacturer named Don, who was an ex-submarine commander from Boise, Idaho. Bill asked me to fly to Denver with him to meet Don in a red carpet conference room so that we could make progress on our strategy. After we concluded our business, Don said, "I need to share something with the two of you. I'm so proud of my son. He spoke at our church this week about being gay and having the courage to talk about coming out. This has strengthened my faith." Bill responded, "Thank you for sharing that, Don. My gay son has been with his partner for three years, and I'm so proud of him." I realized that you never know where you will find allies.

Overall, my managers have ranged from tolerant to supportive. Since I was twenty, I have mentioned Keith's name right away and have never played games with pronouns. When I left HP to join Intuit, I made it clear that I would be out from day one. I helped form Intuit's Pride Network, which began as a group of out leaders and professionals talking about the creation of an employee network. We received approval from the Human Resources director. When we announced the launch, some employees were very vocal in opposing the creation of an LGBT network and posted hateful comments on Intuit's intranet site. The Senior Vice President of Human Resources took me aside to show me the messages. After I read them, she said, "All of the senior leaders, including me, are unwavering in our support of the creation of the Intuit Pride Network, and these comments do not represent the values of this company. We will not be swayed by hatred."

The launch of the network was a great success. We invited the gay CEO of another company to speak. All of Intuit's Senior Vice Presidents attended our two-hour launch to hear our hopes for the network and help us with planning. At the end of the launch, our internal facilitator asked people how they were feeling. Many people around the table expressed gratitude for the support the senior leaders had given by staying through the whole meeting. It really demonstrated how much the company cares about us.

One engineer in his early twenties was visiting from San Diego to attend the launch. He said, "This is my third job since graduation from college, and it is the first time I haven't feared for my safety. I feel so much support." Imagine a brilliant software engineer whose brain is half consumed with worries about safety, while the other half is trying to create software to delight our customers! By freeing people from hateful and discriminatory environments, employee engagement and productivity soars.

> **" By freeing people from hateful and discriminatory environments, employee engagement and productivity soars. "**

I was incredibly proud of our CEO Brad Smith's keynote speech at the Out & Equal Workplace Summit in 2010. He did a phenomenal job and took months working to develop his point of view about what it means to be an ally and the importance of inclusion in the workplace. He created discussion circles with LGBT and ally employees. These included videotaped interviews with LGBT employees, which he was able to review and reflect on. The ending statement in his presentation at the Summit was, "I talk about my support for LGBT employees, and people tell me that it makes me an ally. I thought it makes me a friend."

As it becomes easier to be vocal about our sexual orientation and expectations for inclusion and diversity in the workplace, we also have the responsibility to be role models all the time. In every new hire orientation, accelerated leadership program, and director's college, I start by introducing myself and using a visual journey line, which represents the milestones in my life. I talk about my work at HP, my deep caring for the environment, the fact that I'm a neat freak, and I talk about Keith and how important he has been in my life for the past thirty years. My sexual orientation is transparent from day one, and people joining the company understand that the leadership team expects people to bring their whole selves to work.

After one of these presentations, a young business analyst asked me for career counseling. When he came in to meet with me, he was very nervous and asked, "Are you serious about Intuit being a place where you can bring your full self?" "Of course," I replied, and then I shared my own story about being out of the closet. He relaxed and then said, "I think I'm coming out, and I don't know what to tell my boss or coworkers, and I haven't told my family. I started seeing a guy, and when people ask me about my weekends, I feel I have to be dishonest about who I am and whom I'm seeing. If I tell them that I am gay now, they will think I'm a liar." I explained to him that coming out is a process and that people will understand and appreciate his honesty.

As leaders, what you say and how you say it has a ripple effect through people's lives. Inviting others to be themselves and authentic is powerful. As a leader, I can't presume what the other person's environment is like. I can only guarantee that it will not be an issue at Intuit. Intuit's value of diversity is foundational to the company. Two different CEOs have come up to me and asked me questions about my partner. One even asked if Keith and I have children. We had a wonderful conversation about how children are part of our lives even if we don't have children. Our current CEO, Brad Smith, saw me across the room and came running up to say, "Scott, I just heard the New York Supreme Court just legalized marriage; isn't that great?" I was so surprised, and I found it phenomenal.

> " As leaders, what you say and how you say it has a ripple effect through people's lives. "

There has been a lot of great change, but the fight is not over. In twenty-nine states, we can still be fired for being gay or lesbian. Imagine the lesbian employee in Cary, North Carolina working for Intuit who can't take her part-ner to any office parties because her partner is a schoolteacher. As a teacher, she could be fired the very next day if people found out that she is a lesbian. In thirty-four states, it is still legal to fire someone for being transgender. We have to remember that we have not yet achieved equality. We also have to remember that in many companies and many states, the fear of losing a job or being discriminated against is a huge, life-altering problem. By demonstrating the power of authenticity and the good business results that can be achieved through inclusion, we have the chance to make a difference.

> " By demonstrating the power of authenticity and the good business results that can be achieved through inclusion, we have the chance to make a difference. "

Yvette Burton

Dr. Yvette C. Burton has blazed a unique trail, making contributions to the global LGBT movement in a diverse set of executive roles that span grassroots, government, private industry and philanthropy. Dr. Burton is currently the CEO and Founder of Silent Partner Solutions, a business transformation and leadership development consulting firm. Prior to this role she served as a CEO of a leading global foundation and held leadership positions at the IBM Corporation, where she served as a managing global business development executive, business transformation strategist, and market development research director. At age twenty-six, Dr. Burton was named Director of Lesbian Health in the New York City Department of Health. Dr. Burton is a past board director of the Empire State Pride Agenda, a founding board director of the Audre Lorde Project, and a past co-chair of the Out & Equal Workplace Summit. She has received the Lesbian, Gay, Bisexual & Transgender Community Center's Award for Visionary Leadership and the Metropolitan Church of New York Award for Exceptional Corporate Leadership on LGBT Issues. She was also awarded a Lifetime Achievement Award for Excellence in GLBT Equality and HIV Advocacy by Gay Men's Health Crisis, and a Stonewall Foundation Honor for Outstanding Women.

On September 24, 2008, just weeks prior to the U.S. presidential election, I found myself in Washington, D.C., testifying before the Homeland Security and Governmental Affairs Committee at the invitation of Senators Susan Collins of Maine and Joseph Lieberman of Connecticut. They were co-sponsors of *The Domestic Partners Benefits and Obligations Act*, a law that would give the same-sex spouses and partners of federal employees the health insurance, life insurance, government pensions, and other employment-related benefits and obligations enjoyed by married, heterosexual federal employees. It was an exciting day. I recall wondering in the days prior how I — and how we — had gotten there. I had in mind the larger question of how it had come to pass that the possibility of extending benefits to the partners of gay and lesbian federal employees was a credible debate to be having in America — from kitchens to board rooms to Capitol Hill. I also wondered how it was that I should be the one chosen by circumstance to sit in that chair and offer advice to a Senate committee.

A great deal had changed. Just eight years before, I was working at a large, privately held consulting firm with a longstanding conservative culture. During a meeting there, when an award was presented to a longhaired male employee, the presenting executive remarked that it was the first time he had presented an award to anyone with a ponytail. Women present that day exchanged knowing glances, acknowledging their own invisibility, implicit in the executive's comment. I found the comment irritating, but I also knew as a lesbian that LGBT people were even more invisible. Today, that same firm has been recognized for its accomplishments as an LGBT-friendly employer, and the progress has been real. So how did all this change happen? The explanation for that transformation and for the phenomenon of my participation that day in Washington arises from two areas of historic change. First, a growing number of corporations have come to understand that diversity, inclusive of sexual orientation and gender identity, is good for business. Secondly, more and more LGBT people have chosen to be authentic at work and in the other public aspects of their lives; they disarmed the irrational fears of heterosexual coworkers, and they learned how to coalesce as a group. I have been proud and feel fortunate today to have been among the actors in both of these advances.

I credit the drive to be visible and authentic for turning the tide for working LGBT people. LGBT people have ceased to be abstractions and stereotypes. They have become real people in the eyes of the majority, and this has been pivotal in changing attitudes and making visible the value that we were already bringing to the marketplace.

The story of that evolution is grounded in some influential events and in the character, resolve and skills of many LGBT individuals and allies who, one by one, took the courageous step of coming out at work and sharing the lessons that serve our movement still today.

Where coming out was concerned, I was one of the lucky ones. My personality and family situation delivered me to the workplace in the early 1990s as a confident, out person. I didn't "major" in being a lesbian, nor did I attempt to keep it a secret. Shortly after college, my first serious relationship resulted in my coming out, if you could even call it that. My parents made no fanfare about it, and I did not — then, prior, or at any point — fear being cut off by my family. As a result, I can say that I have never in my adult life been what I would consider closeted. Unfortunately, being closeted for some

> " I didn't "major" in being a lesbian, nor did I attempt to keep it a secret. "

period of time has been the norm for LGBT people; those who are in the closet have often paid a price, although it must be noted that some who have come out have suffered penalties. Still, I observed numerous colleagues who became known for being "hard to get to know." Leaders never felt they really knew them. Despite their skills, they missed out on promotions and plum assignments, at least in part because they lacked the sponsorship that comes only from letting superiors and clients know you well.

This all began to change in the early 1990s, just as I was beginning my career in earnest. Growing numbers of LGBT people made the decision to come out at their jobs and even to form official or unofficial affinity groups within the companies. This was enough of a trend that *Fortune* magazine ran a cover story in December of 1991, entitled "Gay in Corporate America," with extensive, striking photography of gay and lesbian-identified people on the cover and throughout. *Fortune* wrote, "Official or unofficial, there's a group in every large company in the U.S. Most are closeted, like the groups at Hughes and TRW. The president of the company may not know, but they're there." These are the groups and the people who planted the seeds of what Out & Equal is today, and we owe a tremendous amount to them. Through the years, LGBT employees have gone from simply providing discreet mutual support to one another to being business assets to their firms.

> **"Through the years, LGBT employees have gone from simply providing discreet mutual support to one another to being business assets to their firms."**

LGBT visibility increased in part because of the tragic toll of the AIDS epidemic. *Fortune* magazine posited that volunteer work during the early years of the AIDS crisis brought many gays and lesbians out of isolation and in contact with one another, fueling affirmation and organization. The magazine also noted that the imperative of supporting education, research and care moved many executives to decide that life was too short to remain on the sidelines.

Although I was openly lesbian, it was certainly these imperatives that brought me deeper into the community and into contact with a growing number of LGBT people — through my work as a volunteer. It was through New York City's Lesbian, Gay, Bisexual & Transgender Community Center that I became involved in the delivery of critical health services to LGBT community members and families struggling with substance abuse, bereavement and other issues of epidemic proportions in our community.

As more and more gays and lesbians came into contact with one another, we also learned important lessons about working beyond our differences, stereotyping ourselves less often, and seeing our community and allies in broader, less rigid terms — evolving from Gay, to Gay and Lesbian, to LGBT and more. But traversing our differences to build a coalition was not so easy in the beginning. We actually had to learn to allow one another to be our authentic selves, even as we worked together to make that happen in our workplaces and in the larger society.

My background in health and my deep involvement with health service provision through the Community Center led to me being asked to take a position in David Dinkins' administration as Director of Lesbian Health in the New York City Department of Health. Mayor Dinkins was the first and, thus far, only Black mayor of New York City. It was an exciting time, and I was thrilled to bring my skills to his administration. As soon as I was appointed, however, it became clear that many in the lesbian community saw what they considered to be my hetero-normative feminine clothing and hairstyle as signs of inauthenticity, and I was subject to calls for my resignation. These concerns were expressed directly to me and even in letters to the Mayor himself. This was a disappointing scenario: lesbians who were seeking equality were exhibiting zero tolerance for freedom of gender expression. I stayed on at the department, of course, and we went on to design and direct the City's first department focused on lesbian health policy development, ethnographic research and program implementation.

The fact is that being LGBT, or otherwise outside the perceived mainstream of sexual orientation and gender identity, does not inoculate us from the prejudice and bigotry that pervade the society in which we were, each of us, formed. Our workplaces, corporate and otherwise, are awash in these prejudices. We have to be vigilant — but not obsessive — on this point, and we need to approach this in the spirit of aggressive, continuous improvement. Happily, there is ample evidence today that this lesson has been learned.

The other major driver in the progress that we have made so far in becoming truly out and equal in the workplace has been the decision, one company at a time, to extend equal benefits to the partners of LGBT employees and to implement nondiscrimination policies that include sexual orientation and, more recently, gender identity. Once these steps were taken, CEOs discovered tremendous, often unanticipated business productivity value in allowing employees to be themselves. I relish the occasion when one of my clients told me that the fact that I was open with him about my lesbianism made him trust me all the more with his business.

> ❝ CEOs discovered tremendous, often unanticipated business productivity value in allowing employees to be themselves. ❞

In *Here is New York*, E.B. White's famous essay about New York City, White wrote, "No one should come to live in New York unless he is willing to be lucky." I believe this principle applies not only to New York, but also to life in general. And anyone who has read White's entire essay understands that when he wrote the word *"willing,"* he also meant to imply *"prepared."* I was lucky enough to become deeply involved with numerous companies who were going through the process of choosing and valuing diversity and working to invite the best LGBT talent into their organizations. This has led to opportunities for me to contribute to the progress of our movement. I was prepared, and I was more than willing.

My first interview at IBM, during which domestic partner benefits for LGBT partners were mentioned, signaled that IBM would be a different corporate environment where being a lesbian might turn out to be a neutral factor — at the very least. I was particularly impressed, because I felt certain that this policy was not brought up during my interview based on any inkling of my sexual orientation — just that this was systematically part of the IBM recruiting conversation. I knew this was a good sign, but I had no idea what awaited me beyond the knowledge management and business innovation roles for which I was recruited. Who could have anticipated the path that unfolded for me? It included leading IBM's efforts to develop partnerships with LGBT-owned businesses and leading paid consulting engagements to help other clients develop and implement strategies for engaging LGBT market segments and employees — all as part of IBM's Human Capital Management business.

By the time I was invited to testify before the Senate, I was invited not as a lesbian activist or even an IBM executive, but as an individual with deep expertise in human capital management and in the implementation and business implications of domestic partner benefits. After receiving the phone call, I contacted IBM's legal, communications and government affairs teams to inform them of my desire to accept the invitation and to assure them that I would appear as a private person. Instead of giving me the clearance I requested, IBM surprised me by urging me to testify — not as a private individual, but as an IBM executive speaking on behalf of the company.

I feel tremendously fortunate to have been prepared for the unlikely and unanticipated opportunities that were presented to me at IBM, because the LGBT work that I did there on behalf of the company and clients gave me insight into the intersections of human rights and social justice movements, industry, government and policy. In addition, there is nothing more satisfying than seeing the result of one's labors at work in society. When I see the employees of some of my former clients at the Out & Equal Summit, I know that the investments made by their employers and by thousands of individuals who dared to associate their true selves with the value they bring to work every day are paying off — not only for their businesses, but for all of our global society.

" *There is nothing more satisfying than seeing the result of one's labors at work in society.* **"**

Just as I did that September day in Washington, I'm still feeling lucky, prepared, and very much myself. I wish as much for every LGBT person who is looking to build and enjoy a better future for themselves and all who inhabit our world.

Brian McNaught

Named the "godfather of gay sensitivity training" by *The New York Times*, Brian McNaught is considered one of the world's leading educators on lesbian, gay, bisexual, and transgender issues. He has authored numerous educational resources in book and DVD form, including "Anyone Can Be an Ally — Speaking Up for an LGBT Inclusive Workplace," and a Web-based guide for managers on LGBT workplace issues. In 2011, Brian was awarded Out & Equal's Selisse Berry Leadership Award for his many contributions to workplace equality. A popular contributor to national media, including CNN and NPR, he has advised thirty Fortune 500 corporations, writes a weekly blog and newspaper column, and hosts a television program on LGBT history. He lives with his spouse Ray Struble in Fort Lauderdale, Florida, and in Provincetown, Massachusetts.

Our bodies tell us our sexual orientation. Our souls tell us to come out. It's easier to argue with our souls than it is with our bodies.

Like most gay men I've met, I felt physical attraction to men for as long as I have memory. It is not an exaggeration to say that I had homosexual awareness as a child. The excitement I felt was undeniable when I stared at the handsome men who visited our home, appeared on television, taught in school, sat in church, or lay on the beach. Because I was a little Catholic altar boy who wanted

> **"** *Our bodies tell us our sexual orientation. Our souls tell us to come out.* **"**

to be a saint, my excitement was accompanied by fear and shame. Puberty intensified all of my feelings, both pleasant and unpleasant.

I'm going to sound like the grandfather whose stories of walking ten miles in the snow to school always made us roll our eyes as teenagers. We knew we were being told that we had it easier than he did, that life was tougher when he was a child. I don't say my life was tougher than that of young gay, lesbian, bisexual, and transgender (LGBT) kids today, but it was certainly different. It's just as hard for our teenage LGBT students to imagine life without positive role models as it was for me to imagine life without cars or buses to take me to school.

When I came out publicly as gay at age twenty-six, I was fired from my job as a writer and columnist for the Catholic Church in Detroit. Recently, when I received a lifetime achievement award from Out & Equal, I thanked the Catholic Church for firing me, because if they hadn't, I might never have chosen the career of being an educator on lesbian, gay, bisexual, and transgender issues. But it wasn't easy for me when the Archdiocese of Detroit fired me for affirming my homosexuality in 1974. There simply weren't a lot of places to go for support — no gay community centers, gay-identified therapists, no Parents and Friends of Lesbians and Gays, no Out & Equal, and no Human Rights Campaign. No one had the equal sign decal or rainbow flag on their car. Neither had yet been designated as LGBT symbols. There was no GLSEN, GLAD,

GLAAD, Lambda, or any organization with national recognition other than the National Gay Task Force, as it was called at the time. LGBT people made up pseudonyms when quoted in newspapers or when they joined a local gay group. Even the minister of the Metropolitan Community Church (MCC) in Detroit, who was featured in the same newspaper article that got me fired, refused to give his last name.

My parents received threatening phone calls when I came out in the national press, and so did I. The calls I got were also obscene. There was no such thing as email then. The messages I received were delivered in envelopes full of paper with Bible quotes, along with the words "homo" and "fag." The day my name appeared in the *Detroit News* as the founder of the local Dignity chapter, a closeted homosexual parked his car across from where I worked and screamed, "Faggot! Faggot! Faggot! You're nothing but a faggot!"

> **" My parents received threatening phone calls when I came out in the national press, and so did I. "**

There were no resource materials for my parents to read to help them through the public humiliation they felt with my coming out. Nor were there books, TV movies, or educational resources for my colleagues at work. When I decided to start the Dignity chapter, shortly after attempting suicide by drinking a bottle of paint thinner, I took each staff person in the editorial department out to lunch, one by one. The word "gay" was barely known then. "Gay Liberation" began at the Stonewall uprising on June 28, 1969, but there was very little press coverage. Homosexuality was very much the "love that dare not speak its name," as Oscar Wilde once said.

Nevertheless, each of my friends at work, though shocked by the news, was personally very supportive. However, when my homosexuality became public knowledge, and the newspaper dropped my weekly column, everything changed. It was okay for me to be a homosexual, but not to let others know about it. Doing so brought unwanted attention to the newspaper. The day following the announcement that my column had been dropped, several lesbian, gay, bisexual, and transgender students from the University of Michigan picketed outside my office building with signs that said, "Give Back the Column." One of my colleagues opened the door and yelled out, "Which one of you fairies owes me a quarter for my tooth?"

Such an example of verbal harassment in the workplace today would likely result in serious disciplinary action. At the time, it was greeted with laughter by everyone within earshot in the building. Before I was terminated, anti-gay articles had been taped to the walls of the editorial department, and a petition was circulated that said the other employees did not support me. One friend cried because she knew if she didn't sign the petition she would be ostracized and possibly fired.

When I say that it was a different time, I'm not just saying that there were no gay characters on television and that we had to be protected by unhappy police officers when we marched in our very small Gay Pride parades. I'm also referring to the character of the American people. Americans honored spiritual leaders at the time, as well as authors who challenged them to think outside of the box. We may have watched a television show, *The Lifestyles of the Rich and Famous*, but more to be shocked by the ostentatious display than due to envy. We were the country of discovery and the first walk on the moon. We were the country of Woodstock, love-ins, questioning authority, demonstrating for peace, boycotting of non-union lettuce and wine, of Gandhi, folk music, clergy who challenged civil authority, and a Pope who called into question the monopoly that Catholics thought they had on salvation.

My coming out was a spiritual action, not a biological one, nor a political one. My life became political because of my job termination, but when I started the Detroit chapter of Dignity, I did so because, as the song sung by Peter, Paul, and Mary puts it, I felt called to "Hammer out justice. Hammer out freedom. And hammer out the love between my brothers and my sisters all over this land." It was the words attributed to the prophet Jesus that made it impossible for me to hide my sexual identity and to refuse to fight for the lives of others like me: "Blessed are those who suffer persecution for justice sake, for theirs is the kingdom of heaven." In his book *Siddhartha*, the story of the Buddha, Hermann Hesse, and the authors of every popular spiritual book of the day, encouraged us to be authentic, to "Live life deliberately," as Henry David Thoreau aspired. Our national heroes were not bankers who got multi-million dollar bonuses, or men with great abs, or teenagers with great voices. Our national heroes were people who gave their lives for a worthy cause.

When I went on my hunger fast in 1974 in protest of the sins of the Catholic Church against gay people, and with the demand that the Church educate the clergy about homosexuality, such a water-only protest was not unusual. Martin Luther King, Jr., with whom every American was familiar, had done the same, as had Caesar Chavez, leader of the United Farm Workers. Spirituality has guided my political life as an educator on lesbian, gay, bisexual, and transgender issues. Each book I wrote, and each DVD I created, I did to help others be free of the fear and shame I felt as a child. For nearly forty years, each presentation I've made has been preceded by a private prayer that my words help heal and provide hope to others. Since being fired for being gay, I've been asked by major financial institutions and other companies to work with their senior executives on lesbian, gay, bisexual, and transgender issues in India, Japan, Singapore, Hong Kong, Australia, the United Kingdom, Canada, and throughout the United States. The National Security Agency (NSA) has twice brought me in to speak with their leadership. In every one of those settings, I spoke with a prayer that my words would make a positive difference in their lives and in the lives of their colleagues and family members.

Attempts at intimidation were persistent, especially in the beginning. My first public presentation in 1974 was accompanied by the warning that someone was bringing a gun to the church where I was talking. Moments before I spoke at one college, the local bishop called to forbid me to speak. I ignored him. At another college, undercover police were at the airport when I arrived, and sat in the auditorium as I spoke, because a viable death threat had been made. Fundamentalist Christians have harassed me by picketing, leafleting, or sitting in the front row of rooms where I've given talks. One right-wing Catholic group stopped a Mass that was being said in support of me to proclaim on an unfurled banner that, "A Moral Wrong Can Never Be a Civil Right." Outside my apartment mailbox, one person threatened in an anonymous message, "Get out of town McNaught. I hope you die of AIDS."

What none of the people or organizations that have tried to intimidate me has understood is that their rejection never discouraged me. It energized me. It gave me more reasons to believe that the work that I've been doing is much needed.

I don't identify as a theist today, but I still identify myself as spiritual. I know that might be confusing. While I don't believe in a kindly, almighty grandfather in heaven, I continue to be guided by the belief that every bit of positive energy I bring out of myself and into the world has an important positive effect upon all of the living things of the world, today and tomorrow. The book I read each morning with Ray, my spouse since 1976, refers to this positive energy as the "Tao." I like that word better than I do the word "God."

My meditational readings tell me that we create our own happiness and our own suffering. We

> **"We create happiness when we live in, and embrace, the moment."**

create happiness when we live in, and embrace, the moment. We make ourselves suffer when we cling or have expectations. There were days in my life that I hungered for more affirmation and recognition for my work. I created suffering for myself when I did so. I've learned, or am learning, to let go of the work I have done in the past, to have no expectations of the work I will do in the future, and to be grateful for the work I'm able to do in the present, regardless of public affirmation.

I was thrilled to receive the Selisse Berry Leadership Award from the Out & Equal Board of Directors in 2011. To have twenty-five hundred people stand and applaud you, even if many of them have no idea who you are, or what you've accomplished, can be very exciting and affirming. I know that there are hundreds of men and women who have spent many, many years working on lesbian, gay, bisexual, and transgender issues who will never get an award or have their contributions acknowledged. I wish I could make copies of my award and send one to each of them. But I would also need to send a note that reminded them that the award collects dust and will be tossed away when they die. But what doesn't collect dust, and can't be tossed away, is the positive energy we have brought, are bringing, and will bring to the lives of all people, regardless of their sexual orientation, their gender identity, or their gender expression.

> **"** *I know that there are hundreds of men and women who have spent many, many years working on lesbian, gay, bisexual, and transgender issues who will never get an award or have their contributions acknowledged.* **"**

The work we do is our reward. The e-mails we now get thanking us for helping people be better allies, parents, or LGBT people is the reward. And rest assured, those of you who are in your teens, twenties, and thirties, that when you are in your sixties, most LGBT young people will roll their eyes when you tell them that, when you were their age, you couldn't get married or adopt children in every state, or you couldn't bring a foreign partner into the country. They will think you are ancient when you describe how there were no gay or lesbian heroes in the movies or on television and no transgender people in advertising.

In thirty years, Out & Equal may well have accomplished its mission. New organizations will undoubtedly be created to address the newest challenges in the lives of our families. That is the way of life. Each generation has to walk its own ten miles through the snow to school and expect that their stories may be understood as saying, "My life was harder than your life."

It *was* hard, but I have no regrets, only gratitude. I've had a wonderful life of activism as an educator on lesbian, gay, bisexual, and transgender issues. And, it's far from over. I know this because my soul tells me so, and I've learned not to argue with my soul.

Tracie Brind-Woody

Tracie joined Citi in London in 2005 and has been the Chief of Staff for the EMEA Information Services Group since 2009, managing a team of nearly 400 in London, Belfast, and India. She has been an active member of the Citi Pride London network for six years, serving as Co-Chair of the group for three years. She represents Citi on the Gay Women's Network committee, a professional group formed in 2008 that offers gay women working in London's financial sector access to career development and networking opportunities. Tracie currently serves on the Out & Equal International Advisory Board and assisted in planning L-Women at Work, the first pan-European conference focused on advancing the careers of lesbians, bisexual, and transgender women in business. She also helped coordinate the first-ever Out & Equal Global LGBT Workplace Summit in London in 2012. Tracie lives with her wife Claudia in Oxfordshire, England.

When I worked at my previous bank, several people there knew that I was gay, but there was no diversity policy in place at that time, and I never felt the need to come out. I joined Citi back in 2006, and it was six months before I joined the London LGBT network as I settled into life in a new bank and area of business. I attended my first event shortly after joining the LGBT network and was immediately targeted, as one of only a small number of women in the network, to take part in a panel at the Out & Equal Workplace Summit in Chicago. As a new face within my organization, I hadn't felt the need to "come out," but now I had to make a decision, because I needed approval to attend. To that end, I spent three hours writing and rewriting an email to my boss, who was in New York at the time, explaining the situation and outing myself in order to attend the event.

It was a very emotional experience for me to reveal myself fully as a lesbian for the first time in my working environment. It took me those three hours to write and rewrite just that one paragraph. The response from my boss was extremely supportive, even to the point that she acknowledged how hard it must have been for me to write to her. I wish that I had done it many years earlier than I did, but then I do believe that there is an individual time and place for each of us to take that step beyond our personal comfort zone and to move forward and experience being wholly oneself in the working environment. We anticipate people's reactions and, for some reason, are bewildered when we are treated as ordinary people. To anyone who asks, I say it's your decision — timing, location, with whom and how you go about it. Citi and Out & Equal 2006 were the setting for my decision and my time.

> **" There is no hiding for me again, and that's a great feeling. "**

While I did not appear on the Citi panel at the Out & Equal Workplace Summit, I did spend the whole Summit watching and taking in a tremendous experience that was very new to me. The upshot of it all was that I left the Summit as a member of the London LGBT committee, and, around a year later, I became a co-chair of its network in London. There is no hiding for me again, and that's a great feeling to experience and hold.

Where would I be today, if I had not had to make the decision on whether to out myself to my boss to attend the Chicago Summit? Probably still leading a life where some people would know me truly and others would be second-guessing who the real Tracie might be. I would have read about LGBT issues but done nothing more than that.

But I'm not living that life, and for that I'm extremely grateful. It's been a tremendous six years since that time, and I have been extremely lucky to have attended all of Out & Equal's conferences since then in various roles and guises: panelist, session planner, committee member or simply attendee. That first conference was like nothing I had ever experienced before — so many LGBT attendees and allies in one place to discuss issues and share experiences. I declared my intentions before I left Chicago and have been involved ever since: Citi London LGBT committee member for six years, with three as its first woman co-chair; a founding member and Citi committee member for the Gay Women's network for professional women in London, which

> **“ Out & Equal lit the fire that stills burns brightly. ”**

now has more than seven hundred members; and for the last two years, a Citi representative on the Out & Equal International committee with the first pan-European Lesbian event in Amsterdam and the Global Summit in London. And so Out & Equal lit the fire that stills burns brightly, even when the focus has changed in various directions during that time. What can I say — it's been a complete package: I even met my wife through the International committee!

Whilst I've been fortunate to be involved in various associations and activities during the years since Chicago, one of the most important aspects for me is the huge networks of friends and acquaintances that have developed alongside these roles and responsibilities. The network is international, and we are all small pieces of a very large jigsaw puzzle with a common cause, looking to make the world a better and safe place for the lesbian, gay, bisexual, and transgender community.

> *We are all small pieces of a very large jigsaw puzzle with a common cause.*

Liz Bingham

Liz Bingham is Managing Partner for People at Ernst & Young. Based in London, she is a member of the firm's U.K. Leadership Team. She joined Ernst & Young in the corporate restructuring business in 1986 and has enjoyed a varied career, serving clients in many parts of the world and including a variety of leadership roles. Liz is passionately committed to creating an environment where everyone has the opportunity to succeed. Ernst & Young was named Employer of the Year in the 2012 Stonewall Workplace Equality Index, which rates U.K. companies. Liz was a featured speaker at the 2012 Out & Equal Global LGBT Workplace Summit in London.

I first came out to myself in 1992, when at age thirty I met and fell in love with a woman. At the time, I was fourteen years into a reasonably successful career at Ernst & Young and was a senior manager in the Restructuring business. With the benefit of hindsight, I realize now that mentally and emotionally I was somewhat at a crossroads, and I wasn't certain that my career ambition would be fulfilled at Ernst & Young. Probably as a result of these unrecognized feelings, I remained closeted both at work and in many parts of my private life. Two years on, my partner came to meet me after work at our office's local bar, and I introduced her to everyone as my "flatmate." Several weeks later, I had a meeting with my boss, who was a very senior Partner. We spent some time discussing a particular technical issue, and I got up to leave his office as the subject concluded. As I got to the door, he stopped me, asked me to shut the door and return. I did as he asked, but I was pretty freaked out, as we had a worksite culture of open doors, and any closed-door meeting usually meant disaster!

When I sat back down he asked me, "Your friend whom I met the other week: are you and she in a relationship?" I was shocked. This was completely unexpected, and through the turmoil in my head, I realized that I could lie, and I was sure I could do that credibly as I had been doing so for a couple of years. But the overwhelming feeling was that I didn't want to lie, so I told the truth. We had a fantastic conversation, and at the end I asked that he respect my confidence, as my sexual orientation didn't affect my work. His response was another shock. He said, "You are wrong. It does affect your work." I immediately felt I had made a catastrophic error of judgment in discussing my personal life with him until he went on to say, "The fact that you are in a happy, stable, and loving relationship has made you much more effective in your interactions with clients and your team." It was my first lesson in inclusive, authentic leadership. Since that meeting, I quickly gained confidence, and I started my full coming out journey. Each interaction built my confidence, and I flourished personally and professionally. My coming out to my boss took place eight years before I came out to my parents, but by then I was in a very different space, buoyed with confidence and certain of the support of my friends and colleagues. Needless to say, my parents were fabulous, loving and supportive, and I think they, too, could see how I had grown as a person happy in her own skin.

My advice to others is to own your personal journey, and you will find the right time and the right way that suits you, and seek out allies in your network who will back you and support you in realizing the power within you.

> " Own your personal journey, and you will find the right time and the right way that suits you, and seek out allies in your network who will back you and support you in realizing the power within you. "

In 1994, when I first came out at work, the firm didn't have well-articulated diversity policies. The corporate values were of the firm being a meritocracy, which was probably "'90s speak" for Diversity and Inclusion, but policies and procedures were a bit thin on the ground! So there was nothing formal that gave me any encouragement to come out I had to find that inner strength myself, and I genuinely believe that my boss's question originated in his personal desire to create an inclusive environment.

Since then, our policies and procedures have become much more evolved as we continue on our journey to inclusive leadership for everyone, regardless of background. However, I also believe that you can have all the policies in the world, but if the "tone from the top" does not set and support the diversity agenda, the policies really won't matter much, because inclusive leadership is behavioral, *not* written. Our philosophy at Ernst & Young is that people will be most engaged at work and therefore more productive and positive if they can be themselves in the workplace. The senior leaders of the firm globally, as well as in the U.K., are passionate advocates of this principle — not just because it is the "right thing to do," but because it makes good business sense. I have been actively encouraged to engage internally and externally around the diversity agenda, and the relationships we as a firm have with organizations such as Out & Equal and Stonewall are truly valued in the same way that we value relationships with our largest global audit clients.

Since my coming out in 1994, my career at the firm took on a sense of purpose and gave me the confidence and certainty that my career ambition could be fulfilled at Ernst & Young. Since that time, my career accelerated, and I am now a Senior Partner, a member of the U.K. firm's Leadership Team (the executive board), with responsibility as Managing Partner for People & Talent. I think of my career as very much consisting of two halves, pre-coming out and post-coming out.

In the last few years, I have started to better understand the importance of role models in a business context. When I grew up in the firm, I had virtually no female role models and no gay role models at all! It has been that dawning realization that as an out gay senior woman, I have a responsibility to role model inclusive behaviors and to coach, guide, mentor and encourage those around me, regardless of gender, sexual orientation, ethnicity, or background.

> **" To be a role model, I didn't have to be perfect; I just needed to be authentic. "**

One of the revelations for me, which took time to sink in, was that to be a role model, I didn't have to be perfect; I just needed to be authentic. I have taken every opportunity to deliver on this, not just in Ernst & Young's business, but with other organizations, public sector, private sector or third sector.

In my current role as Managing Partner for People & Talent in the U.K. & Ireland, I accept, with a degree of trepidation, that my voice is amplified and that I have a duty to use my leadership position unselfishly and honestly. In recent years, I have worked a lot with Stonewall in the U.K., supporting them at their workplace conferences, sharing thought leadership and connecting strongly with that organization's advocacy of LGBT equality in the workplace. I have also connected and worked with the Gay Women's Network; Interlaw, which is LGBT for the legal profession; and L-Women at Work, the first European conference for Lesbians, held in Amsterdam in 2011.

I have had the privilege to work with Out & Equal both with this book project and with the 2012 London Summit, and I genuinely consider all of these opportunities to be a privilege. I am in equal measure pleased and proud that I can contribute while also gaining a huge personal satisfaction from joining a global agenda that continues to take giant leaps in support of LGBT rights while also taking incremental steps towards equality in every sphere. In the summer of 2012, I appeared at the European Commission to address an audience of ambassadors and policymakers of African, Caribbean, and Pacific countries, as well as European parliamentarians, on LGBT equality in the workplace. I did not expect that to be an easy audience for obvious cultural, political, and religious reasons, but then nobody said that being an advocate and role model would be easy. In fact, it's the tough gigs that make the most difference in the long run.

Jamison Green

San Francisco-based author and educator Jamison Green is an internationally
recognized leader in transgender law,
policy, theory and education. Consulting
with businesses, governmental agencies,
and professional/educational organizations to improve the health, safety, and
civil rights of gender-variant people, his
services have been vital to the imple-

mentation of transgender-inclusive benefits at several major corporations, including IBM and Genentech. Jamison serves on the
Out & Equal Transgender Advisory Committee and is a longstanding partner in training on behalf of the transgender community.

There was no closet that could hold me, not if I was to earn
a living at all. Before I could bring my body and my gender into
congruency, my coworkers had no doubt that I was different. Though
I was designated female at birth and labeled myself as such because
I didn't know how to do otherwise, I didn't look or behave like a
woman, and I found it constitutionally impossible to wear women's
clothing. Many coworkers assumed I was a lesbian, simply because
of my masculine appearance and without knowing that I did have

a female partner. I came out as lesbian to a few coworkers in the late 1970s and early 1980s, but for the most part I kept my personal life private until my partner and I decided to have a child. In 1984, when my partner became pregnant using Assisted Reproductive Technology, I began to advocate for domestic partner benefits at my company — for *any* unmarried couple — and outed myself in the process. I was told that we were ahead of our time.

I was forty years old when I transitioned from female to male (in 1988), so I had already had more than fifteen years of work experience. No one warned me that I would not be able to use my own health benefits because of broad exclusions for transsexual treatment or history. Just as with the domestic partner issue, I knew I didn't deserve to be discriminated against, and if it was happening to me, it must be happening to thousands of other similarly situated people who didn't deserve it either. I began to use all my spare time to educate and advocate for transgender and lesbian/gay/bisexual equality, health, and social safety, not just in the workplace context, but also throughout the social sphere. The workplace, though, was always a touchstone: at my company, everyone understood how important it is that people be judged fairly in the work environment — and how important it is to be able to have a workplace at all, rather than get forced out because of discrimination

> **"** Once I transitioned to male, no one thought there was anything unusual about me any longer. **"**

Once I transitioned to male, no one thought there was anything unusual about me any longer, which actually made me a very effective spokesperson. I used my suddenly ordinary appearance and my corporate management experience as leverage to gain both access and trust as I spoke publicly about the unusual topic of transsexualism and the damage inflicted by homophobia. I was one of the first trans activists to advocate that trans people not be forced to live in "stealth" — forced to hide or change jobs or invent a false past in order to be accepted.

I refused to exchange a lesbian closet for a transsexual one. I worked to help draft and pass San Francisco's gender identity and expression nondiscrimination ordinance in 1994, which went into effect in 1995. As soon as that measure became a reality, I began to advocate for San Francisco City and County employees to have the health benefits they deserved: coverage for transgender medical procedures and treatment. I saw that if we could establish a precedent in San Francisco, we could then cite the City's experience and demonstrate that it didn't cost the municipality anything to include trans people's health care in group insurance plans. This example could help convince other employers to demand trans-inclusive policies from their insurance carriers and administrators.

> **" It didn't cost the municipality anything to include trans people's health care in group insurance plans. "**

Somewhere in the mid-nineties, I met Selisse Berry. Out & Equal didn't exist yet, but Selisse was already working hard to provide diversity training to businesses, and she contacted me to learn how to incorporate transgender concerns into her trainings. When Out & Equal was formed, I was invited to share my advocacy and policy recommendations through many Bay Area events. In those early days of the Out & Equal Workplace "movement," most lesbian and gay people didn't care about transgender issues and didn't understand how our concerns were related. But the Out & Equal organization kept the faith: wherever people were forced to trade their authenticity for their livelihood, Out & Equal stood firmly on the side of our freedom to be who we are and to bring our whole selves to work.

Throughout my working life, I have found that job performance and social skills — the ability to work collaboratively and ensure that one's own actions contribute to the organization's success — could overcome a variety of phobias and prejudices among one's coworkers. In the past, there were plenty of times when I felt it wasn't appropriate — or I feared management or colleagues' reactions — if I were to share information about my partner (when I was a lesbian), or about my transsexual history (once I had one!). However, I could rationalize that behavior only so long. It always took a toll on me. But I was never complacent, because I was too unusual prior to my transition to a male body, and after my transition, I simply knew too much about homophobia and prejudice to remain silent. I didn't make a big issue of my trans-ness, but gradually, as I became more comfortable within myself, I learned not to worry about what others thought, and I learned how to balance my own needs with the demands of my workplace.

> " If your coworkers can rely on you, and they like and appreciate you, they will support you even if they don't always understand you. "

Workplaces often provide moments when an individual contributor can shine, but the primary activities at most job sites are collective and collaborative. If your coworkers can rely on you, and they like and appreciate you, they will support you even if they don't always understand you. I've been lucky, I know, that most of the white-collar jobs I've had have placed me with predominantly well-educated and thoughtful people who have been willing and able to adapt to new information. I was also lucky in the blue-collar positions I had earlier in my career. In those settings, I learned that job skills, a willingness to help one's coworkers, and a sense of humor are absolutely crucial to ensure survival. I've been lucky. But I've encountered far too many trans people who have not been so lucky, and their struggles have motivated me to speak out against the injustices that they have faced.

In the mid-1990s I started traveling to Europe, reaching out to as many trans people as I could find, asking them to meet with me so I could learn about their lives. Were their concerns the same as ours in the U.S.? Were they able to get the health care they needed? Were they afraid to let people know their histories? Were they concerned at all about collaborating to define human rights, civil rights, or workplace rights for trans people in their countries? I appeared in more than a dozen documentary films, spoke at conferences, advocated for medical and legal reforms. By the early 2000s, I had been invited to lecture and appear in local media in nearly a dozen countries in Europe and the Far East. In 2004, Vanderbilt University Press published my book, *Becoming a Visible Man*, which brought me even more recognition as a thought leader in the trans community and among professionals whose work impacts transgender and transsexual people.

From 2002 through 2007, I served on the Human Rights Campaign Business Council. (Selisse Berry, Out & Equal's Founding Executive Director, was also a member when I joined.) There I influenced the changes in the Corporate Equality Index to drive transgender acceptance in the workplace, and I helped develop many of the educational resources HRC offers on their website. I loved serving on the Business Council, so it was painful for me to have to resign after the HRC board — against the advice of the *entire* Business Council — sanctioned Barney Frank's proposal to drop gender identity and expression from the Employment Non-Discrimination Act (ENDA), which was then under consideration in Congress. This opened a rift and a festering wound in the LGBT world, where many still believed that transgender people had no place and that our T issues held the LGB majority back. The transgender community and many of our allies (including Out & Equal and more than three hundred other educational and civil rights organizations) expressed their strong response to HRC's divisive and damaging action. And the watered-down ENDA still didn't pass. Many transgender people and organizations refused to work with HRC after that. But I believed that if we were to gain access to health benefits, the Corporate Equality Index was still the strongest mechanism we had to drive change in the insurance industry by creating corporate demand, and so I've continued to consult with HRC to help them do more to leverage transgender equality. Out & Equal's Workplace Summit is the premier educational venue to spread the word about this work and encourage others to take on its challenges.

I've been honored to receive numerous awards — for work that I would do without recognition. But the best prize I ever got was the opportunity to meet Heidi Bruins when she co-chaired the Out & Equal Summit in 2001. She and I married in 2003, and now Heidi and I indulge our advocacy interests with mutual support. Would I do it all again? You bet! I'd just want to meet Heidi sooner!

Heidi Bruins Green

Heidi Bruins Green is a learning and development professional who balances the quirky pleasures of a twenty-plus-year career in accounting/finance and her newer career, begun thirteen years ago, designing training for a cloud-based financial management software company. A driving force behind Out & Equal Workplace Advocates' Bisexual Advisory Committee, Heidi has delivered work-

shops on bisexuality in the workplace at the Out & Equal Workplace Summit for eleven years. She started volunteering to help program the Workplace Summits in 1996. Heidi lives in the San Francisco Bay Area with her husband, Jamison Green, whom she met at the 2001 Out & Equal Workplace Summit in Cincinnati.

When I started identifying as a lesbian in 1981, I was in denial. Like many people when they first realize and consummate a same-sex attraction, I conveniently "forgot" my history of good relationships with men as I embraced my new, sexy, radical lover. I declared myself a dyke, considered my past unenlightened, and leapt into the world of women loving women. It wasn't until my second significant relationship with a woman that I reclaimed all of my history and got comfortable with myself as a woman who loves people, whatever the configuration of their genitals. As Lani Ka'ahumanu wrote, "It's not the plumbing, it's the electricity."

Once I started dating women, I didn't consider men as possible partners for a long time. It was the late '90s when I next dated a man. I've been an activist my whole life, participating in civil rights marches, door-to-door canvassing in presidential campaigns, grassroots organizing to keep abortion clinics open. So when I came out, I jumped right into the politics of the gay rights movement, as it was then called. I was in a lot of battles, but my work with Procter & Gamble is something I'm really proud about.

I started at the Sacramento plant of Procter & Gamble in 1989. In less than two years, I was promoted and relocated to Cincinnati, where I lived for twelve years. In making the move from California to Ohio, I knew I was not headed to a socially enlightened place. When I was offered the promotion, I told my manager that I would only be willing to go if they would also relocate my partner. The process took the company six months and approval from a senior vice president, but they ultimately paid all our moving costs.

The year after I moved to Cincinnati, two-thirds of the city's voters passed an anti-gay ordinance that was devastating to the community. I was crushed and hurt, and at a women managers' retreat the day after the election, I told everyone there that I felt personally attacked and as though I could not trust any of them, since two-thirds of the city had supported this hateful denial of me. Most of the managers there said they had not voted for the ordinance. I'm sure some women were not being truthful, but I hope my revealing my personal pain made them think.

I had already started meeting socially with other lesbian, gay, and bisexual employees by then; Procter & Gamble had no transgender employees at the time. We started to develop strategies about how to form a group at work. Most people in the social group didn't want to get involved, but we had a core group of six. We plotted our timing: a diversity department was being created, and we targeted its assistant director. We got a meeting and came in with our requests.

The assistant director was visibly shaking in the meeting. We were probably the first LGB people that he was aware of knowing. We asked for a formally recognized ERG, inclusion of LGB issues in diversity training, and domestic partner benefits. The meeting took place in 1993; the ERG was allowed to form in 1995 under the name GABLE/P&G, and domestic partner benefits were implemented in 2001. They were announced by the Senior Vice President of Human Resources at the 2001 Out & Equal Workplace Summit. When I left the company in 2003, LGBT issues were still not addressed in corporate diversity training. The stated reason was that LGBT diversity was important enough to warrant its own training. In translation, this meant, "We don't want to teach this in regular sessions that are given throughout the company." Because of GABLE's constant pushing and advocacy, Procter & Gamble eventually took on issues like Cincinnati's anti-gay rights ordinance, which was finally defeated after I left.

I had openly identified as bisexual for many years at that point. Being bisexual wasn't easy at Proctor & Gamble. Not because of the straight people I knew: it was the lesbians who were hardest on me. Lots of "micro-aggressions" were visited on me when I started dating a bisexual man on our leadership team. We received lots of teasing about being "breeders" and comments on what we did in bed. This behavior was not something that the two lesbians on the team had to endure, and they had gotten together with both of them cheating on long-term partners! I stopped getting invitations to women-only events and heard such comments as, "Oh, you wouldn't want to come if you couldn't bring him."

Many years ago, my mother, who is the only person I have ever met who actually read both of Kinsey's studies in their entirety, said that she boiled down what Kinsey said to this: 10 percent of people are gay, 10 percent of people are straight, and everyone else is somewhere in between. Kinsey didn't use the word bisexuality, but that's what he meant. My mom's belief was that 80 percent of the people in the world are bisexual, and while the math may be much more complicated, I believe there is a lot of essential truth in that sentiment.

Like Kinsey, many researchers ignore bisexuals when studying sexuality or sexual orientation, so it's actually difficult to find hard data on bisexuality, especially from the experience of bisexuals themselves. Since 2001, I have led workshops on the experiences of bisexuals in the workplace at the Out & Equal Workplace Summit and other venues, and I would comb the literature for data I could cite to my information-starved audiences.

> **" Many researchers ignore bisexuals when studying sexuality or sexual orientation, so it's actually difficult to find hard data. "**

At the 2009 Out & Equal Workplace Summit, I was disheartened when I approached a well-respected company that does market research on the LGBT community about collaborating to find out what the bisexuals they had in their data were saying. I was told that they only analyze their data for what the lesbians and gay men have to say. It wasn't worth their time to search out the infinitesimal number of bisexuals!

That was the final straw for me! It was clear that bisexuals and transgender people were going to have to do our own research. My husband had recently conducted the most exhaustive study to date on the sexual health and perspectives of transmen, so I was emboldened to take on conducting research on bisexuality myself.

I decided I needed both sponsorship and bi community support, so I reached out to many bi activists and leaders and was gratified at the outpouring of support and time to help me create a survey. Out & Equal was the first organization to commit to sponsorship, and then the Bisexual Resource Center and the American Institute of Bisexuality signed on as well. I also contacted an old friend from my days on the GABLE Leadership Team to help with the data. Dr. Nick Payne was Procter & Gamble's company statistician for many years. He had retired and was in a second career as a statistics professor at the University of Cincinnati. Nick's involvement brought both the opportunity to evaluate correlations in the data and the chance to have an Institutional Review Board-certified survey. The certification makes the results publishable academically and gives them credibility in corporate circles as well. With all those elements in place, I was ready to launch my survey.

I sent the survey out to the bi community in as many directions as I could. I asked all the leaders to send it to everyone they knew. I forwarded the link to bi organizations. Out & Equal sent the link to ERGs. These efforts were all undertaken to contact bisexuals willing to share their workplace experiences. I got more than fifteen hundred responses back from fifty-three countries on six continents, though most respondents were from the U.S. and the U.K.

> **Bisexuality is not a "stop on the way" to being either gay or straight, but, instead, a distinct sexual orientation.**

This story isn't about my study's findings, but about my life experiences, so I won't dive into the details, but the survey confirmed some things I believed about bisexuals' workplace experiences, while other data surprised me. Most bisexuals are monogamous; many are more comfortable being out to straight people than to gay men or lesbians; and bisexuality is not a "stop on the way" to being either gay or straight, but, instead, a distinct sexual orientation, quite separate from monosexuality.

Very few bisexuals are willing to be openly involved with the LGBT community. Some avoid doing so because of hostility from monosexuals, but most see ERGs as simply irrelevant to our lives. As a bisexual, I feel like an afterthought in the LGBT community, just one of the letters, and one that no one else is particularly interested in getting to know. Most ERGs have only a few, if any, bisexuals, and this seems to justify the benign neglect. However, if Kinsey and my mother are even somewhat right (and data from many sources say they are), then our ERGs are missing a lot of potential members. We could be stronger, more diverse, and more powerful.

Even from otherwise enlightened friends, I hear distrust of bisexuals. It's still typical to hear, "She's going to leave you for a man." If your partner is going to leave you for someone else, the genitals involved are not the primary issue, right? I also observe the rejection of bisexuals in different-sex relationships and the hostility implicit in regarding and treating us as allies rather than members of the community.

We have a *long* way to go in LGBT circles to understand bisexuals. I see Out & Equal embarking on that journey, and it gives me hope.

Silvy Vluggen

Silvy Vluggen is IBM's Global Lesbian, Gay, Bisexual and Transgender (LGBT) Program Manager, with worldwide responsibility for the development and implementation of the company's LGBT policies and programs. Based in Paris, France, she also manages external relationships for the LGBT constituency and has worldwide responsibility for Cultural Intelligence, enhancing the  cultural awareness level of IBM staff and helping to ensure that every employee is capable of achieving results in a multicultural environment. Originally from Maastricht, the Netherlands, Silvy has been at IBM since 1993 and was part of the company's Software Group before joining the Human Resources organization. Prior to her current role, she served as IBM services manager for Europe, the Middle East, and Africa.

While IBM has been a global company since its inception more than 100 years ago, globalization has spurred more corporations to establish offices in various international locations. IBM, which does business in 170 countries, has made extensive efforts to enact diversity initiatives in these settings. As IBM's Global LGBT Program Manager, I work with senior leaders around the globe to focus on our strategy to face challenges connected with IBM's LGBT constituency.

IBM is a globally integrated enterprise, which means that nearly every employee is likely to interact with people from other countries and cultures. We take cultural differences into account. While we value local cultures and respect local opinions, cultural reasons cannot stand in the way of deployment of our global diversity programs.

In some countries, local laws pose huge challenges to workplace equality. Homosexuality is still illegal in almost eighty countries and is punishable by death in seven. While we strive for global consistency in our LGBT programs, local laws impact which programs we are able to develop. But regardless of location, IBM's equal opportunities policy is never negotiable. A particular country wanted to modify the policy and remove the words "sexual orientation, gender identity and expression." However, IBM policy is truly global and our statement stands wherever we do business, anywhere in the world.

> **"** *Regardless of location, IBM's equal opportunities policy is never negotiable.* **"**

The diversity work at IBM has produced some remarkable results. Workplace equality has become a reality for an ever-increasing number of LGBT individuals at IBM over the past two decades. IBM has more than fifty LGBT employee resource groups in locations around the world. We have been able to raise awareness and create programs in nations where homosexuality is still illegal or was until very recently. We have established a local employee resource group for LGBT employees and have also rolled out domestic partner benefits.

When homosexuality became legal in India in 2009, I immediately reached out to IBM's local, India-based Human Resources group to discuss implementing domestic partner benefits. The local HR department asked for more time, because Indian culture was not yet ready to integrate this change. We worked with the local HR and management team to prepare the organization for the change, to allow society to catch up and adopt the new legislation that had decriminalized same-sex relationships. As a result, the company's domestic partner benefits were implemented in India in 2012.

We provide reverse mentoring to local management on LGBT workplace issues all around the world. We have also hosted LGBT Business Leaders Forums in Poland and Italy. Clients are invited to these events, which focus on sharing best practices for LGBT workplace equality and raising awareness of the challenges faced by the LGBT community.

Each initiative IBM takes to increase LGBT inclusion makes the company a great place for LGBT employees to work. We work with openly LGBT executives at sites around the world, who act as role models and actively participate in our LGBT diversity efforts. These out executives mentor our high-potential LGBT employees so that they can advance to executive positions in the future. We also give employees the opportunity to self-identify on a voluntary basis. Among other things, this system allows the company to identify and develop a pipeline of high-potential LGBT employees.

> **We are also building a community of straight allies around the world because there is power in numbers.**

We are also building a community of straight allies around the world. This is particularly important, because there is power in numbers. As a minority group, the LGBT community needs a stronger voice in order to convince the majority and reach full equality. In order to strengthen our ally base, IBM's out executives reverse mentor the country general managers around the world on LGBT issues. In addition to this, we have an army of almost three hundred LGBT employees who serve on a voluntary basis to reverse mentor first-line managers around the world including managers in growth markets like India, China, and Brazil.

Handling workplace transitions of our transgender employees is always a very rewarding experience. When they first come to me, people are often very fearful about discussing their transition. Once they see our policies and the programs we offer, they are relieved. I personally talk to transgender employees as often as they need, so that they can feel reassured that their job with IBM is safe. We educate both management and peers on the topic and provide opportunities for them to ask questions, so that they can really understand. I have never heard a negative comment from any of our staff, and all of our transgender employees have shown a lot of gratitude for how well the transition process proceeded in the work sphere.

> " Handling workplace transitions of our transgender employees is always a very rewarding experience. "

I also manage IBM's global participation in the Out & Equal Workplace Summit, from defining the partnership with Out & Equal to coordinating the details of rounding up fifty of our employees from around the globe to attend the Summit. IBM leverages the Summit as a leadership development opportunity for our high-potential LGBT employees. They always return to work extremely energized and motivated to take action and serve as role models for the LGBT constituency at their location. IBM has partnerships with several LGBT organizations around the world, but none of them is so closely aligned with our own internal goals and objectives as Out & Equal.

I am immensely proud that IBM is on the forefront of LGBT workplace equality. We serve as a role model for many other corporations. I receive a lot of benchmarking and speaking requests — too many to honor, and they demonstrate the number of corporations that look to us as a model for diversity. This makes me proud to be an IBMer and so grateful to be doing this work full time. I would like to see a world in which LGBT people are treated with dignity in every single country. The first step is to make workplace equality a reality for lesbian, gay, bisexual, and transgender people across the globe.

> **❝** *I would like to see a world in which LGBT people are treated with dignity in every single country.* **❞**

Kevin Jones

Kevin Jones joined Out & Equal Workplace Advocates as Deputy Director in February 2009 after nearly twenty-five years in the corporate world, most recently as a managing director in risk management for Citigroup in New York City (NYC). During his eleven years at Citi, Kevin worked closely with the Office of Workforce Diversity on issues specific to LGBT inclusion and was the founding co-chair of the company's national and metro NYC employee resource groups. Kevin serves on the Human Rights Campaign Business Council and the Board of Directors of True Child, an action tank of leading experts that promotes gender transformative approaches to reproductive health, gender-based violence, and educational achievement. Kevin serves on advisory boards, including the Stonewall National Museum & Archives and Equal India Alliance. He is in a registered domestic partnership with his partner of more than sixteen years, Tony De Sousa, and lives in Northern California.

Until the fall of 1992, I was out to only a few very close colleagues at work. That changed when my then-partner of five years was diagnosed with AIDS and I felt compelled to discuss my sexual orientation with my manager. I was a Vice President in charge of loan operations at Barclays Capital in NYC, and I had to let people know that there were things going on at home that might require me to be away from the office on short notice. Coming out to a wider circle of people at my workplace was not something that I relished, but I felt I did not have much choice. As it turned out, the horrible things that I imagined might happen at work did not. My coming out experience was very positive, and, in retrospect, it allowed me to remove an important source of stress in my life at a time when I was confronting more important challenges.

When I accepted a position with Citibank in 1997, I expected to be out from the start. I was a bit surprised that the bank did not have employee resource groups, let alone a Pride group. I proceeded with caution but soon met some LGBT employees representing Citibank at an LGBT business expo. I was thrilled and quickly became involved with a small group of people who were meeting unofficially outside of work. Doug Robinson was leading the group, which was working to obtain domestic partner benefits at Citibank. He quickly became a role model and mentor to me on LGBT workplace equality — and a good friend.

> **The lack of domestic partner benefits struck me as patently unfair.**

He encouraged me to become involved, and I jumped right in. The lack of domestic partner benefits struck me as patently unfair. It was an injustice that affected me personally, and I wanted be a part of changing it. We met regularly with representatives from Human Resources on the topic. We created a photo album with pictures of Citibank employees who identified as lesbian or gay and discussed the ways in which they were affected by the lack of health benefits. We hoped this would put a human face on the issue.

We also reached out to colleagues at other corporations such as IBM, Chase, and MetLife to learn how they had achieved success or had developed strategies for obtaining domestic partner (DP) benefits. We formed Gay & Lesbian Employee Groups (using the unattractive acronym "GLEG") as a forum for discussing best practices in achieving DP benefits. It was an exciting preview of the work that would ultimately come to be my passion.

Following the Citibank-Travelers merger in 1998 to form Citigroup, progress around LGBT workplace inclusion began gathering steam. Gail Natoli was named Citi's first Chief Diversity Officer and was a remarkable ally. She worked with her colleagues in Human Resources to ready the company to add domestic partner benefits, and we anticipated that they would be announced near the end of 1999.

> " The breakthrough came when one of Citi's businesses framed the offering of domestic partner benefits in clear monetary terms. "

Then we hit a wall. Someone important remained unconvinced. The breakthrough came when one of Citi's businesses framed the offering of domestic partner benefits in clear monetary terms.

The City of San Francisco decided that they would only contract with companies that offered domestic partner benefits. The Municipal Finance Division outlined the lost business opportunity with San Francisco if Citi did not offer DP benefits. Citi then began offering DP benefits in early 2000.

I learned several important lessons in those early years when working within corporations: change can take time; cultivating allies is invaluable; developing a clear business case is imperative; and a rational, respectful and persistent approach will get results.

The year 2000 marked some other transformational events for me. Citi held its first corporate-sponsored Pride Month event that June, featuring a presentation by Witeck-Combs Communications that highlighted the opportunities in marketing to the LGBT community. Enter my next friend and mentor on LGBT workplace issues, Bob Witeck. Among the many points that Bob and his business partner Wes Combs made during the presentation, Bob said one thing that would change my life: "There is an event this September in Seattle called Out & Equal. You should go." So I took a week of vacation, headed to Seattle with Tony, and attended my first Out & Equal Workplace Summit, where I saw the amazing work that Selisse Berry was doing on LGBT workplace equality — work that I was eager to join.

> " Change can take time; cultivating allies is invaluable; developing a clear business case is imperative; and a rational, respectful and persistent approach will lead to change. "

My first Out & Equal experience opened my eyes to many things, but my clearest memory involves learning about the issues of discrimination endured by transgender employees. I was particularly moved by a panel discussion that debated the wisdom of including gender identity in the Employment Non-Discrimination Act (ENDA). At that time, proposed federal legislation included only protections based on sexual orientation, due to the political calculation that a fully inclusive bill would never pass.

The panel included Dana Rivers, a transgender woman who had been fired from her job as a teacher in Southern California. Upon hearing Dana's compelling story, I knew then that I wanted to work for full inclusion and equality of all parts of the LGBT community. It is a commitment that I have since tried — not always as successfully as I might have liked — to keep central to my work. It was that first Out & Equal experience that led to my support of the inspirational Riki Wilchins and Gina Reiss at GenderPac and True Child.

I also left that first Workplace Summit understanding the importance and power of employee resource groups. I was determined that Citi needed to move toward formal recognition of ERGs. That became a reality in 2003, and the advance was one of many at Citi due to the advocacy and leadership of Ana Duarte-McCarthy, who had become the company's Chief Diversity Officer, a position that she still holds. I do not think that I can describe how much I cherished working with Ana. She has accomplished amazing things in her role at Citi as a consistently remarkable and effective ally of the LGBT community. It was with great personal pride and respect that I watched her receive the Out & Equal Champion Award in 2007.

We had some great successes at Citi in the realm of diversity for the LGBT community. Citi began sponsoring the Out & Equal Workplace Summit in 2003. In 2004, Citi joined a business coalition supporting a bill to stop the unfair taxation of people in domestic partnerships and added gender identity to its global nondiscrimination policies. The list of accomplishments goes on. Personally, my involvement in Citi's diversity efforts gained me great visibility before senior executives, which definitely helped my career.

Advancing workplace equality for lesbian, gay, bisexual, and transgender employees was immensely rewarding for me. Over time, it became more important to me than my day job. By 2008, I had an opportunity to volunteer for a severance package, and I had reached a point in my career where doing so was financially feasible for me. I decided to leave Citi to look for a job where I could merge my profession with my passion.

A few months later, when Out & Equal announced that they were recruiting for a Deputy Director, it was the perfect opportunity. Every day, I am now able to work for LGBT equality in workplaces across the United States and around the world. It has been inspiring to watch the evolution of workplace equality over the past thirty years since I began my career. Companies are making advances more quickly than I could have dreamed possible when I first entered the workforce. Yet for all our progress, so much more remains to be done.

It has been a privilege to be a part of this change and to have met and worked with people (too many to name) who are truly heroes. Some of my story — the best part of our story — is yet to be written.

> " *Every day, I am now able to work for LGBT equality in workplaces across the United States and around the world.* "

Bob Witeck

Bob Witeck served in the U.S. Senate for nearly a decade, and later as Senior Vice President at Hill & Knowlton Public Affairs. In 1993, he co-founded his own firm, and he serves today as President of Witeck Communications, Inc. working with major companies and nonprofits on a broad range of LGBT issues and communications strategies.

In the mid-1970s soon after college, like many recent graduates I found myself perplexed as I weighed my future career and grad school options. Without a solid plan in mind, I decided to come back home to Washington, D.C., and consider landing a job on Capitol Hill.

In 1938, each of my parents first arrived in Washington at the height of the New Deal and in hindsight, just as the nation's capital began preparing for the threat of war. The city was alive with possibilities especially in public service. While my father completed law school, he began his own career in federal service. By 1950, he had earned an appointment to the professional staff of the Senate Appropriations Committee where he stayed for the next quarter century.

To be honest, although my father thrived on a Senate staff, and we were surrounded by the political culture in the city, my own ambition to work in Congress seemed lukewarm at best. When younger, though, I had actually imagined having my own career in politics.

However, as my same-sex attractions and identity began to form, that possibility began to seem more and more remote. If gay, surely I could never run for public office, nor be open and honest at all with others. From where I stood, there were no hints that lesbians and gay men were welcome in the political arena any more than other walks of life. In fact, this prospect appeared much worse and far less hospitable.

For many young men and women, who considered themselves bisexual, gay or lesbian, at that time, the choices were painfully clear as we launched our careers. We simply had to keep our cards close to our chests, avoid bringing our personal lives into the office, and above all, make sure never to share too much personal information with our coworkers or our boss about how we spent our weekend or the people we were dating.

With the rules understood, I took a shot and applied for a couple of staff openings in Congress. Although I am a lifelong Democrat, I found a very promising spot on the staff of Oregon Senator Bob Packwood, a liberal Republican. Looking back nearly four decades, this simple bipartisan culture was more the rule than the exception it now seems. At that time, both parties in Congress included members who held diverse philosophies and ideologies. Moreover, Congressional staffs also seemed to enjoy a reasonable degree of bipartisan cooperation.

In Washington's culture, and especially on the Hill, the governing though unnamed philosophy remained "Don't Ask, Don't

Tell." For most of us, we rose in the ranks and achieved professional status by covering our past, shielding our present, and avoiding speculation on the future. Dishonesty truly was the best policy.

In my first staff position, I was assigned the role of a junior legislative assistant. However, given my gift and love of writing, within a couple years, I was named assistant press secretary as well. Lucky for me, that was also the moment when I became an eyewitness to history in ways that I could never have imagined as a young gay Senate staffer.

The year was 1979. At that time, over thirty years ago, there was no federal law banning employment discrimination for sexual orientation or for gender identity. Today, in 2012, tragically that remains true. What is remarkable, of course, is my belief that 1979 was the first year and the first moment in Congress that this glaring injustice was ever officially recognized.

> **" The year was 1979. At that time, over thirty years ago, there was no federal law banning employment discrimination for sexual orientation or for gender identity. Today, in 2012, tragically that remains true. "**

On the morning of September 18, 1979, Senator Packwood and the other members of the Senate Finance Committee arrived to begin a confirmation hearing for a Presidential appointee. Facing the last year of his term in office, President Jimmy Carter named Florida Governor Reubin Askew to be a member of his cabinet and to serve as our nation's Trade Representative. Governor Askew's positions were well known because of his outspoken support for Anita Bryant's efforts in Dade County, Florida, to deny "homosexuals" employment rights and specifically in 1977, to ban homosexuals from teaching in public schools. Not surprisingly, most of the confirmation hearing was consumed with discussion about America's trade priorities. There were no real surprises during the questioning.

An unusual moment arose, however, when three gay civil rights leaders were permitted to speak in opposition to Askew's nomination. Under Committee rules, none were permitted to directly question Governor Askew at the hearing. Senator Packwood, however, did have that power. He intended to use it.

Packwood began by asking Governor Askew whether he had said these reported words, "*I would not have a homosexual on my staff.*" For one of the first times in Congressional history, a Member of Congress raised an issue about the civil rights of gays and lesbians. The official hearing record reports the Governor's reply: "Yes sir, I did. I said a known homosexual, and I would not."

The Senator then asked if that was his present position, and Askew confirmed it was true. Packwood followed up again and asked Askew whether it was his position to "not have a homosexual" on his staff. Askew responded, "I would not have a known homosexual on my staff, simply, Senator, by virtue of the tremendous problems it presents in dealing with public constituencies."

Packwood asked, "If I understand your answer, to the extent that you can, within the bounds of the law, you intend to follow the policy as Special Trade Representative of not hiring known homosexuals?"

Askew responded, "Let us put it this way, Senator, that I would follow whatever the personnel policy of the Federal Government is, but in the selections I have made thus far — and I have very little flexibility in hiring — I have not, and would not."

Over thirty years ago, a nominee for Cabinet rank declared that he was perfectly within America's laws and customs to deny jobs to individuals, despite their obvious talents, qualifications and fitness, simply because of their sexual orientation. Given the year, and the lack of any major disqualifying traits, apart from his then politically acceptable bigotry, the full Senate soon confirmed Governor Askew, trusting President Carter's cabinet choice. It is very hard today, however, to imagine this same scenario with a cabinet designee for any future President knowing that an overwhelming majority of all Americans agree that it is simply not fair to discriminate in the workplace so outrageously.

For me personally and for so many more of us, it was kind of a wake-up call too. Before that moment, I honestly did not know how my own boss felt about working with gay people — and had merely remained by his side and hiding in plain sight. It was as though a giant burden had lifted and reassured me that my fears were unfounded.

As assistant press secretary, I was just as happy to receive a phone call from the *Washington Blade* and to report the unprecedented exchange at the Senate hearing. I was especially happy to know that my boss felt that basic civil rights protections belonged to all of us — a philosophy he specifically reinforced by agreeing to cosponsor the first, bipartisan federal gay civil rights bill of that session along with his colleagues, Ted Kennedy, Paul Tsongas and Lowell Weicker.

> " It was actions like those I witnessed in the Senate that gave me and many others the courage to be open in our own lives and to become lifelong advocates for equality. "

It was thinking like that and the long-ago campaign by Governor Askew's Florida ally, Anita Bryant, that motivated Harvey Milk to enter not just city politics but also the national stage to change hearts and minds by first changing laws. It was actions like those I witnessed in the Senate that gave me and many others the courage to be open in our own lives and to become lifelong advocates for equality.

I have not worked on Capitol Hill for over two decades now. However, I remember how valuable those early years were for me to champion boldness and to conquer my fears. Regrettably, however, it also reminds me how achingly slow our political system can be — given that our Congress has not yet passed federal employment nondiscrimination legislation. Until that day, it seems that men like Governor Reuben Askew remain free to exercise their bigotries and biases and to stand in the way of a fair and open workplace for all.

> **"** *Corporate America has long known that basic fairness is good business.* **"**

Corporate America has long known that basic fairness is good business. Today, over 90 percent of Fortune 500 companies have precisely the same nondiscrimination policies that include sexual orientation, and more than a third cover gender identity. The nation can and must benefit from their best practices.

For me, it was the start of a satisfying career that reminds me every single day that it's never too early (or too late) to do the right thing.

Frank Kameny

Frank and Me
By Bob Witeck, President of Witeck Communications, Inc.

Frank Kameny was a lifelong gay rights pioneer. After being fired and then barred from federal employment in the 1950s, he fought for several years to get his job back. Kameny and a friend established the Washington, D.C., branch of the Mattachine Society in 1961. He has received numerous awards for his efforts, including the LGBT Workplace Equality Pioneer award from Out & Equal in 2007. In October of 2011 Frank Kameny passed away, and shortly after an asteroid was named in his honor.

In June 2012, the heavens above us shone more brightly as a previously uncharted asteroid was named in honor of the late Dr. Franklin E. Kameny thanks to a fellow astronomer. My only regret, of course, was that Frank, a lifelong star-gazer, did not live long enough to witness it.

Kameny's life and struggles to achieve equality for lesbian, gay, bisexual and transgender people did not always win him universal acclaim on Earth, however this very rare, celestial memorial is testament to the monumental civil rights work he began nearly six decades ago.

Growing up in the Washington, D.C., area in the 1950s and 1960s, I feel very lucky that I not only shared Dr. Kameny's hometown but also later, his friendship. As a teenager then, I have to confess that his courage, certainty and honesty were frightening to me. In 1969, as I entered my senior year in high school, every silent and paralyzed fiber in my body told me I was attracted to boys. This was a secret so deep and so disturbing to me that I couldn't bring myself to talk about it with anyone. Not my parents, or my six brothers and sisters who attended parochial school with me. And certainly none of my friends or fellow students.

I should add that, although the historic Stonewall demonstrations had just occurred months earlier, their inspiration and consequences were still too fresh to reach me at my home in Arlington, Virginia.

At a time when America was populated more by gay bars than by gay-straight high school alliances (and with the Internet still years from launch), it's not surprising that few teenagers found any channels of support, understanding and truthfulness about being gay. Instead, in our public library, I discovered a few clinical texts and a scary book or two about the risks of being a homosexual. If you've ever seen "Little Britain" perform, I really did feel like the "only gay in the village."

With luck and by reading our newspaper, I discovered there was a group in Washington, D.C., called the Mattachine Society, which advocated ending discrimination against homosexuals. From time to time, I read reports about a stubborn and impatient activist named Dr. Franklin Kameny, who served as Mattachine's leader.

I steeled my courage one day, with a pocketful of coins, to walk to the shopping center near our home and find an out-of-the-way pay phone. I looked up the phone number for the Mattachine Society and when I dialed, to my horror and joy, Dr. Kameny answered.

I cannot recall whether he identified himself or not, but over the years, I realized that the phone was in his home and my phone call was among hundreds or perhaps thousands he answered over the years. Many were calls from young men and women like me who were lost, afraid and most of all clueless.

With that brave call over four decades ago, and my timid first step, I believe Frank Kameny was actually the first openly gay man with whom I'd ever spoken. I don't recall all or even much of what we said, except for the sense of confidence I soon felt that told me I was not alone. For some of us, that's truly a life saver. Frank was especially proud of having coined the phrase, "Gay is good," and for the few minutes we spoke that day, I think that was his gift to me.

> **"Frank was especially proud of having coined the phrase, "Gay is good," and for the few minutes we spoke that day, I think that was his gift to me."**

As a native Washingtonian, and like many of us near and very far, I have felt Frank's influence over a long life and his rightful claims to our civil rights history as well as his years of friendship. Remarkably, his life's work and legacy began by righting one fundamental wrong: his 1957 firing from federal employment because of his sexual orientation.

Like Rosa Parks, Frank found the "back of the bus" hateful, confining and demeaning, not to mention unlawful. When first hired as a government astronomer, and following his military service in World War II and the doctorate he earned at Harvard, Frank could not have been more ably equipped or more enthusiastic to help lead America's space exploration.

However, when the federal government labeled him "unsuitable for employment" because of his homosexuality, yet trained well as a scientist, he was powered by irrefutable logic. When combined with his self-taught legal acumen and his gifts as a polemicist, he transformed his rejection and exile into victory.

Franklin Kameny is properly credited with many milestones, including bringing an aggressive strategy and convincing messages to the nation's LGBT rights struggle. Kameny and his colleagues, Jack Nichols and Barbara Gittings, brought the first public protests to official Washington with a picket line at the White House in April 1965. Later, and with support from New York's Mattachine Society and the Daughters of Bilitis, the pickets expanded to the Pentagon, the U.S. Civil Service Commission (which presided over Frank's dismissal) and to Philadelphia's Independence Hall.

Will history remember Frank and honor his giant contributions as we commend other civil rights pioneers? The good news is that in the past decade, many of us became aware that Frank Kameny rarely discarded any paper or memento that crossed his hands or his sight. In Frank's own words, he called himself a "pack rat." In his home in northwest Washington, Dr. Kameny stored boxes and piles of correspondence, reports, newspapers, photographs and other records. If any idiosyncrasy defined Frank, it was his prodigious, almost obsessive personal repository of knowledge about LGBT

> " Kameny and his colleagues, Jack Nichols and Barbara Gittings, brought the first public protests to official Washington with a picket line at the White House in April 1965. "

civil rights and civil wrongs. While the twenty-first century dawned with the digital age in full view, Frank's world was almost entirely one of paper and written records.

Consider also that Dr. Kameny had not held a full-time job since his humiliating firing in the mid-1950s. Instead, he dedicated his life to full-time advocacy and consequently, his very means to live were extremely modest. In his later years, he repeatedly relied on generous friends and devoted followers to help make tight ends meet and to help cover the costs of remaining in his own home too.

In 2006, therefore, a few committed volunteers joined with Frank to respond to his needs and the community's resources by starting the nonprofit Kameny Papers Project. In this way, and with Dr. Kameny's pride and approval, many boxes of papers and a number of his original picket signs were formally appraised, and ultimately given as a life gift to the Library of Congress and the Smithsonian.

To achieve transparency and to ensure that Dr. Kameny made all informed decisions about his legacy, these materials then were lawfully purchased by a circle of generous individuals along with several leading LGBT civil rights groups including the National Gay & Lesbian Task Force, Human Rights Campaign, and the Log Cabin Club, among others. This was done with great care to compensate Dr. Kameny directly for his life's work and on his behalf, to forever preserve the historic contributions he led to America's civil rights record. Fortunately, some of his remaining artifacts and papers were also gifted to other LGBT collections and archives around the country.

How can any of us forget Dr. Kameny's story now that many of his papers are preserved in the Library of Congress and some of his earliest picket signs enshrined at the Smithsonian? Remarkably, his artifacts have been included in a public exhibit entitled "Creators of the United States." Like our earliest patriots, founding fathers and defenders of liberty, Dr. Kameny surely is among the inventors of our "more perfect union." When alive, Dr. Kameny had the singular honor to visit his artifacts and papers — and to witness, over a year's time, how the Library's cataloguers miraculously transformed nearly sixty boxes of now safeguarded letters and documents into a searchable and retrievable public archive for future historians, students and writers.

For sure, those papers and signs are archival treasures, and merely symbols of the giant actions he took in life. Yale law professor

> "*How can any of us forget Dr. Kameny's story now that many of his papers are preserved in the Library of Congress and some of his earliest picket signs enshrined at the Smithsonian?*"

William Eskridge compared Dr. Kameny to Rosa Parks, Dr. Martin Luther King and Thurgood Marshall when eulogizing him last year on Capitol Hill and reminding us:

> *"For decades, Frank Kameny inspired and actively participated in every major campaign for lesbian and gay rights — from repealing or invalidating consensual sodomy laws, to revoking state employment discrimination against gay people, to creating affirmative laws barring discrimination because of sexual orientation, to recognizing lesbian and gay marriages and families. In every campaign, the Gay Is Good idea has prevailed or soon will prevail."*

Fast forward to 2009 and instead of picketing outside the White House, Dr. Kameny then found himself an honored guest in the Oval Office to witness President Barack Obama signing the *Matthew Shepard Hate Crimes Act*. And within a year, he also sat in the front row to watch the President's repeal of *Don't Ask, Don't Tell*.

To think this journey began in 1957 with an official letter that read, "Dear Dr. Kameny: It is necessary that you return at once to the Army Map Service… within 48 hours of receiving this Letter." The matter-of-fact letter followed the civil service guidelines that classified individuals like Dr. Kameny among "homosexuals or sexual perverts not suitable for Federal employment."

> **"** The matter-of-fact letter followed the civil service guidelines that classified individuals like Dr. Kameny among "homosexuals or sexual perverts not suitable for Federal employment." **"**

Dr. Kameny promised to follow every avenue to "its end." Over fifty years later, while vindicated by the government's reversal of their employment ban, at last he also earned a heartfelt apology for that long-ago humiliation. In 2009, Office of Personnel Management Director John Berry, the highest openly LGBT leader appointed by President Obama to head up the modern-day civil service, invited Dr. Kameny to accept his apology along with the nation's most prestigious award for distinguished public servants, the Teddy Roosevelt Award. Frank Kameny embraced John Berry and replied emotionally, "Apology accepted."

While paying tribute to Dr. Kameny's life, John Berry also remembered the child in each of us, and the fear and hiding that imprisoned us as LGBT people. Like me, John grew up in the 1960s realizing his secret was a heavy burden:

> *"I knew that I was interested in public service. But my hopes were held in check, because I also knew that prospects for gay men in public service were both limited and difficult, filled with fear and public loathing. Frank Kameny freed us from that fear.*

"His life cleared the path that I and countless others followed into public service. His unrelenting and unceasing fight for gay rights enabled other Americans to step out of the closet and into the full light of equality. But most importantly, his long battle, and eventual triumphs, show the miracles one man wrought upon the world."

" In 2009, Office of Personnel Management Director John Berry, the highest openly LGBT leader appointed by President Obama to head up the modern-day civil service, invited Dr. Kameny to accept his apology along with the nation's most prestigious award for distinguished public servants, the Teddy Roosevelt Award. "

Every single day, as progress accelerates around us, I feel that many of us are reminded of the child within, and the early anxieties and panic of being different, being alone and fearing discovery. Today, I hope every person, whether gay or straight or bisexual or transgender, appreciates and acknowledges Frank Kameny's example, along with many others, knowing how much he achieved to make all our lives better and the world a far safer and accepting place.

History of Out & Equal Workplace Advocates

Out & Equal Workplace Advocates

Out & Equal Workplace Advocates is the world's largest nonprofit organization specifically dedicated to creating safe and equitable workplaces for lesbian, gay, bisexual and transgender people. The journey to becoming Out & Equal began with the convergence of several currents of LGBT advocacy. The foundation of Out & Equal's success has been collaboration and creating synergy between like-minded groups and individuals.

One of the streams leading to the creation of Out & Equal began in the late 1980s when a group of San Francisco activists contacted the United Way of the Bay Area (UWBA) to discuss issues affecting lesbian, gay, bisexual, and transgender people. Since 1922, the UWBA has raised money through workplace campaigns to support local nonprofit organizations. LGBT activists approached the UWBA because, at the time, none of these funds were being used to support LGBT organizations. Their initial discussion with the UWBA was followed by several years of community pressure and persistence.

In 1992, the United Way of the Bay Area became the first United Way in the country to include sexual orientation in its own equal employment policy. The UWBA went a step further and required its nonprofit constituents to implement LGBT non-discrimination policies in order to receive United Way funding.

Many Bay Area organizations were willing to comply, but were unprepared to develop new LGBT worksite policies and practices. Activists saw an opportunity to educate local organizations by developing an LGBT diversity training program and approached the leadership of the United Way to begin a joint effort. A group of LGBT volunteers compiled curriculum from around the country and worked with the United Way's task force on LGBT issues to create *Building Bridges*, a training program that fosters increased awareness of LGBT issues in order to develop a healthier and safer workplace.

> **" Activists saw an opportunity to educate local organizations by developing an LGBT diversity training program, and approached the leadership of the United Way to begin a joint effort. "**

Selisse Berry was hired as Building Bridges' director in 1996 and began to certify volunteer Building Bridges trainers and offer LGBT diversity training to nonprofit organizations. Selisse initially worked out of the Pacific Center in Berkeley, California, running the new training program and building coalitions with other LGBT organizations. She was the only staff person, working with a tiny budget.

The Pride Collaborative

By 1997, Selisse Berry had moved Building Bridges to United Way offices and was intent on expanding the LGBT diversity training program's client base to include businesses and corporations. She began to examine existing LGBT resources and sought out groups and individuals championing workplace equality in corporate environments. She met with United Way's CEO, Tom Ruppanner, to lay out her vision for a more comprehensive LGBT employee support organization. Ruppanner supported Building Bridges' proposed expansion beyond diversity training and the addition of new programs.

Throughout the 1990s, LGBT employees in Fortune 500 companies began advocating for equal rights in American workplaces. In June of 1994, organizers sent an invitation to the San Francisco Bay Area LGBT employees from a variety of companies to join in an informal gathering in Redwood City. Much to the surprise of the organizers, more than two hundred people showed up. The organizers realized that there was real potential for LGBT employees to make a significant impact in the business world and started a volunteer-led organization called AGOG: A Group of Groups. AGOG's mission was to convene corporate LGBT employees to advocate for domestic partner benefits and employee resource groups (ERGs).

> **"** *There was real potential for LGBT employees to make a significant impact in the business world.* **"**

Another coalition, Progress, was formed a year later to bring together ERG leaders from across California to develop their leadership skills. Progress hosted leadership development summits in Sacramento, California, in 1995 and in Dallas, Texas, in 1997. The conferences focused on developing more effective leaders to advocate around LGBT issues in the workplace.

Selisse began to network with the leadership of AGOG and Progress. As director of Building Bridges, she invited them to meetings at UWBA to discuss ways they could support each other's work. All three groups had limited resources and time, yet had an abundance of contacts, skills and enthusiasm. AGOG and Progress were entirely volunteer, made up of highly motivated Fortune 500 employees with full-time jobs. Building Bridges, even with its slender nonprofit budget, had the only paid staff member, Selisse, who could dedicate all of her time to organizing for workplace equality. The three groups saw value in merging their resources and expertise.

Selisse brought the three groups together to discuss the priorities of a new merged organization. The discussions were lively. In the beginning, Building Bridges members favored prioritizing LGBT diversity workplace training. AGOG members preferred to network with ERGs to facilitate communication and ensure best practices. Progress members thought leadership development and annual events would help LGBT employees become better advocates for making change in their workplaces.

After seven or eight months of meetings, Selisse noticed that participants were starting to use the word "we." When she began hearing that magic word, she knew that Progress, Building Bridges, and AGOG members had started to envision the future as a team.

> **" In 1998, Building Bridges, AGOG, and Progress joined forces and decided to move forward together as the Pride Collaborative. "**

In 1998, Building Bridges, AGOG, and Progress joined forces and decided to move forward together as the Pride Collaborative under the fiscal sponsorship of UWBA. The Pride Collaborative maintained the activities that each participating group had pioneered. It offered an annual leadership conference, ongoing Building Bridges diversity training and bimonthly networking opportunities called Pride Power Breakfasts.

Pride Power Breakfasts provided informal gatherings for LGBT employees to network, feel a sense of community, and learn about workplace equality and leadership development. Selisse approached several corporations to request that they provide conference rooms for the breakfasts and items for the event's informal raffle. Individuals who attended the LGBT networking breakfasts tossed their business cards into a hat for the prize drawing; the business cards helped Selisse build a database and a community. These Pride Power Breakfasts formed the basis for the extensive Regional Affiliate network that would later develop under Out & Equal Workplace Advocates.

Each breakfast had a different topic and keynote speaker or panel addressing a variety of issues including: coming out at work and in job interviews; how to create LGBT employee resource groups; maintaining ERG meeting attendance; and how to engage allies and executive sponsors in LGBT advocacy work. The Pride Power Breakfasts welcomed up to one hundred people at each event, and offered a combination of networking and sharing best practices.

Out & Equal in the '90s

Beginning in the early 1990s, a small group of employees at Pacific Gas & Electric hosted a conference called *Out & Equal in the '90s*. The first conference was held at City College of San Francisco.

The event was such a success that the National Gay and Lesbian Task Force and Stanford University joined the *Out & Equal in the '90s* conference as cosponsors. The next conference was held in Cupertino and the 1994 conference in Denver to increase participation and broaden geographic representation. The 1996 conference returned to San Francisco and included a pre-conference event for executives and human resources professionals. The final *Out & Equal in the '90s* conference was held in 1997 in Rochester, New York.

An organization called Colleagues assumed the planning and implementation of the workplace conference in 1997. Founded in the spring of 1996 at the National Gay and Lesbian Task Force's *Creating Change* conference, Colleagues was an umbrella organization comprised of LGBT employee resource networks from across the country. Many of these networks were from AT&T

and its spin-off companies. Their employee resource groups were called *League*. More than fifty people from across the country met and agreed to form a national organization, which they named Co-Leagues or *Colleagues*.

Out & Equal Workplace Advocates

Selisse and the board of the Pride Collaborative began conversations with the leadership of Colleagues in 1999. A shared mission prompted the two groups to join together to combine their strengths and resources. As a result of the collaboration with Colleagues, the Pride Collaborative announced its new name at the Workplace Summit in Seattle in 2000: Out & Equal Workplace Advocates.

> **"** The Pride Collaborative announced its new name at the Workplace Summit in Seattle in 2000: Out & Equal Workplace Advocates. **"**

In 2004, after years of being supported by the United Way of the Bay Area, Out & Equal Workplace Advocates became an independent 501(c)3 organization. Anne Wilson, CEO of UWBA, was wonderfully supportive, both during Out & Equal's tenure at UWBA and as the organization prepared to step out on its own. By 2006, Out & Equal moved into new office space in the heart of San Francisco's Financial District. There were only six people on staff, but the annual Workplace Summits had already become so successful and professional that people assumed Out & Equal had a staff of one hundred.

Out & Equal Workplace Summits

The Out & Equal Workplace Summits are the most visible manifestations of Out & Equal's work. The annual Workplace Summits are labors of love that unite the LGBT community and carry the message of inclusiveness and equality to corporations, communities, and individuals. "They encourage us and motivate us to continue to make change in our companies and organizations," says Selisse Berry. "Most importantly, they inspire us to be proud of who we are."

> " There were only six people on staff, but the annual Workplace Summits had already become so successful and professional that people assumed Out & Equal had a staff of one hundred. "

Each Summit is packed with information, resources, educational opportunities and best-practice sharing, all designed to impact global workplaces. From the beginning, the priorities set for the Workplace Summits have been crystal clear. Selisse has always felt strongly that the gatherings must offer an exceedingly professional experience and celebrate true diversity. In that spirit, the annual Workplace Summit is intentional about hosting speakers and workshop leaders who represent diverse racial and cultural backgrounds and include women, bisexual and transgender people. Out & Equal's unwavering support and gratitude for allies is clear in its programs and presentations. The Summit celebrates the importance of the arts within the LGBT community and consistently showcases entertainment as part of the Summit experience. Last but not least, Out & Equal Workplace Summits place a great deal of emphasis on being together and having fun!

> " The annual Workplace Summits represent diverse racial and cultural backgrounds and include women, bisexual and transgender people. "

The first Out & Equal Workplace Summit took place in Atlanta in 1999 and celebrated the theme, "Workplace Equality in the New Millennium." There were approximately two hundred people at the event and a palpable feeling of excitement and possibility was in the air. Keynote speakers included Virginia Apuzzo, former assistant to the President for White House Management during the Clinton Administration; IBM Chief Diversity Officer, Ted Childs; Elizabeth Birch, HRC's Executive Director; and Allan Gilmour, Chief Financial Officer of Ford Motor Company.

During the Summit, Ms. Apuzzo and Raytheon software engineer Louise Young joined Selisse Berry in discussing the importance of recognizing the workplace as one of the places where societal change occurs. Ginny and Louise suggested giving recognition to exemplary companies and at the second Workplace Summit in Seattle, Washington, Out & Equal introduced the Out & Equal Workplace Awards, commonly referred to as the *Outies!* The Outie Awards recognize individuals, groups and employers making great strides towards equality. The Outie Awards have become highly sought-after and prized commendations.

> **" The Outie Awards recognize individuals, groups and employers making great strides towards equality. "**

In addition to presenting the Outie Awards for the first time, the 2000 Workplace Summit also welcomed Kathy Levinson, Former President and Chief Operating Officer of E*Trade as a keynote speaker. Other prominent speakers included Microsoft Director of Diversity Santiago Rodriguez and Urvashi Vaid, former director of the National Gay and Lesbian Task Force.

The 2001 Summit was scheduled for Cincinnati, Ohio, but was moved to Northern Kentucky when the Cincinnati City Council approved an anti-LGBT ordinance. Out & Equal refused to bring its conference and money to a location that did not support equality for the lesbian, gay, bisexual, and transgender community. The Workplace Summit was held across the river in Kentucky and was a huge success, featuring lesbian activist Mandy Carter; LGBT liaison to President Bill Clinton, Julian Potter; Mike Wilke, Founder of the Commercial Closet; and a panel discussion by Kodak executives.

The 2002 Workplace Summit was hosted at Disney World in Orlando. Howard Dean, the Governor of Vermont, and Patricia Ireland, the former president of NOW, inspired a crowd of more than four hundred. One plenary panel discussed transgender issues at American Airlines, while another focused on international issues facing LGBT employees around the world.

In 2003, former Texas Governor Ann Richards and entrepreneur Mitchell Gold joined retired NFL player Esera Tualo at the podium for the Summit in Minneapolis, Minnesota, to discuss challenges and hopes for the LGBT community before a crowd of six hundred attendees. The 2004 Workplace Summit in Tempe, Arizona, featured Estée Lauder's Senior Vice President of Global Communications, Sally Sussman, along with tennis champion Billie Jean King.

Judy Shepard, the mother of Matthew Shepard, was a keynote speaker at the 2005 Workplace Summit in Denver, Colorado, and shared her hopes that the United States will one day become a safe environment for lesbian, gay, bisexual, and transgender people. Tammy Baldwin, openly lesbian Congresswoman from Wisconsin, actor B.D. Wong and Tim Gill of the Gill Foundation gave inspirational keynote speeches. Between 2004 and 2005, the number of participants nearly doubled — jumping to more than eleven hundred. Political humorist, Kate Clinton, emceed

> " The United States will one day become a safe environment for lesbian, gay, bisexual, and transgender people. "

the Summit's Gala Awards Dinner for the first time. Kate was so popular at the Gala, she has continued to be part of every Summit since then and has become a close friend of the organization.

The 2006 Summit in Chicago, Illinois, presented another spectacular line-up of speakers including actor George Takei, best known for his role on *Star Trek*; Nina Jacobson, the former president of Buena Vista Motion Pictures Group; Yolanda King, human rights activist and daughter of Dr. Martin Luther King, Jr.; and Richard Florida, author of *The Rise of the Creative Class*.

The 2007 Workplace Summit in Washington, D.C. presented former NBA player John Amaechi, LGBT activist Chrissy Gephardt, MTV and Logo executive Brian Graden, and musicians and civil rights activists Toshi Reagon and Dr. Bernice Johnson Reagon. The conference welcomed nearly twenty-four hundred attendees. Frank Kameny was honored that year with a lifetime achievement award for his advancement of workplace equality with the federal government.

> **" 2008 marked the first time a CEO of a Fortune 500 company addressed the Workplace Summit in a plenary speech: Don Knauss, the CEO and President of The Clorox Company. "**

2008 marked the first time a CEO of a Fortune 500 company addressed the Workplace Summit in a plenary speech: Don Knauss, the CEO and President of The Clorox Company. The lesbian, gay, bisexual, transgender, and ally crowd at the Austin, Texas Convention Center welcomed him warmly. Participants also heard from media entrepreneur Ariana Huffington; the former Ambassador to Romania, Michael Guest; Carson Kressley, an openly gay actor from *Queer Eye for the Straight Guy*; and author and media commentator Keith Boykin, a former Clinton White House Aide. During the Summit, Hurricane Ike hit the gulf coast of Texas, which fortunately did not affect Austin, but created quite a "stir" throughout the Summit.

During the 2009 Out & Equal Workplace Summit in Orlando, Florida, John Berry, the highest-ranking openly gay man in the Obama Administration, delivered an inspirational keynote speech connecting the struggle for LGBT rights to the civil rights and disability rights movements. U.S. Secretary of State Hillary Clinton sent her recorded congratulations to the Gays & Lesbians in Foreign Affairs Agencies for winning the Outie Award for Employee Resource Group of the Year. In a keynote speech, Sharon Allen, chairman of Deloitte LLP and one of the most influential businesswomen in the world, said that individual companies have to make advances in LGBT support and nondiscrimination regardless of legislation. Other speakers sharing insights included Emmy-winning actor Leslie Jordan and internationally acclaimed author and civil rights legal scholar Kenji Yoshino.

" Individual companies have to make advances in LGBT support and nondiscrimination regardless of legislation. "

The 2010 Workplace Summit in Los Angeles included an insightful address from Equal Employment Opportunity Commission Commissioner Chai Feldblum, who spoke about equality and the legal implications of a fully inclusive, national Employment Non-Discrimination Act (ENDA). She said that ENDA's passage "would mean that we could live our lives openly and honestly at work." Country music star Chely Wright engaged the audience by relating her coming-out journey, including a significant crisis in 2006 due to the pressure of hiding her sexual orientation. Since coming out, she said she wanted to use her "public capital in a way that could best facilitate change and understanding." Intuit CEO Brad Smith's remarks were warmly received as he spoke of being an ally to the lesbian, gay, bisexual, and transgender community. "Someone told me that my support for the LGBT community makes me an ally," Smith said. "I always thought it makes me a friend."

> **"Someone told me that my support for the LGBT community makes me an ally," Smith said. "I always thought it makes me a friend."**

In 2011, Kathy Martinez, U.S. Assistant Secretary of Labor for Disability Employment Policy, discussed recent advances for the disability and the LGBT communities at the 2011 Summit in Dallas. She reminded everyone of the importance of advocating as a community: "Alone we can do a little, but together we can do so much." Sander van't Noordende, Group Chief Executive of Accenture, related his experience of coming out in the work arena and declared that diversity and equality must go hand in hand. "For us as leaders, it's about making sure we have the right spirit in our companies," he said, "and making sure we have the commitment to lead the journey towards equality step by step, relentlessly."

> **"Alone we can do a little, but together we can do so much."**

Wes Bush, CEO and President of Northrop Grumman, spoke of how LGBT inclusion helps drive commercial success, "You have to have diversity in your leadership, in the way you think about constructing your company — or any enterprise — to attract and retain the very best talent." The CEO of JCPenney, Mike Ullman, also spoke and JCPenney maintained a visible presence at the Summit with their popular fashion show.

Andy Cohen, Bravo TV 's Senior Vice President, conducted an onstage interview with actress

> " *LGBT inclusion helps drive commercial success.* "

and choreographer Candis Cayne. Prime time television's first transgender actor to play a recurring transgender character, Cayne closed with a high-kicking performance of the classic song, "I'm a Woman." Out & Equal Founding Executive Director Selisse Berry spoke about the great change that has occurred in workplaces around the world and the importance of coming home to ourselves in the journey towards becoming truly out and equal.

In preparation for that same Summit, Out & Equal staff conducted the final site visit at the Hilton in Dallas. During the visit, Selisse Berry was given the choice of the Ronald Reagan or the Margaret Thatcher suite. She pointed out to hotel management that neither leader was a good match for Out & Equal's constituency, or for a conference focused on LGBT workplace equality. Both world leaders neglected the LGBT community, especially during the devastation of the AIDS epidemic, and opposed all kinds of workers' rights. The hotel responded and, for the duration of the Summit, they renamed the rooms; one was the Del Martin and Phyllis Lyon suite, and the other was renamed the Harvey Milk suite. That said a lot — not only about their interest in securing the business generated from the Summit, but also about their willingness to support equality.

This turn of events was a huge change from the first Out & Equal Workplace Summit experience in 1999. That first year, just hours before the conference began, the production crew was in the process of setting up the microphones when they realized that Out & Equal is a lesbian, gay, bisexual and transgender organization, and they packed up their equipment and left. The hotel was scrambling, Selisse organized a corps of volunteers, and they swung into action and got the job done. Despite the inauspicious beginning, the Summit was a fantastic experience, and the atmosphere memorable.

Ever since that first Summit experience, Out & Equal has provided pre-conference diversity training to the site's staff — whether the Summit is at a convention center or hotel. These sizable trainings involve a cross-section of the venue including security, housekeeping, the front desk, managers, and others. With these trainings, each Workplace Summit is truly an opportunity to forward Out & Equal's commitment to creating safe and equitable workplace environments for lesbian, gay, bisexual, and transgender employees.

Out & Equal Regional Affiliates

After a number of successful Workplace Summits, Out & Equal constituents began to ask how they could bring the energy and enthusiasm they felt at the Summits home with them. "Our Pride Power Breakfasts in the Bay Area had become ongoing successful events," says Selisse, "and the desire to extend 'that summit feeling' made me see the breakfasts as a model for a Regional Affiliate program." During the same time period, Out & Equal began working with the leaders of GLEG: Gay and Lesbian Employee Groups in New York. GLEG was a gathering of LGBT Employee Resource Groups, similar to AGOG in San Francisco. Following a series of conversations, Out & Equal invited GLEG to become its first Regional Affiliate in 2001 and to help determine the process for future regions to do so, too. Out & Equal now has

> " Out & Equal now has Regional Affiliates around the country and continues to explore opportunities for international affiliates. "

Regional Affiliates around the country and continues to explore opportunities for international affiliates.

Regional Affiliates organize a variety of networking and educational events. The Houston affiliate recently organized a panel with NASA entitled "Out in Space." The New York Finger Lakes Affiliate in Rochester, NY, organized a Northeast Corridor Regional Conference and invited workshop leaders from the national Summit to present. Dallas plans large gatherings, including a big wine-tasting event every year. The Chicago affiliate organizes several events during Pride Month at different companies. San Francisco hosts a "Hot August Night" in cool, foggy August that mixes networking with an educational component.

Out & Equal Executive Forum and Leadership Celebration

The first annual Out & Equal Executive Forum was held in 2008 to address the unique needs of top-level executives who are lesbian, gay, bisexual, and transgender. The forum was born out of conversations with many senior executives. When these successful individuals met with other top executives, they often found that they were the only LGBT people at the table. Conversely, when they were among LGBT colleagues, they were frequently the only top-level executive in the room.

Out & Equal decided to bring these talented individuals together to discuss their unique needs, and also explore how they could have a greater impact on behalf of the LGBT community, in their organizations, and the world. Christie Hardwick accepted the role of facilitator and created a curriculum

> **"** Out & Equal decided to bring these talented individuals together to explore how they could have a greater impact on behalf of the LGBT community. **"**

for that first forum, which was wildly successful, and the forum continues to be a haven for senior and emerging executives each year.

Since 2008, the Executive Forum has culminated in a special celebration gala dinner in San Francisco. The Out & Equal Leadership Celebration coincides with the Executive Forum and recognizes organizations and individuals who have taken the lead on fundamental issues of equal rights, both in and out of the workplace. The winners and honorees are true role models and advocates who encourage businesses and individuals to become involved through their leadership. Past winners have included Houston Mayor, Annise Parker, and civil rights icon Julian Bond.

Out & Equal's Global Presence

Out & Equal's global expansion began with increasing numbers of international participation in the annual Summits. Because Out & Equal constituents largely represent global companies, expanding its outreach beyond U.S. borders seemed a logical next step. Beginning in 2003, Selisse has been intentional about expanding LGBT workplace equality globally and has taken advantage of a number of international speaking opportunities.

> **"** Since many of Out & Equal's global constituents regularly attend Summits, the organization began to identify ways that Out & Equal could support the efforts beginning to take place globally. **"**

Recognizing that leveraging the role that global companies play in LGBT workplace equality is invaluable. To that end, Out & Equal encourages U.S.-based constituents to expand their LGBT policies globally. Out & Equal's ongoing dialogue with international colleagues and friends began in Europe and Canada and expanded to India, Latin America, Asia and other parts of the world. Since many of

Out & Equal's global constituents regularly attend Summits, the organization began to identify ways that Out & Equal could support the efforts beginning to take place globally.

In Barcelona, Spain, in 2007, Selisse was invited to speak at a daylong symposium for LGBT business leaders, which was sponsored by alumni of the business school struggling with LGBT issues. In a country where marriage equality is legal, many LGBT people are still not out at work. The LGBT people present shared their experiences of significant homophobia in the business community there.

In London, Selisse talked with many European Out & Equal constituents about beginning an international affiliate program, similar to the Regional Affiliates in the U.S. She also attended business forums alongside European gatherings of Euro Pride and the Out Games. In 2009, Selisse presented at the business forum in Copenhagen, Denmark, and later traveled to Warsaw, Poland, in 2010, to speak at the business forum there. After the forum, participants marched in the Euro Pride parade and were cognizant of walking on behalf of local residents who might live only a few blocks away but who could not join the Pride events out of fear of discrimination

The Out & Equal Board of Directors determined to make global expansion part of the ongoing mission of the organization in 2010. A Global Advisory Committee was formed bringing together thought leaders to discuss global LGBT workplace issues. In the summer of 2011, they gathered in Rome for the LGBT Business Forum during Euro Pride.

One of the groups represented in Rome is called Parks, after the American civil rights icon Rosa

> " A Global Advisory Committee was formed bringing together thought leaders to discuss global LGBT workplace issues. "

Parks, and is headed by Ivan Scalfarotto. In 2003, Ivan attended the Out & Equal Workplace Summit in Minneapolis. The Summit was a life-changing event for him, and afterwards Ivan vowed to start something similar to Out & Equal in Italy. Ivan's dream became a reality in 2010, when he returned to Milan and established Parks to advocate fairness for the LGBT community in Italy. Membership in Parks is normally restricted to corporations, but in May of 2012, Selisse was greatly honored to be inducted as the first individual member of this courageous organization.

At the Global Advisory Committee meeting in Rome, IBM executive Claudia Brind-Woody proposed Out & Equal as the leading convener for the Global Business Forum during World Pride in London the following summer, with IBM as presenting sponsor of Out & Equal's first-ever Global Workplace Summit.

Out & Equal's Global LGBT Workplace Summit

Out & Equal brought together people from around the world to consider ways to build greater equality in the workplace for LGBT people and allies with the first Global LGBT Workplace Summit in London. The Global Summit offered two days of plenary sessions, panels and workshops. More than three hundred and fifty lesbian, gay, bisexual, and transgender global executives, leaders and allies from twenty-six countries attended the conference. Participants from more than eighty corporations, organizations, and government agencies shared best practices and discussed strategies for creating workplaces where LGBT people are safe, accepted, and valued.

As presenting sponsor, IBM was a leading contributor to the conference planning discussion along with employees from Citi, Ernst & Young, Lenovo, Bank of America, Deloitte and Accenture. Several Nonprofit partners including Parks from Italy; Denmark's Q-Factor; Equal India Alliance; Kaleidoscope; and Pride at Work Canada participated in the planning of the event.

Tennis legend Martina Navratilova, one of the Summit's many notable speakers, said that coming out is essential to educating society and ending discrimination. "Go home," she implored, "and come out to your preacher, come out to your teachers, come out to those at your post office. When we make it personal, it's harder for people to be prejudiced."

> "Go home, and come out to your preacher, come out to your teachers, come out to those at your post office. When we make it personal, it's harder for people to be prejudiced."

In his keynote address, Harry van Dorenmalen, the Chairman of IBM Europe, expressed similar sentiments, adding, "The personal is powerful; when you are genuine and sincere, you can have a powerful impact." Saying that the workplace equality movement is at a crossroads, he suggested several tactics for moving forward, including the recommendation that LGBT people cultivate and mentor allies: "Straight allies can be really good ambassadors... Find one or two straight allies around you and help these people using reverse mentoring."

The first evening of Out & Equal's first Global Summit featured a significant opportunity for dinner at the House of Lords. Ken Batty kindly helped arrange the event through Lord Philip Norton, a leading constitutional scholar. One of the evening's dynamic speakers was Anna Grodzka, the first openly transgender Member of Parliament of the Republic of Poland.

> "Straight allies can be really good ambassadors."

The plenary sessions featured a variety of speakers including Vladi Luxuria, a former Member of the Italian Parliament and a transgender activist. "Things have changed. The world we live in today is better than the world that people like me lived in in the past," she told the gathering. "At work, we as transgender feel that we need to show not only the ability to deserve this job, but that we have the dignity and the right to have a place in society." Luxuria urged her listeners, "Do anything you can do to make this world a better one."

> **"Do anything you can do to make this world a better one."**

Michael Cashman, a Member of the European Parliament and Chair of the U.K. Labour Party's National Executive Committee, asked attendees to continue pushing corporations to use their influence in promoting LGBT equality. "As activists and politicians, we can never win this alone," he told the crowd. "We need your global companies to win arguments with governments to change their rules and approaches. Only together can we attain equality and maintain it."

> **"Only together can we attain equality and maintain it."**

Out & Equal Today

While the Out & Equal Workplace Summits receive most of the limelight, Out & Equal is much more than those events. Out & Equal Workplace Advocates has grown to a staff of more than twenty people and continues to further workplace equality through diverse programs and approaches: events, diversity training, Regional Affiliate programs, monthly online Town Calls, LGBT CareerLink, and the world's largest registry of LGBT employee resource groups. It is striking that today's mandate carries forward the vision of the four organizations — AGOG, Progress, Colleagues, and Building Bridges — that came together to become Out & Equal; every single hot topic and outreach idea they battled over at their first retreat continues to inform the work Out & Equal does today.

> " Out & Equal has a robust training and professional development department. "

The organization has a robust training and professional development department. It provides networking opportunities through its Regional Affiliate program and Employee Resource Group registry with two hundred and fifty participating LGBT employee resource groups. Out & Equal also provides leadership development opportunities for both established and emerging executives.

The Building Bridges diversity training program serves private and public sector clients, as well as nonprofits; the program offers both "LGBT 101" and more advanced trainings. Building Bridges works primarily with private companies but has also conducted trainings for the EEOC, public libraries, and federal prisons. Online training resources include webinars, such as "Building Bridges Toward LGBT Diversity," "Dialogues on Gender Identity," and "Developing a Strong LGBT Ally Program."

Pat Baillie, the Director of Training & Professional Development, oversees the department and hosts the monthly Town Call series, with guest speakers addressing current topics in an hour-long conference call format. Designed for busy working professionals and employee resource group members, the interactive learning experience features presentations on wide-ranging topics including LGBT data and survey findings, professional development, tax equity and marriage equality. Out & Equal also offers print materials and online resources such as Twenty Steps to an Out & Equal Workplace.

Out & Equal Associate Director of Career Services Julie Beach offers career advice to diversity candidates and manages

Out & Equal's LGBT CareerLink. This professional networking site and job board links diversity-friendly employers with top LGBT talent. The site was created when several employers asked Out & Equal for a direct recruiting route to the LGBT workforce.

> " Out & Equal's leadership team is committed to bringing equality to more workplaces and more employees around the world. "

Out & Equal's leadership team is committed to bringing equality to more workplaces and more employees around the world. According to Kevin Jones, Out & Equal's Deputy Director, "The biggest challenge is to figure out how to grow not just arithmetically, but exponentially. There are so many more workplaces in the U.S. and around the world where the conversation about workplace equality still needs to happen and change needs to take place.

> " Out & Equal keeps moving forward, motivated by the need for equality and inspired by the transformation happening as a result of the energy, passion, and commitment of our ally and LGBT community. "

Out & Equal can be a part of it, and that's the opportunity and the challenge."

Out & Equal is committed to workplace equality for LGBT employees around the world. The organization is constantly seeking new ways for companies to have an impact on work environments and societies where being lesbian, gay, bisexual, or transgender is still illegal. And of course, there is still an immense amount of work to be done in the United States. Out & Equal remains committed to the task, creating opportunities for peer-to-peer learning and fostering a spirit of education and exchange.

In an effort to reach audiences across the United States and around the world, Out & Equal has expanded its services into the virtual arena so that people who may not be able to attend a Workplace Summit or who live in another part of the world can access online resources for workplace equality. Some of these initiatives include hosting virtual conversations with employee resource groups and Regional Affiliates around the globe. Out & Equal is in the process of creating international affiliates and is committed to everyone bringing their whole self to work regardless of where they work or where they live.

Founding Executive Director Selisse Berry remains steadfast to the task: "Out & Equal keeps moving forward, motivated by the need for equality and inspired by the transformation happening as a result of the energy, passion, and commitment of our ally and LGBT community."

Resources

The 20 Steps to an Out & Equal Workplace

Out & Equal Workplace Advocates has developed a list of tools and best practices to create equality in the workplace for lesbian, gay, bisexual and transgender (LGBT) employees. These 20 Steps have helped many employers create more equitable workplace environments where everyone can be both "out" and "equal" at work.

EQUAL POLICIES AND BENEFITS

1. Include sexual orientation in global nondiscrimination and anti-harassment policies.
2. Include gender identity and expression in global nondiscrimination and anti-harassment policies.
3. Recognize same-sex couples and their families with full, equal access to all company benefits.
4. Ensure that global health coverage includes complete health benefits for transgender employees.

TALENT MANAGEMENT & PROFESSIONAL DEVELOPMENT

5. Establish and support LGBT employee resource groups.
6. Recruit, hire, and offer mentoring to LGBT employees through tools such as LGBTCareerLink.

7. Provide professional development experiences specifically for LGBT employees.

8. Track recruitment and career development metrics for LGBT employees who choose to self-identify.

WORKPLACE CLIMATE

9. Provide diversity training with specific reference to LGBT issues, such as Out & Equal's Building Bridges Training, for all employees.

10. Use anonymous climate surveys to measure effectiveness of LGBT diversity policies and programs.

11. Include LGBT diversity objectives in management performance goals.

12. Communicate routinely to all employees how the organization supports its LGBT workforce.

COMMUNITY COMMITMENT

13. Support nonprofit groups working for LGBT equality.

14. Sponsor and encourage visible participation in LGBT cultural events.

15. Include LGBT images in marketing and advertising strategies.

16. Include LGBT-owned businesses in supplier diversity program objectives.

ADVOCACY & CORPORATE RESPONSIBILITY

17. Be a visible role model for LGBT workplace equality in the community.

18. Support public policy efforts that protect LGBT workplace equality.

19. Actively oppose any attempts that would limit or restrict LGBT workplace equality.

20. Share leading practices on LGBT workplace equality by supporting the Out & Equal Workplace Summit.

About Out & Equal

Founded in 1998 by Executive Director Selisse Berry, Out & Equal Workplace Advocates is the leading champion for fully-inclusive workplace equality that convenes, influences and inspires global employers and their lesbian, gay, bisexual, transgender (LGBT) and allied employees. We believe that workplace changes can lead to broader cultural changes through the passion, wisdom, and energy of like-minded individuals and organizations. It is our vision that all LGBT people should be free to be open, authentic, and productive at work.

Our Programs

Out & Equal provides a range of year-round programs designed to educate and empower LGBT individuals in the workplace, including:

Out & Equal Workplace Summit — Our annual conference brings together thousands of lesbian, gay, bisexual, and transgender people (LGBT) and allies to create inclusive work environments.

Out & Equal Executive Forum — A two-day conference where senior executive leaders and emerging executives come together to learn from one another and share their best practices.

Out & Equal Leadership Celebration — An annual event recognizing organizations and individuals who have taken the lead on fundamental issues of equal rights, both in and out of the workplace.

LGBT Diversity Training — Out & Equal offers a range of training programs and services to corporations and organizations of all sizes.

Out & Equal Town Call Webinar Series — A free monthly one-hour webinar featuring guest speakers presenting on current LGBT topics.

Out & Equal LGBTCareerLink — Offers diversity-friendly talent recruitment for employers and LGBT job candidates online.

Regional Affiliates — Affiliates host networking and educational events, work with the national office to coordinate local training sessions, and bring together employee resource groups (ERGs) from a wide range of corporations and local businesses. Each affiliate is organized and led by its local Leadership Council.

Employee Resource Group Registry — The largest online community of LGBT ERG leaders.

Business of Change — A digital platform which provides LGBT nonprofit organizations and potential corporate supporters or sponsors with tools they can use to form fruitful partnerships.

To learn more about our programs, events and services visit us online: **www.OutandEqual.org**.